Flight Surgeon

**Complete and Unabridged
Diary
of
Medical Detachment, 1943-1944
242nd Medical Dispensary
Eighth Army Air Forces
381st Bomb Group
Station 167
Ridgewell, Essex, England**

by

**Lt. Col. Ernest Gaillard, Jr., MD
USAAF-MC (Ret.)**

**Compiled & Edited
by
William N. Gaillard**

The Oath...

The following statements are included in all military oaths for enlisted men and officers:

"...I will support and defend the Constitution of the United States against all enemies, foreign and domestic; that I will bear true faith and allegiance to the same;"

(enlisted men) "...I will obey the orders of the President of the United States and the orders of the officers appointed over me, according to regulations and the Uniform Code of Military Justice, so help me God."

(officers) "...I take this obligation freely, without any mental reservation or purpose of evasion; and I will well and faithfully discharge the duties of the office upon which I am about to enter, so help me God."

1stBooks – rev. 06/28/05

ISBN: 1-4107-4672-0 (e)
ISBN: 1-4107-4671-2 (sc)

Library of Congress Control Number: 2003094405

Printed in the United States of America
Bloomington, Indiana

This book is printed on acid-free paper.

Cover Graphics by Stefan McDonald

Dedication...

For my father and mother, Lt. Col. Ernest Gaillard, Jr., MD USAAF MC (Ret.), and Mignonne Nash Gaillard, who actually lived to tell the tale—and for all the brave men of the 381st Bomb Group who did not...

Yes; quaint and curious war is!
You shoot a fellow down
You'd treat if met where any bar is,
Or help to half a crown

Thomas Hardy
The Man He Killed, Stanza Five
Poems of the Past and Present, 1902

MEDICAL HISTORY AAF STATION 167[1]

This history is prepared in accordance with HQ Eighth Air Force Memorandum 25-16, beginning 4 June 1943.

INTRODUCTION:

In the compilation of this history, the day-by-day events have been largely ignored and have been only included when the events of the day have contributed some interesting fact or set of circumstances that might be contributory to the understanding of the medical history of the group.

The detailed description of the evolution of sanitary procedures, the treatment of combat crew casualties, the treatment of psychiatric casualties and problems of administration are presented in a general way using all the available data and facts and figures presented when helpful. After the presentation of most of the factual material, there appears a commentary on current practices, procedures and suggestions on medicines, which would probably make the medical department a more efficient and useful adjunct to the Air Forces.

Separate headings are presented, which are complete studies and can be used without any reference to the remainder of the material presented.

The authors of this work are:

- Major Ernest (NMI) Gaillard. Jr., O-330166, MC
- Captain Louis G. Ralston, O-479721, MC
- Captain Ralph M. Wymer, O-478018, MC
- Captain Bernard E. Cohler, O-382023, MC
- Captain George J. Pease, O-1609307, MC
- 1st Lt. Joseph V. Fick, O-1543431, MAC

242nd MEDICAL DISPENSARY (AVIATION)

The squadron medical detachments are pooled to form one large detachment, which renders medical service to all personnel on the station. Station Sick Quarters are located on a hill well away from the flight line and easily available to evacuation from the base (AAF Site 14). Herein are located two wards, one for officers and one for enlisted men, a crash room for emergency surgical procedure, a sick call room, pharmacy, medical supply store room, a small laboratory, offices of the Surgeon and the administrative branch of the detachment, and a decontamination center in duplicate arrangement.

---

[1] The entire narrative of this particular introduction, **"MEDICAL HISTORY AAF STATION 167",** through the last two words "emergency treatment" was extracted and copied verbatim from the 381st Memorial Association's Website, http://www.381st.org, under the menu heading "Ground Commands", re: 242nd Medical Dispensary Tenant Command.

The dental department is set up in the former WAAF Site Sick Quarters, which is located in AAF Site 12. Here is also located an additional ward, which takes care of any overflow of patients from station sick quarters, and which is used for cases of venereal disease and other contagious diseases.

The medical detachment operates as a pseudo-independent organization having its own living site for enlisted personnel. This is composed of two barracks adjacent to the main sick quarters installation. An acting detachment commander has been appointed through whom the enlisted men receive the duty assignments, passes, etc.

The medical service of the base has been divided into different categories with a specific officer in charge of each; for example, Captain Wymer has been designated Equipment Liaison Officer, acting as liaison between the medical Department and the Group equipment office. In this way the status of the equipment is known at all times and a close check can be made of the various first-aid kits on the aircraft. So, too, in the case of base medical inspector, venereal disease control, respiratory disease control, etc.

Daily sick call is handled by all of the medical officers, as is the ward work, one officer being in charge of the wards for a week at a time. The medical officers rotate M.O.D. duties daily.

MISSIONS: Two flight surgeons attend each briefing and see the planes off on the mission. The medical department issues candy rations to each combat crewmember going on the mission. Coffee and cookies are also given out before take-off by the ambulance drivers and first-aid men.

When the planes return from a mission, five ambulances are stationed at the control tower and the receiving end of the runway to receive casualties. At least two medical officers are present with these ambulances, which, in addition to the regular first-aid kits, also have a surgical kit, which can be used for emergency treatment.

From the *Makers of the Realm* by Sir Arthur Bryant:

"However skilful a man may be in writing—however natural his style—no one can write history naturally. The array of facts, which the historian has first to collect, is far too great. In my own work, I generally find that for perhaps a single paragraph I may have forty or fifty typed or hand-written slips of paper—extracts and notes from letters, books, and documents. And the sense and truth of all these have somehow to be worked into that paragraph. It's like a jigsaw puzzle. However carefully one may have arranged one's material, however thoroughly one has mastered it, to get it all down in the right and natural order is a most difficult business. That's the fun of writing history—it's a test, like everything else worth doing, of effort, endurance and infinite patience."

Infinite patience, indeed...

Additional Notes to the Reader:

This is, for all intents and purposes, a medical war diary with many anatomical and numerous, dated technical, military terms and acronyms for which some of you may be unfamiliar. Obviously, this isn't medical school or the Army and we can't expect you to have a copy of *Gray's Anatomy*, the *U.S. Army Manual*, or the *Uniform Code of Military Justice* from 1943 handy at all times to understand this narrative. So, and without going too far overboard, I compiled a brief glossary at the end in a separate section for the convenience and accommodation of the modern reader.

Also, again, kindly bear in mind the nature of the text itself: it is a medical WAR diary. Additionally, and for purely clinical reasons, several B&W photos were taken of individuals returned from bombing missions over enemy territory who were either KIA, WIA, or IIA (that's Killed in Action, Wounded in Action, and Injured in Action to you and me). These pictures, quite frankly, are more than a little disturbing and gruesome, even by today's jaded, "Hollywood" standards of gratuitous blood and gore. After wrestling with the notion for several weeks, I chose to re-bury these disquieting images back into Dad's original diary where they belong; the sensitivities of the surviving, immediate family members and descendants—and, simply, out of common decency—far outweighing any academic or perverse, prurient interest here. I have enclosed some other, never-before-seen photos, however, from the time and place that will give you some idea of the flavor of life on an American Army Air Force base in England during the early forties. These are from both the diary and the family photo album.

Remember, these records were transcribed from the commander's holographs and banged out on a Remington, Royal, or Smith-Corona manual typewriter (about the size of today's refrigerated beer box) by an army *(sic)* of reasonably well-educated, sergeant clerks who were not only the word processors, but the word-processing *programs* as well. Each had their own styles and notions of grammar, punctuation, diction, syntax, and, most interestingly of all, spelling. This was especially evident in the spelling of certain cities and regions in the admirable geographies of France, Germany, Czechoslovakia, and Poland—the latter two nations' languages having this more-than-marginal predilection for consonants. You get the picture and so did I. I made corrections where I could, sounding out both my Webster's and Hammond's Pronouncing Gazetteers from 1939, as some of these towns and villages no longer even exist.

Item Last: A copy of this diary got out, obviously, through either the use of contemporary carbons or mimeographs (those non-coms!), and has appeared elsewhere. However, shortly after my mom died and we had to sell the house, we discovered the actual war diary underlineoriginals/underline (two volumes, no less) after having been effectively sequestered from my sister and me for some sixty-odd years. As children, we'd heard about them, but never actually saw them. In addition to the typed, onion-skin originals on hand, they also contained Dad's reports, letters, analyses, secret or restricted documents, hand-penned headnotes, annotations, strikethroughs, corrections, embellishments, modifications, and additions as he mused and pondered each day's original transcribed account returned to his possession as commander for the final edit. These supplementary, significant entries are more than a little interesting and I dovetailed them in as best I could.

Ostensibly, if you are a physician/MD, Nurse, or EMT, or other health care professional, you will find this account to be of particular, instructive benefit relative to today's medicine; and, if you're not, you'll enjoy it anyway simply for the marvelous adventure that it tells. It is to be savored by all.

Acknowledgments...

To begin with, and for obvious reasons, I would like to thank the two individuals to whom I dedicated this modern version of the diary: my late British mother and my not-so-late American father—the first for having had me and the second for having penned this chronicle in the first place. Had they not met in England, married, and actually survived World War II to eventually return to the United States, my sister and I would still be wafting and drifting around somewhere in the astral plane between the Horse Latitudes and the City of Dis. Fortunately, Cheryle and I haven't the foggiest idea of what either place looks like, the both of us having had the extraordinarily good fortune of having been whelped in the second half of the twentieth century. Incidentally, that was Mom talking to us: we were either whelped or spawned, not born—and not brought up, but, rather, *dragged* up. That's the Old School Tie for you.

And, more than appropriately, to my sister, Cheryle, for having perennially hosted my father for the last three-odd years since my mother's death—and for putting up with my artistic quirks, excitements, short temper, fits of paroxysm and pique, irritatingly muttering of the text to myself during my many substance edits, drinking all her whiskey, and keeping odd hours at her house during my bi-weekly sojourns in San Diego to help her tend to my ailing father—and not to mention her having to read my run-on sentences.

To my aunt, Ellen Nash Holmes (Mom's sister), for having provided surrogate, maternal moral support to me all my life, for having had my cousin, Robin, the brother I never had, and for allowing me to openly maraud my way into her husband's armed services photo album from the Royal Navy, Fleet Air Arm for the English Page. After all, we must remember that World War II, or, the "1939-1945 War", was prosecuted and *won* as a truly "Allied" endeavour.

To my former roommate, John F. Chordas of Redondo Beach, California, for having unwillingly consented for me to usurp his dining room table and kitchen (I just went ahead and converted them without his permission anyway) into my own personal inner sanctum during the early, excruciating research and scanning of the original diary text for *Flight Surgeon*. He had to suffer the same throes of exasperation and annoyance as my sister; however, one hundred miles to the north and in a far, far smaller space. Thanks, John.

To my good friend of nine years, Stefan Grant McDonald, whose artistic proficiency and aptitude with Adobe Photoshop quite literally put a spin on my propellers, vapor trails off my wingtips, cajoled the weatherman to order a convincing ten-tenths undercast, provided for more brightly-colored, American Armed Forces insigniae; and rendered an otherwise prosaic, frightfully tedious and dreary shell into something actually worth the occasional ogle and gawk—that quintessential "coffee table book" book cover.

And to Coco King, Megan M. Dowling, Terese Bisignano and Steven E. Wohn for the compliments, booze, lunches, dinners, haircuts, make-overs, sleep-overs, moral support, gentle banter, dangling conversation, silly questions about WWII, pin money, and Internet access; to my children, Joshua and Isabelle Gaillard, for my abiding and undying desire to thrive and actually get the finished MS to the publisher on time; to Bob "Ball Turret Gunner" Gilbert, my former co-worker at Hughes Helicopters, Incorporated, good friend of over twenty-odd years, and technical advisor who actually served with my dad in the 381st Bomb Group during the war; and to *all* those others around the nation, and together with the *United States Air Force History Support Office* at Bolling AFB, Washington, D.C., without whose prompt, invaluable, and consummately professional, military assistance this book would have been, at the very best, incomplete.

Thanks to all of you—I owe you in spades.

Foreword...

Over forty years ago, my sister, Cheryle, and I would sit around on the living room floor of our then-new house in La Jolla, California that Mom and Dad had finished building in 1952. We had 45's and two-speed LP's, and we listened to Elvis, Buddy Holly, Perry Como, Gene Autry—or David Seville and the Chipmunks and Spike Jones. Thank God my sister and I each had our *own* record players as well, and in our own *rooms*; it kept peace in the house.

We also sat on the living room floor in front of our old, RCA Victor, black-and-white television. It had this fuzzy screen about the size of a large Frisbee, manual analog controls (*you* were the remote), and accented by a beautiful, blonde wood cabinet. It had a dial tuner with right of entry to just twelve VHF stations of which we could only get six with our rabbit ears—the rest were in L.A. A rooftop antenna was not only out of the question, but, also, to my mother's proper, English sensibilities, garish. And, yet, there was always something on—like *The Mickey Mouse Club, Buffalo Bob, Howdy Doody,* Johnny Weismueller *Tarzan* movies, *Francis the Talking Mule, Buck Rogers, Roy Rogers, Hopalong Cassidy, Sky King, Seymour's Monster Rally, Moona Lisa*—or *Sugarfoot* or *Cheyenne* or *Rawhide*, or that new show, *Bonanza.*

Occasionally, we also watched the *de rigueur* war movies with John Wayne, Humphrey Bogart, Robert Taylor, Richard Widmark, Noel Coward, Alan Ladd or Randolph Scott. And it was always those action war flicks that "got" to me and my little, pint-sized comrades-in-arms: *Sands of Iwo Jima, Sahara, Bataan, Take the High Ground, Run Silent, Run Deep, Flying Leathernecks, Pork Chop Hill, In Which We Serve, Mrs. Miniver, The Enemy Below, Operation OSS, The Dam Busters,* and, one of my favorites, *Twelve O'clock High.* We were our parents' World War II soldiers, sailors, marines and combat pilots, and we knew all these movies by heart.

Always at about that war-movie time, my mom or dad or their buddies, or my aunts and uncles from England, or their buddies, would saunter in, point to the TV and alternatively say things like, "They got that part right", or "Oh, *jolly* good show", or they'd <u>all</u> shake their heads and say, "No, no, uh-uh", or, "Well, that's not *quite* accurate—but at least they're not being silly", and we were hungry to know. We wanted war stories and they always told them to us. If it wasn't crawling through the other sands of Tarawa or Taipan, it was flying over the ball bearing plant at Schweinfurt dropping ordnance, or dogfighting with Göring's *Luftwaffe* off the white cliffs of Dover.

We always thought our English family war veterans sounded funny because as kids we really couldn't understand them. It wasn't a bath, it was a *bawth*; it wasn't quinine water, it was *quinéen*; and, "you can call the <u>race</u> anything you want to, but the hat's a *bowler*", etc. My uncle, Denis John Holmes, for example, was in the Royal Navy's Fleet Air Arm and flew this horrible thing called a Swordfish. It was this dated, archaic-looking, carrier-deployed bi-plane with fixed landing gear cradling a largely dysfunctional torpedo (roughly the same length as the tailboom section of the fuselage), and cooked along, seemingly, at about 3½ knots buffeting a mild headwind. This is what the English Crown sent out to sink the German Navy.[2]

---

[2] The Crown even had the impudence to send the Swordfish out to harass the *Bismarck.* Well, we all know what happened to the *Bismarck.*

Later on, Denis also introduced the Swordfish to the *Japanese* Navy in the waters off Ceylon (now, *Sri Lanka*). Amazingly, he survived the war unscathed. He used to always joke that the enemy couldn't shoot him down because he "moved too slow".

In 1960, when I was about eight years old, I said to him, "Uncle Denis, the *Blitz* must have been simply horrible!" to which he vaguely replied, sated with silk cravat, briarwood pipe and brandy snifter, and with that quintessentially insouciant, avuncular and infamous British penchant for understatement: "Yes————uh, J-J-J-Jerry could be *rawther* tiresome". Jerry could be rather *tiresome*? That was it? That was my WAR story? *Huh?*

And when they'd finally leave the room, they'd invariably sign off with that hale and hearty, "You kids really have <u>no</u> idea of what we went through during the war and what we did without and the number of our friends who got killed". This time, though, it was payback time and "us" kids' turn to say, "They got that part right".

Later on, when I was about seventeen years old, the realistic drama, all-star cast, made-for-something movie, *The Battle of Britain*, debuted in 1969 on one of the then-three major television networks. I remember my mother and father being riveted and mesmerized and watery-eyed in front of our brand-new, Packard-Bell color console. I walked in and said, "What's up?" and without even looking at me they reiterated (yet again), "You kids have no idea...", shortly followed by the pithy criticism, "Billy, this is *good*; this is how it really happened there." And they were right—it *was* good—and we had no idea of what happened there and never, ever would. It wasn't our time. It wasn't Vietnam.

During the "Big One", as my generation likes to call World War II, Dad was an army flight surgeon. As former ROTC at the Universities of Kentucky and Louisville, the military had his "pickle" and he was now conscripted into the Army. He was physically wrenched out of his physician's residency at Rhode Island Hospital in Providence, and ordered to active duty shortly after Pearl Harbor. Completed internship or no internship, doctors were being selectively drafted for the war effort in order to tend to the dead, dying and wounded that were certain to come their way as the prosecution of global war took its inexorable course. Once in, he was able to choose the Air Corps and was immediately reassigned to the Schools of Aviation Medicine and to Randolph and Lackland Fields, Texas. He'd always wanted to learn how to fly.

After several months of long-term and intensive, supplementary training, they deployed him off to jolly, old England via a southbound train after having landed at some unknown, miserably cold airdrome in Scotland. Arrival date at Station 167, Ridgewell, Essex, England was 04 June 1943. This station was the headquarters of the US Eighth Army Air Forces, 381st Bomb Group–Heavy (the "Mighty 381st") comprising four bombardment squadrons of B-17 bombers. It also contained eight, subordinated tenant commands of which the medical detachment was designated "242nd Medical Dispensary". There were approximately 7,000 personnel assigned to the station at the time after either co- or reassignment with the 432nd Air Service Group, Number Three Group Bomber Command, 90th Squadron, Royal Air Force. In other words, we partially shared this station with our English, allied hosts. Our grown-up guys at the time couldn't understand them either.

His operation there (and in the air) lasted from 04 June 1943 to 02 October 1944. He had met and eventually married my mother the previous January 18th when he was ordered reassigned to the huge military hospital complex much farther west at Cirencester in Gloucestershire where, eventually, my brother, Garnet Nash Gaillard, was born in 1945.[3]

This lasted until near war's end when his medical skills were conscripted and put to the test once again on the Continent in one of the liberated death camps in Germany (*Buchenwald*), and then treating both the especially hateful, civilian injured and wounded population in bombed-out, Allied-occupied Berlin. These were two things he never talked about—and especially *Buchenwald*. So, if you don't think war is indeed an equal opportunity tragedy, just ask any American flight surgeon who's been around the block, and he'll tell you.

This diary that tells the tale in words, never-before-seen pictures, and forgotten headlines covers that specific period—and what a tale it is. As you plow through it, and with the obvious exception of both its occasional comic relief, and in deference to those who actually lived it, you have to pause for a moment, put it down, lay your index finger across your upper lip with your elbow on your knee, and shake your head in unconditional astonishment thinking, "This couldn't have happened—and certainly not on this scale; the casualties were just too high". But it did happen. It could *not* have been made up.

Vera Brittain, to illustrate an example, wrote and later published her signature work, *Testament of Youth*, in May 1933 about her family's experiences during World War I, what the English call the "Great War". Not everyone from her publisher at Victor Gallancz, Ltd. to her friends to her fair-weather acquaintances would simply believe what she had written: it was too tragic, too appalling, too horrid, too expensive in terms of, literally, life and limb, and too heart wrenching—and all too true. Twenty years after that first armistice, the Lost Generation gave way to the "Greatest Generation" of Studs Terkel, and, latter-day author, Tom Brokaw, but with one common thread: that frightful calamity of all-out war and its terrible, across-the-board cost in requisites of men, munitions, money and shattered families.

This is that story again, however, from the *American* perspective, and with none of Vera Brittain's beautiful verse patterns or flowery, baroque phraseology that comes of an inherent and exquisite, native command of the English language; just that inclement, day-by-day, pedestrian grind of an American air combat bomb group on British soil trying to stay alive, useful and sane in the face of world history's greatest, all-out serial conflict.

In brief, clinical compass, this, too, was their "testament of youth".

William N. Gaillard
Redondo Beach, California
April 2005

---

[3] In fact, it was so far west as to be less than thirty miles due northeast from the source of the Thames River itself.

Flight Surgeon

Lt. Col. Ernest Gaillard, Jr., MD USAAF MC (Ret.)

DIARY OF MEDICAL DETACHMENT

STATION 167

BEGINNING 04 JUNE 1943

****

04 June 1943 — The Medical Detachments of the 381st Bombardment Group (H) includes Hq., 532nd Squadron, 533rd Squadron, 534th Squadron, and 535th Squadron, arrived at AAF Station 167 by train after landing in the UK at a more northern post in Scotland. Station Sick Quarters had previously been occupied by the RAF and taken over by the Medical Detachments of the 330th Service Squadron, 100th Service Group and Hq. Squadron, 312th Service Group, and operated by the combined Medical Detachments of above-mentioned groups. The 381st Group Surgeon, Major G.P. Schnabel, who accompanied the Flight Echelon, has not yet arrived at this Station. Patients from the advance party were being cared for in the Station Sick Quarters and several were admitted from the new arrivals to the Station.

Station Sick Quarters are located on a hill well away from the Flying Line and easily available to evacuation from the Base. The physical lay-out is such that three Nissen Huts with connecting hall-ways house a ward containing 14 cots for enlisted men, a smaller ward containing 3 cots for Officers, a Crash Room for minor surgical procedures, duty room, and auxiliary rooms for storage of supplies. (2). Sick call, Pharmacy and Medical Supply store room, the Surgeon's Office, and Dental Department, Kitchen and Boiler Room. (3). Decontamination Center in duplicate arrangement, which are used in part for overflow and emergency patients. Only cases of minor illness or injury will be cared for in Quarters if the duration of confinement is thought not to require longer than seven to ten days.

Roster of Medical Personnel as of this date:

Headquarters

Cpl. Maurice E. Lemasters
Pfc. Michael W. Spack
Pfc. Stanley A. Johnson

532nd Bombardment Squadron

Cpl. Wallace V. LeBlanc
Cpl. Frank Boroviak
Pfc. William Mammay
Pfc. Robert Ball
Pfc. Eugene Kelly
Pfc. Durell W. Wayland
Pvt. Francis Knight
Pvt. Raymond Lashure

533rd Bombardment Squadron

Sgt. William C. Stone
Cpl. Joseph Babich
Cpl. William Piech
Pfc. Marshall Miller
Pfc. Malcolm F. Robertson
Pfc. Charles Denning
Pfc. William Berrells
Pfc. J.D. Arlin Atchison

534th Bombardment Squadron

Sgt. Homer B. Stamp
Cpl. Olaf C. Ostenson
Cpl. August Psikal
Pfc. Jack Austin
Pfc. William Greene
Pvt. John A. Raab
Pvt. Edward F. Lorenz
Pvt. Anthony J. Goral

535th Bombardment Squadron

Sgt. Howard W. Brown
Cpl. William H. Bassett
Cpl. George M. Hench
Pfc. Maynard O. Payne
Pfc. Edward Gonynor
Pfc. Harvey G. King
Pfc. Charles J. Timonore
Pfc. James H. Quaintanoe

330th Service Squadron

Sgt. Henry H. Thomas
Cpl. Aulton D. Smith
Cpl. Ranzy Pierce
Cpl. Carroll Gambill
Pfc. Andrew Joerger
Pfc. Joseph Manning
Pvt. Forrest Stansbury
Pfc. Emil Bukachezski

312th Service Group Headquarters

Sgt. Donald A. Lockwood
Cpl. Milton O. Patterson
T/5 Clarence G. Earman

Pfc. Arthur W. Reder
Pfc. Edward M. Standel
Pfc. Willare H. Sharitz
Pvt. Brian F. Karlovich
Pvt. Martin R. Prendergast
Pvt. Joe E. Coleman

Officers:
Medical:

532nd Bomb Squadron
1st. Lt. Bernard E. Cohler

533rd Bomb Squadron
Capt. Louis G. Ralston

534th Bomb Squadron
Capt. Ralph M. Wymer

535th Bomb Squadron
Capt. Milton H. Bland

330th Service Squadron
Capt. Cornelius J. Dwyer

312th Ser. Gp. Hq.
1st Lt. W.G. Fessler

Officers:
Dental:

Hq. 381st Bomb Gp.
Capt. Leslie F. Crones

312th Ser. Gp. Hq.
Capt. Lee Scholnik

5 June 1943 — Major Hall, Surgeon 4th Bombardment Wing, visited the Station and outlined and discussed briefly the Medical Set-up and reports required in this Theater of Operations.

The Detachment of the 12th Evacuation Hospital, Braintree, England was visited in the afternoon for the purpose or learning the correct procedure of admitting patients requiring evacuation from Sick quarters.

6 June 1943 — Major Schnabel arrived this P.M. and took up the duties of Station Surgeon.

8 June 1943 — The greater portion of the Flight Echelon, led by Lt. Colonel Nazzaro, arrived this P.M. It was a beautiful and welcome sight to see the formation.

10 June 1943 — Routine Medical duties are proceeding smoothly. Organization of the Detachments has been satisfactory. Sick call has been set-up and held daily in the following sites, in addition to Station sick-quarters: Site #1, #3, and WAAF Site #1. First Aid Stations have been set up in the Picquet Hut in each Site and are to be manned during Air Raid alerts.

19 June 1943 — A case of Scarlet Fever of moderate severity was discovered in the ward containing other patients, who were immediately quarantined or isolated for seven days. New admissions were cared for in the auxiliary space of the Decontamination Center.

22 June 1943 — The first raid of the Group was staged early this A.M. Two aircraft with crews are missing in action and two aircraft, which were severely disabled, crash-landed in England. Six members of Lt. Shenk's crew were wounded in action and all hospitalized at 12th Evacuation Hospital, Botesdale, England. One man, Sgt. Kinley V. Lindsay, AEG, 533rd Bomb Squadron, was admitted to our own Sick Quarters. Apparently only one man, of the six hospitalized, received severe injuries.

S/Sgt. Arnold B. Lorick, Tail Gunner, 533rd Squadron, was killed in action and his remains were returned to this Station and will be forwarded to Brookwood Cemetery for internment.

S/Sgt. Julius D. Sosby, Tail Gunner, 535th Bomb Squadron, returned in a state of acute emotional shock and was admitted to Sick Quarters — sedative therapy instituted.

Complete list of men missing in action:

DESTINATION: Antwerp, Belgium

532nd Bomb Squadron (H)

B-17F #42-30016 — "Iron Gut Gert"

Name	Squadron	Rank	Position
Horr, E. F.	532nd	1st Lt.	P
Roberts, W.R.	532nd	2nd Lt.	CP
Griffith, G. P.	532nd	2nd Lt.	N
Hoover, C. L.	532nd	2nd Lt.	B
Mandell, R.N.	532nd	S/Sgt.	RO
Chapin, G. A.	532nd	S/Sgt.	TTG
Henry, C. P.	532nd	Sgt.	BTG
Jones, A. A.	532nd	S/Sgt.	TG

| Clark, H.R. | 532nd | S/Sgt. | WG |
| Hodson, E. I. | 532nd | S/Sgt. | WG |

533rd Bomb Squadron (H)

B-17F #42-29984 — "Little Chuck"

Martin, J. J.	533rd	1st Lt.	P
Marsh, R.J.	533rd	F/O	CP
Long, H. R.	533rd	2nd Lt.	N
Hoag, W.W.	533rd	2nd Lt.	B
Goswick, Hugh F.	533rd	Sgt.	RO
Lantto, J. S.	533rd	S/Sgt.	TTG
Fornaro, L. J.	533rd	S/Sgt.	BTG
Geary, B.	533rd	Sgt.	TG
Witts, G. W.	533rd	S/Sgt.	WG
Hutchison, J. B.	533rd	Sgt.	WG

Complete list of men killed in action:

Name	Squadron	Rank	Position
Lorick, Arnold B.	533rd	S/Sgt.	TG

Complete list of men wounded in action:

Name	Squadron	Rank	Position
Sosby, Eulis D.	535th	S/Sgt.	TG
Lindsay, Kinley W.	533rd	Sgt.	AEG
Sinclair, John D.	533rd	T/Sgt.	ROG
LaBuda, Mitchell J.	533rd	S/Sgt.	AAEG
Bardsley, George C.	533rd	S/Sgt.	AROG
Sloan, James F.	533rd	S/Sgt.	AG
Brinton, Charles W.	533rd	S/Sgt.	AAG
Williams, George C.	533rd	2nd Lt.	B

Aircraft lost in crash:

533rd Bomb Squadron (H)

B-17F #42-30021 — "No Name"

23 June 1943 — During the process of loading 300# bombs on B-17F of 533rd Bombardment Squadron, a severe explosion occurred followed about 15 – 30 seconds later by another bomb explosion. Accident occurred about 1108 at dispersal site #13. This was followed by a fire of severe proportion.

Twenty-two enlisted men, and one officer, who was in a neighboring plane, were killed instantly, and one aged man, a British civilian construction worker, was fatally wounded, dying a few minutes after arriving at Station Sick Quarters. One EM, Pfc. Glen W. Burkland, received a fractured leg, comminuted and compounded, was evacuated to Sick Quarters where first aid was rendered and a Thomas' leg splint was applied before evacuation to Detachment 12th Evacuation Hospital, Braintree, England.

W/O Nutt, and Lt. Alexander, standing by the tail of an adjacent plane, were blown to the ground and, several yards from the plane, received blast injury, mild, to chest and sprained left ankle, respectively, and were admitted to Quarters. Also, 3 British civilians received minor abrasions.

A careful survey of the area involved revealed no living injured other than those listed above, and three others who received minor cuts and abrasions who were cared for at Sick Quarters and returned to duty. As soon as the area was declared safe by the Ordnance Department, the work of removing and identifying the bodies and remnants of bodies proceeded. This required many hours, and covered a large area surrounding the scene of the blast. Ten soldiers known to have been at the scene of the explosion have been unidentified and are unaccounted for. Thirteen bodies or portions of bodies of soldiers were positively identified; the mutilation and charring of the remains made the task extremely difficult.

Aircraft lost in explosion:

533rd Bomb Squadron (H)

B-17F #42-30024 — "Caroline"

Complete list of men killed by explosion:

Unidentified Bodies

Name	Sqdn.	Rank
Smulowitz, Louis*	533rd	Sgt.
Bohlander, Ervin*	533rd	T/Sgt.
Ashcraft, Robert M.	533rd	Pfc.
Jerkins, Melvin L.	533rd	Cpl.
Foerstel, Milton J.	533rd	Cpl.
Fiamma, George (NMI)	533rd	Cpl.
Feeley, Charles A.	533rd	Cpl.
Allen, Roger H.	533rd	Cpl.
Neel, Joseph L.	533rd	Cpl.
McDufee, Guy (NMI)	533rd	Cpl.

*Combat Personnel

<u>Identified Bodies</u>

Tull, Paul L.*	533rd	2nd Lt.
Kristapavich, Joseph J.*	533rd	Sgt.
Harris, Elwood R.*	553rd	S/Sgt.
Lintgen, James J.*	533rd	S/Sgt.
Langolf, Christian*	533rd	Sgt.
Egan, Mitchell J.	533rd	S/Sgt.
Collins, Dennis L.	533rd	Sgt.
Sproha, Joseph F., Jr.	553rd	Cpl.
Main, James A.	553rd	Cpl.
Bongiorno, Henry	533rd	Sgt.
King, James H.	533rd	Cpl.
Wilton, Charles H.	533rd	T/Sgt.
Madden, Elmer F.	553rd	Cpl.

Hunwick, John T.   Civilian (British)

*Combat Personnel

<u>Complete list of men injured by explosion:</u>

Alexander, James H.	533rd Quarters	1st Lt.
Nutt, Joseph L.	533rd Quarters	W/O
Burkland, Francis H.	533rd Hospital	Pfc.
McCabe, Francis H.	Civilian (British) Hospital	
Garwood, R.A.	Civilian (British) Hospital	
Hasty, James	Civilian (British) Hospital	

Early in the afternoon, our planes went off on their second mission over occupied France. Due to the fact that our planes did not meet the rest of the Group at the rendezvous point, they returned without reaching their target. No casualties or deaths with the exception of three men who obtained 1st degree frostbites, hands.

Phillips, Guy F.	534th	S/Sgt.	AEG
Gregory, Paul A.	534th	S/Sgt.	AG
Bassinger, Robin L.	534th	S/Sgt.	AAEG

24 June 1943 — The remains of the victims were transported by two ambulances to Brookwood Cemetery, Surrey, England for internment.

WAAF Site #1 Sick Quarters occupied and Scarlet Fever contacts removed to same.

25 June 1943 — Our 3rd raid of the Group took place today, with the following casualties.

Complete list of men missing in action:

DESTINATION: Hamburg, Germany

B-17F #42-30027 — "No Name"

Name	Squadron	Rank	Position
Schrader, R.I.	533rd	1st Lt.	P
Hamilton, John H.	533rd	Capt.	CP
Rogers, E. J.	533rd	2nd Lt.	N
Samara, E.G.	533rd	2nd Lt.	B
Cutting, W.K.	533rd	S/Sgt.	TTG
Yarnell, W.W.	533rd	S/Sgt.	RO
Kurnafil, Stephen	533rd	Sgt.	WG
Pruiett, C. A.	533rd	Sgt.	BTG
Frisby, L. E.	533rd	S/Sgt.	TG
Leidecker, Ted W.	533rd	Sgt.	WG

Complete list of men killed in action:

Tieman, Ivan J.	534th	S/Sgt.	BTG

Complete list of men wounded in action:

Everett, Arthur J.	535th	S/Sgt.	AAEG
Prodresky, John W.*	534th	S/Sgt.	WG
Riddle, Lloyd C.	534th	S/Sgt.	RO

*This EM was on a plane that landed at a Base near Ely. EM was removed to Hospital, Ely Airdrome, England (RAF). The other two EM's received 2nd degree frostbites and have been grounded.

S/Sgt. Charles W. Brinton, WIA the 22nd, succumbed to gas infection, which developed subsequently.

26 June 1943 — The 4th raid of the Group took place today. Due to a heavy overcast, the planes were unable to see their target; therefore, returned without dropping their bombs. No men were MIA or KIA.

DESTINATION: Paris, France.

Complete list of men wounded in action:

Coucher, Shirley E. ("Quarters")	533rd	S/Sgt.	TTG

Quarantine lifted on Scarlet Fever contacts.

28 June 1943 — The 5th mission was staged today, with the following results:

DESTINATION: St. Nazzaire, France.

Complete list of men wounded in action:

Name	Squadron	Rank	Position
Hendricks, Landon C.	533rd	Capt.	P
Kapuska, John P.	533rd	T/Sgt.	TTG
Vina, Daniel A.	534th	Sgt.	TG

No MIA or KIA. Two Medical Officers, Capt's. Bland and Ralston, were flown to RAF Airdrome at Portreath to take care of any wounded, as gas carried on the mission would not permit return to the home base. Fortunately, only minor injuries were sustained and no aircraft were lost.

29 June 1943 — Sgt. Robert U. Anderson, ASN 33093949, 7th Sta. Compliment Squadron, was accidentally and fatally shot with a Thompson Sub Machine Gun in his barracks this P.M. (Shot by friend, Sgt. Miller)

Raid over France this P.M. resulted in no casualties. (6th raid of Group)

30 June 1943 — Ground has been broken and foundation poured for an addition of Officer's ward of Station Sick Quarters. This will give, when completed, additional space, which is sorely needed.

1 July 1943 — The 82nd Headquarters & Headquarters Squadron, Detachment "A" arrived from Station 109 today with 1 Medical Officer, 1 Medical Administrative Officer, and 8 Enlisted Men. This Squadron will replace the 312th Service Group Headquarters Squadron, which is moving out.

Roster of Officers and EM in 82nd Hq. & Hq. Sqdn.

Officers:

| 1st Lt. | George J. Pease | Medical Officer |
| 2nd Lt. | Joseph V. Fick | Med. Adm. Officer |

Enlisted Men:

Sgt.	Joseph C. Hannigan	31077484
Cpl.	John Divito	36305334
Cpl.	Joseph M. Melancon	14025080
T/5	Butler, Marvin D.	34343105
T/5	Estes W. Helms	38044380
Pvt.	Charles Hoehn	36316801

| Pvt. | Henry R. Trusky | 39305659 |
| Pvt. | Anthony Giordano | 32357108 |

Seven Enlisted Men were promoted one rank.

3 July 1943 — The 312th Service Group Headquarters Squadron departed today. Transferred to 4th Wing.

List of departing Medical Personnel

Officers:

| Capt. Lee M. Schnolnik | Dental Officer |
| 1st Lt. W.G. Fessler | Medical Officer |

Enlisted Men:

Sgt. Donald A. Lockwood	34271961
Cpl. Milton O. Patterson	14131474
T/5 Clarence G. Earman	34271640
Pfc. Arthur W. Reder	33305525
Pfc. Edward M. Standel	31038490
Pfc. Willard H. Sharitz	33213757
Pvt. Brian F. Karlovich	13054051
Pvt. Martin R. Prendergast	31202527
Pvt. Joe E. Coleman	34139014

4 July 1943 — One plane lost in today's raid, and the following crewmembers are carried as missing in action. Remainder of Aircraft and crews returned safely. (7th Mission)

DESTINATION: Le Mans, France.

Complete list of men missing in action:

B-17F #42-29928 — "No Name"

Name	Squadron	Rank	Position
Ballinger, Olaf M.	533rd	1st Lt.	P
Carah, John M.	533rd	2nd Lt.	CP
McConnell, Paul H.	533rd	2nd Lt.	N
Williams, George C.	533rd	2nd Lt.	B
Lane, John K.	533rd	T/Sgt	RO
Gromstal, Byron J.	533rd	T/Sgt.	TTG
Wackerman, Albert G.	533rd	S/Sgt.	BTG
Bauscher, Harry W.	533rd	S/Sgt.	RWG
Owens, Francis E.	533rd	S/Sgt.	LWG
Howell, William C.	533rd	S/Sgt.	TG

6 July 1943 — Bicycle accidents have been responsible for many minor injuries, also occasional serious injuries, requiring evacuation to a Hospital in past several weeks. The frequency of accidents is increasing almost beyond reason.

Lt. Colonel Wright, Major Stone, and Capt. Sutton, Hq. Eighth Air Force Medical Department visited. Questions asked regarding progress amid problems of Station were asked and answered. Crash room inspected. Colonel Wright called on Colonel Nazzaro before leaving Station.

About 1630 hours, enlisted personnel began reporting to Hospital with history of nausea, vomiting, and diarrhea. This continued off and on until about 2400 hours, with total of about 25 to 30 cases. History of illness beginning about 1430 to 1630 hours, and associated with severe nausea, and diarrhea now characteristic.

Thorough investigation of food problem at the Consolidated Mess for the noon meal was investigated. Meal consisted of Beef and Vegetable Stew, which was canned, and no evidence of spoilage existed; string beans, also canned, spinach and potatoes, steam cooked. There seems to be some rumor of an addition of a small quantity of sausage (canned, Vienna style), which was added at the last minute. The sausage was supposed to have been previously opened, whether this is actually the case, and when the can was actually opened is a problem to which no satisfactory answer is available.

7 July 1943 — All patients have come through their trouble in good shape. Except for 2 cases who seemed pretty well exhausted, there are complicating factors. No history of other possibilities regarding the food problem exists. Possibilities of dirty mess kits or faulty washing have been considered, also, possibility of dirty containers used in serving food. No conclusions have been deduced, as the facts do not seem to bear out any single possibility or clue.

It has been decided to make entries of early sanitary inspections, whether of any scope or not, to have some idea of the condition of various places over period of time. So little is being done to remedy the situation it is pitiful.

Site #6 — Enlisted combat crew site ablution is very dirty. Paper and dirt are littered over the floor, toilets have not been scrubbed, and no basins are present for washing. There is no hot water because no coal is available. Some coal shortage exists, and it seems coal for heating water was removed by personnel living in the site for heating huts. Fuel sufficient for heating huts is not available at this time. Explanation for dirty condition of huts and ablution is that brooms, brushes, etc. are not available.

Site #3 — Washroom has no hot water for same reason stated above.

Site #7 — Has no hot water as the containers have not been set up.

Communal Site — EM bathhouse has very little hot water. Temperature of water was 80° F. Many of the showers are leaky, and it is presumed that much of the hot water leaks out as well as large quantity being used. Showers are dirty and have not been scrubbed satisfactorily at any time.

11

10 July 1943 — Eighth raid of the Group took place this morning over the outskirts of Paris. Target was obscured, so no bombs dropped. Major Schnabel accompanied Group on Mission.

11 July 1943 — Today, Major Schnabel left to attend school at the Eighth Air Force Provisional Medical Field Service School, Station 101. He expects to be gone approximately two weeks. Capt. Bland, Surgeon, 535th Squadron, was appointed acting Group Surgeon during his absence.

15 July 1943 — A Medical Board interview was held this morning to determine the sanity of Pvt. William R. Ruth, ASH 20309703, 330th. Service Squadron.

Members of the Board:

Capt. Milton H. Bland - - - President
Capt. Louis G. Ralston- - - Recorder
Capt. Ralph M. Wymer

Decision:

1. Sane.
2. Impression - Constitutional psychopathic state.
    A. Pathological liar.

14 July 1943 — At approximately 0030 and 0350 today, Air raid alarms were sounded throughout the base. Enemy aircraft flew over, and dropped bombs in the vicinity of this Station, however, no bombs actually dropped on our Base. The Medical Detachment assembled at the Station Hospital both times prepared for the emergency that might arise.

The 9th raid of the Group took place this A.M. with the following results:
DESTINATION: Amiens, France

One plane is missing in action — Lt. Holdom and crew — 535th Bomb Squadron.

One plane exploded enroute to target — exact cause as yet unknown. This plane was flying over Rattleden, England when the explosion occurred. Six members of the crew, which included the Pilot and Co-Pilot, were killed instantly.

The other four members of the plane were blown out of the plane and parachuted to safety. These men were immediately removed to 12th Evacuation Hospital, Diss, for treatment. Two of the men were returned to this Station, T/Sgt. Robert L. Potts, RO, 533rd Bomb Squadron, who was put in quarters, and T/Sgt. Richard J. Hanna, LWG, 533rd Bomb Squadron, who was uninjured and returned to full duty. The other two men, 2nd Lt. Donald F. Hamm, –B– 533rd Bomb Squadron, and 2nd Lt. Frank E. Cappel –N– 533rd Bomb Squadron, were kept at the 12th Evacuation Hospital for treatment.

Captain Bland went to Diss immediately with two ambulances to get the bodies of the six deceased men. The party arrived back about midnight, and the bodies were put in the morgue.

Complete list of men missing in action:

B-17F #42-30011 — "Widget", "Chug-a-Lug"

Name	Squadron	Rank	Position
Holdom, Robert J.	535th	1st Lt.	P
Gravelyn, Robert H.	535th	2nd Lt.	CP
Bechter, William A.	535th	2nd Lt.	N
Phillips, James A.	535th	2nd Lt.	B
Coleman, William R.	535th	S/Sgt.	TTG
Craver, William L.	535th	S/Sgt.	RO
Pryor, Morris E.	535th	Sgt.	RWG
Pulliner, Raymond J.	535th	S/Sgt.	BTG
Fossan, Kenneth L.	535th	S/Sgt.	LWG
Scollon, James B.	535th	S/Sgt.	TG

B-17F #42-3211 — "T.S." (Tough Shit), 535th BS, belly-flopped on final approach to base; aircraft total loss, no KIA or IIA.

Complete list of men killed by explosion:

B-17F #42-3223 — "Red Hot Riding Hood"

Hedin, Charles E.	533rd	1st Lt.	P
Burroughs, William D.	533rd	2nd Lt.	CP
Thomas, Vivian M.	533rd	S/Sgt.	TTG
MacDonald, Stewart (NMI)	533rd	S/Sgt.	BTG
Marhefke, Clifford J.	533rd	S/Sgt.	RWG
DeCosmo, Edward J.	533rd	Sgt.	TG

Complete list of men wounded by accident:

Name	Squadron	Rank	Position
Hamm, Donald F.	533rd	2nd Lt.	N
Cappel, Frank E.	533rd	2nd Lt.	B
Potts, Robert L.	533rd	T/Sgt.	RO

Major Reuter, dental surgeon, Eighth Air Force arrived today to visit our Station. He seemed quite satisfied with the Dental Surgery being done at this Station; however, felt that another Dental Surgeon was necessary.

15 July 1943 — Captain Pease took the bodies of the six deceased men to Brookwood (American Military Cemetery) today.

16 July 1943 — The planes took off on their 10th raid today. There were no casualties, whatsoever.

DESTINATION: Hanover, Germany.

18 July 1943 — Major Schnabel returned this A.M., and assumed command of the Medical Detachment. He was attending school at the Eighth Air Force Provisional Medical Field Service School, Station 101, for the past week.

19 July 1943 — Approximately 50 men, mostly from the new M.P. organization, just arrived, and a few from 2 Bomb Squadrons, reported attacks of mild diarrhea. No patient was acutely ill or suffered any particular discomfort. Symptoms were characterized by a moderately urgent diarrhea of some 5 to 6 times. No admissions were made to hospital. No sequelae were present.

Lt. Cohler surveyed the situation and felt that meat brought in on the afternoon of 17 July 1943 and used at the noon and evening meal of 19 July 1943 was responsible. This meat comes frozen in 40-pound packages and requires several hours to thaw—even after unwrapping. Hence, it is felt that this is probably not the source. The enlisted men, however, still refer to it as "embalmed beef". Thorough check of other possibilities brought no clues.

At approximately 1430 today, a red air raid alarm was sounded. Personnel of the medical detachment were already at their emergency First Aid Stations rehearsing the Medical Defense Plan, since a "dry run" had been scheduled for that time. The white signal was given at 1450. There was no enemy activity over this station.

20 July 1943 — The afternoon mail brought a report of water sample, taken 7/7/43, from First Medical General Laboratory. Report states specimen was 2 days in transit, not potable bacteriologically, test reveals evidence of fecal contamination, and colony count is very high.

Inquiring into the nature of collection reveals the sample was obtained from the Consolidated Mess, and no attempt was made to sterilize the tap before sample was taken. This together with the delay in transit is believed to be the cause the difficulty.

Thorough inspection of all mess halls was done earlier in the day. In general, it was felt that slight relaxation of efforts to maintain cleanliness has occurred. In general, all waste containers were quite dirty, both inside and out, and no effort has been made for several days, at least to wash them all. Three containers at the Consolidated Mess were of such long standing that fermentation had taken place. Proper authority has been advised of this situation on several occasions. During past several days, weather has been mild, and hordes of flies are present at every mess hall. Fly spray is not available and flypaper available in insufficient quantities.

In the Officer's Mess, many personnel with long, dirty fingernails were found. The latrine was dirty and vegetable and flour sacks were found on the floor. Request was made to place these sacks on elevated platforms, e.g., pallets.

In the Combat Mess, the storeroom floor was sloppy and the room dirty. Pot and pan room was very untidy, and several containers were very rusty. Latrine was extremely dirty.

At Consolidated Mess, many personnel were found with long fingernails with much dirt beneath. One man serving meat was spearing the slice with a fork and pushing it off with his rather dirty thumb. Garbage containers were very dirty, three with fermenting material, and hordes of flies hovering about the outside of the dirty containers. Many smoked hams, unwrapped, were piled in a sink, which happens to be in a room used as a storeroom.

21 July 1943 — Thorough investigation of the water and sewage disposal systems has been made and there is no evidence or reason to suspect there has been any breakdown in the system. Water lines have been previously tested to 80# per square inch and have been found to be adequate. The supply comes from an artesian well on the base and is not chlorinated. The system is overtaxed in that it is almost impossible to keep up with the demand. If the tank is filled during the night, and the pump operated continuously during the day, the demand is met, but the tank will have about one foot of water remaining at the end of the day. There is considerable particulate material in the running tap water at all times, and usually a light brownish color. It is felt that the supply in the well often becomes so low that a washing of the well bed occurs causing the discoloration and aspiration of the foreign material. A new well has been dug and pump house now being erected. Pumping equipment is not available, however, and delivery date is as yet uncertain. Additional samples of water have been submitted.

A board of officers was convened under the provisions of Section VIII AR 615-360.

Consisting of:

Lt. Col. Ralph G. LaRue, AC	President
Major G.P. Schnabel, MC	Medical Officer
Capt. M.D. Joyce,	

appointed 19 July 1943, by Par. 4, SO #27, Hq., Sta. 167, to investigate and determine whether or not Pvt. William R. Ruth, 330th Service Squadron, should be discharged prior to expiration of his term of service. Board adjourned pending report of psychiatrist, which was thought advisable in the case.

22 July 1943 — Additional water samples have been taken during the past 2 days, one sent to 1st Medical Lab, the other to 121st Station Hospital at Braintree. Further investigation has not discovered any information that would lead to suspect difficulty arising from the water supply. Sewage disposal plant is operating satisfactorily. Direct contamination is not thought to be a possibility in as much as the well is on the highest portion of the Base and well drained, and the disposal plant on a decidedly lower elevation and far from the water supply.

The Clerk of Works advises that the supply of water comes from an artesian well. At present, it is not chlorinated. A purifier, softener, and chlorinator have been ordered, it is understood, but no delivery date has been established.

No difficulty or illness has arisen since the receipt of the water sample report.

24 July 1943 — Lt. Chadwick, VC, 1st Wing, made an inspection of the mess halls and Q.M. storage. Recommendations – none. Consulted regarding water supply problem and no recommendations other than thorough investigation of system and testing or additional samples.

Board of Officers mentioned in entry of 21 July 1943 reconvened to consider psychiatrist's report and disposition of case of Pvt. William R. Ruth, Jr. Psychiatrist reports findings of Constitutional Psychopathic State, inadequate personality, and criminalism. Board recommended discharge under provisions Section VIII AR 615-360.

The Group participated in combat raid over enemy territory, i.e., southeastern coast Norway, placing 21 ships in the formation. There were no abortions and 20 ships returned with no injured personnel. Lt. Osce V. Jones and crew, 535th Bomb Squadron, failed to return. Information received later in the day, via radio, indicated that the ship had landed in Sweden and the crew interned. The airplane was known to have suffered considerable damage.

List of men missing in action (Interned in Sweden):

535th Bomb Squadron (H)

B-17F #42-3217 — "Georgia Rebel"

Name	Rank	Position
Jones, Osce V.	1st Lt.	P
McIntosh, George B., Jr.	1st Lt.	CP
Guertin, Arthur L.	2nd Lt.	N
Nevius, Charles W.	2nd Lt.	B
Nicatra, Joseph (NMI)	T/Sgt.	RO
Haynie, James E.	S/Sgt.	TTG
Newcomb, Charles W.	S/Sgt.	BTG
Early, Shannon B.	S/Sgt.	LWG
Haugen, Alfred E.	S/Sgt.	RWG
Kelleher, Maurice M.	S/Sgt.	TG

25 July 1943 — Group participated in raid over Hamburg, Germany in which three ships failed to return. Capt. Alexander's ship was seen to turn back from a point described as being deep in German territory. Lt. Moore's plane was damaged and part or all of the stabilizer shot away.

Whether crewmembers bailed out or not is not known. Lt. Owen's ship was hit between #1 and #2 engines and seen to burst into flames.

The smoke seemed momentarily to disappear, then burst out again, involving the greater portion of the wing. It was believed the crew bailed out.

One crewmember, T/Sgt. Warren G. Heintz, a radio operator, returned in a critical condition the result of anoxemia. Same difficulty was experienced by the ball turret gunner and his oxygen system, and the radio operator was trying to help him out by passing the bottles of O_2. During the process, the radio operator lost out and became himself the victim of lack of oxygen. Upon arrival at the Base, the patient was cyanotic, breathing shallowly, with weak pulse and unconscious. O_2 administered improved his general condition. His hands were very cold, but not believed frozen. He was hospitalized.

The following are the crewmembers missing in action:

B-17F #42-30153 — "No Name"

Name	Squadron	Rank	Position
Alexander, Joseph E.	532nd Bomb Sqdn.	Capt.	P
Crowley, William C.	532nd Bomb Sqdn.	2nd Lt.	CP
Wemmer, Jack W.	532nd Bomb Sqdn.	2nd Lt.	N
Hellman, Harold	532nd Bomb Sqdn.	1st Lt.	B
Orin, George H.	532nd Bomb Sqdn.	T/Sgt.	RO
Nance, James C.	532nd Bomb Sqdn.	T/Sgt.	TTG
Garvan, Peter D.	532nd Bomb Sqdn.	S/Sgt.	BTG
Johnson, George R.	532nd Bomb Sqdn.	Sgt.	TG
Ferens, Walter F.	532nd Bomb Sqdn.	Sgt.	WG
Heist, James E.	532nd Bomb Sqdn.	Sgt.	WG

B-17F #42-30013 — "Lethal Lady"

Name	Squadron	Rank	Position
Moore, William R.	532nd Bomb Sqdn.	1st Lt.	P
Wendte, Dale G.	532nd Bomb Sqdn.	2nd. Lt.	CP
Dreiseszum, Philip P.	532nd Bomb Sqdn.	2nd Lt.	N
Houck, James H.	532nd Bomb Sqdn.	2nd Lt.	B
Usher, Edward W.	532nd Bomb Sqdn.	T/Sgt.	RO
Ivey, John E.	532nd Bomb Sqdn.	T/Sgt.	TTG
Fortier, William L.	532nd Bomb Sqdn.	S/Sgt.	WG
Kralick, Joseph G.	532nd Bomb Sqdn.	S/Sgt.	WG
Zahm, Edgerton P.	532nd Bomb Sqdn.	S/Sgt.	BTG
Watkins, John M., Jr.	532nd Bomb Sqdn.	S/Sgt.	TG

B-17F #42-29976 — "Sad Sack"

Owen, Jack H.	532nd Bomb Sqdn.	1st Lt.	P
Bohan, William E.	532nd Bomb Sqdn.	2nd Lt.	CP
Bascon, Liston A.	532nd Bomb Sqdn.	2nd Lt.	N
Ronzio, Frank	532nd Bomb Sqdn.	2nd Lt.	B
Slater, Roy L.	532nd Bomb Sqdn.	T/Sgt.	RO
Lindenmeyer, William E.	532nd Bomb Sqdn.	T/Sgt.	WG
Winn, Charles K.	532nd Bomb Sqdn.	S/Sgt.	BTG
Asher, Clarence C.	532nd Bomb Sqdn.	S/Sgt.	WG
Rector, Kenneth K.	532nd Bomb Sqdn.	S/Sgt.	TTG
Cummins, Robert L.	532nd Bomb Sqdn.	S/Sgt.	TG

26 July 1943 — Another raid was conducted over Hamburg, Germany having a different target within the city area than in yesterday's engagement. Twenty-two planes took off, four spares returned, and two aborted, plus 16 returned. No ships were lost.

Lt. Sidney Novell, a navigator of 535th Bomb Squadron was struck in the antero-medial surface, left thigh, 6" below inguinal ligament, cutting the artery and vein, and extending upward into the thigh toward inguinal ligament – by piece of flak 2" long by 3/8" to ½" in diameter. Patient lived but a short time.

Lt. Hester, a Bombardier, had his fingers frostbitten the result of a break in the Plexiglas of the nose. This is not considered serious. Lt. Roraback, a navigator of 534th Sqdn., was struck in the face by Plexiglas of nose and his eyes filled. No damage to cornea is found, but there is severe bruising. Patient's condition considered satisfactory.

27 July 1943 — T/Sgt. Heintz, injured 25 July, is gradually improving. It seems as if his speech is a little thick, which may be due to bruising of the tongue and/or cerebral involvement. The tongue shows some bruising on the tip and adjacent sides, and it is not known whether this is the result of freezing or biting. Several areas of the face and forehead have evidently suffered mild frostbite or suffered some bruising during his fall. Nothing of any importance. Lt. Rorabach's condition is satisfactory, and he is comfortable.

28 July 1943 — The Group participated in a raid scheduled to go to an installation near Kassel, Germany. The combat wing Commander aborted the wing before the target was reached and the planes returned. There were no casualties.

Report of water sample sent to 121st Station Hospital, collected 22 July 1943 came this date. Reported potable bacteriologically.

29 July 1943 - Physical inspection of the command was conducted this date. The Group participated in a raid conducted over enemy territory at Kiel. Two members of Lt. Tucker's crew were injured. S/Sgt. James R. Klingenberger suffered a wound of the lateral surface, right leg above the ankle. Sgt. Grover S. Bonsall suffered a penetrating wound of the lateral surface of the right leg 6" below knee joint and an abrasion of right elbow.

Both patients were injured the result of an exploding 20mm cannon shell, and both were hospitalized at 121st Station Hospital, Braintree. Neither were considered critical. One ship crash-landed at Snederton-Heath with mechanical difficulties and some ship damage. All planes have returned. One crewmember suffered a frostbite of the face, 2nd degree.

30 July 1943 — The Group participated in a raid over Germany in which Kassel was bombed, the Group leading the combat wing. Upon returning, personnel reported very heavy enemy action from flak and fighters, and examinations of planes certainly substantiate this. Two planes returned with props of engine each feathered, one with a tire blown out from cannon fire, and one hydraulic system shot and no brakes. One ship failed to return. One crewmember was slightly injured.

Personnel on ship missing in action:

B-17F #42-3100 — "No Name"

Name	Rank	Squadron	Position
Post, Robert F.	Major	532nd Bomb Sqdn.	P
Humason, Guerdon W.	1st Lt.	532nd Bomb Sqdn.	CP
Casalay, Alfred (acting)	2nd Lt.	532nd Bomb Sqdn.	TG
Hames, Leroy N.	2nd Lt.	532nd Bomb Sqdn.	N
Tsialas, William G.	2nd Lt.	532nd Bomb Sqdn.	B
Kithcart, William H.	Sgt.	532nd Bomb Sqdn.	TTG
Parker, Albert L., Jr.	T/Sgt.	532nd Bomb Sqdn.	RO
Fabiano, Frank	S/Sgt.	532nd Bomb Sqdn.	BTG
Anderson, Walter J.	S/Sgt.	532nd Bomb Sqdn.	WG
Robbins, Harold E.	Sgt.	532nd Bomb Sqdn.	WG

This raid ended the sixth in seven days for the Group, which is the heaviest operational schedule ever maintained. I feel the men have withstood the strain well, and while very tired are definitely not jittery. They need a rest and change now. Subsequent events will tell the story. The loss of the 532nd Squadron CO was a blow to this squadron particularly.

I believe that they will be adjusted to the loss in a short time, however, as they must have realized that some squadron CO would be shot down sooner or later if they continued to participate in raids. Probably the reason it has not happened before is because the frequency of participation has been regulated by official order.

1 August 1943 — Inspection made this A.M. of messes.

Officer's Mess and Club: Service court dirty, i.e., broken dishes and tin cans are piled in the corner, as well as scattered about garbage rack. Spillage of vegetable waste, coffee grounds, and other garbage has made the area unsightly. Latrine in the mess is not clean. Lavatory is crusted with dirt, and toilet has not been scrubbed in some time. Storage rooms are clean and contents put away. Kitchen and dishwashing room are satisfactory. China, glassware, and utensils are clean.

<u>Consolidated Mess</u>: The floor throughout the entire kitchen is very sloppy, slightly greasy, and slippery. It seems a failing or perhaps mania to have the kitchen floor awash the greater part of the time. On the floor near sink for washing pots and pans were two grease- and waste-filled containers, which were extremely sloppy. Material emptied into the containers missed the mark and large portion landed on both sides of the containers at the floor. Floors in both sides of the eating portion were wet and sloppy to walk in. The food storage rooms were clean and dry stuff put away. The meat preparation room was clean, except for a pool of bloody water in the center, which had drained off the frozen meat and had not been removed. Food cooking appeared to be of good quality and savory, chocolate cake was unusually tasty looking.

<u>Combat Crew Mess</u>: This mess is in the process of being moved to the new communal site, which is closer to combat crew personnel. This mess is not open today. Officers are fed at the Club and EP at the Consolidated Mess. The present Airmen's Mess is to be used for a PX and bar for enlisted personnel.

2 August 1943 — Airmen's Mess opened in the new communal site this morning. Some difficulty in getting settled down was experienced, but on the whole, I think it was accomplished very smoothly. Facilities are a little better in that they are a little better arranged and more convenient. The long distance from the kitchen to the officer's section has been eliminated.

4 August 1943 — There have been no operational missions since 30 July. Combat crews have been able to leave and rest, and are now engaged in training and test flights and ground school.

Lt. Colonel Streeter, Wing Surgeon, visited the Station, accompanied by Lt. Colonel Ryan, MC and Major Davis, AC (Wing Inspector). The Station hospital was thoroughly gone over by these officers. The Consolidated Mess was visited next, and a good many unsatisfactory conditions were found:

1) Floor over kitchen was wet and sloppy.
2) Garbage can was left in the mess kitchen.
3) Floor of flour storage in back was wet, 2 sacks of flour on the floor, one of which is probably spoiled, and other kitchen utensils stored with the flour.
4) Improper segregation of wastes — trash, broken china, metal and paper placed in same container. Grease can ¾ full of water.
5) Trench dug near northwest corner of mess hall partially filled with water and breeding mosquitoes.
6) Drain between west wing and kitchen wing on north side stopped up and running over leaving a large pool of foul smelling liquid.

The officers then proceeded to the Airman's Mess in the new compound site, now operating in its third day. Conditions were deemed satisfactory for this short period of operation.

8 August 1943 — Inspections were made and the following found:

Latrine in briefing room is quite odoriferous, and pails poorly cleaned. To toilet paper. Latrine near operations building was also dirty, papers and trash on the floor, toilets, and washbasins not washed and no toilet paper.

Combat Mess is running much more smoothly and facilities are better than at former location. Disposal of metal and paper not very well worked out as yet, as there is considerable confusion about the service entrance. In general, mess was clean. Dirty linen was piled in a hamper in one storage room, had overflowed onto the floor, and had considerable odor.

Consolidated Mess shows a great deal of litter and poor coordination. The floor was sloppy and wet, making a great deal of muddy tracks all over the kitchen and supply section. Garbage was poorly separated; particularly metal, paper, and glass.

Large shower building in communal site needed policing. Many shower heads were leaking, and hot water temperature 62° F. Recommendation has been submitted for use of shower building in new communal site.

Officer's Mess was in fair condition. Latrine was dirty (I have never seen it clean). Some silverware & china were greasy and dirty. Dish washing room was untidy, with lots of rags and utensils laying around.

10 August 1943 — Lt. Vernon Chadwick, VC visited the station and went over the mess hall for possible causes of the occasional diarrhea.

Watching the men wash mess kits it appears that there is very little being done towards thoroughly washing the kits. Not enough soapsuds are in the water, and it is not of sufficient temperature.

Dishwasher was operating at 150° F, and personnel were introducing cold water for increasing the pressure of the machine. Whether this is a defeat or a poor operating procedure remains to be seen.

11 August 1943 — A few officers eating in Combat Mess developed mild diarrhea this morning about 0430 hours. The evening meal at the Combat Mess was blamed (as usual). The meal consisted of meat and vegetable stew, a canned preparation shipped from the States, potatoes, creamed peas, jam, bread, butter, and cooked dessert.

The meat dish was prepared during the afternoon and served at the 1800 hr. meal 10 August. I am unable to find any item of the diet to which a cause might be assigned. So far as I am able to determine, no other eating or drinking factors are involved. Thorough inspection of the mess does not bring anything revealing. It is possible the dishwasher is being operated at a temperature inconsistent with proper sterilization. A temperature of 180° F minimum is recommended.

The Combat Mess itself was in good shape.

Consolidated Mess has improved over yesterday. The floor is still a little sloppy making a poor appearance. Storerooms were clean. Some mess personnel were dirty, i.e., dirty clothing and fingernails. One man slicing cooked meat was wearing an apron approaching the black shades.

Officers' Mess kitchen was in a hubbub due to installation of additional sink.

Communal site latrine was fairly clean and general appearance improved. Hot water temperature was a scalding 62° F and many showerheads are leaking a steady stream.

Sergeants' bathhouse, however, was extremely clean and well policed, which answers that age-old, perennial question, "Now, precisely, WHO is it that runs the Army, anyway?

10 August 1943 — During the late afternoon and evening, the water was unusually cloudy, having a brownish color. The men feel that this was the source of the diarrhea, particularly in light of the peculiar taste and color. This assured only in combat crewmembers, and upon investigation, I find probably 25 to 30 from 4 squadrons were affected. If then, it is a water problem, why were no others involved? No one was seriously affected and none hospitalized.

12 August 1943 — Going more thoroughly into the problem of diarrhea, which began early yesterday about 75 Officers and Men were found to be involved. Many were affected who did not report on Sick Call. Many reported moderate cramping and several were still having diarrhea today, more than 24 hours after the onset. A few additional cases have developed since yesterday. A few combat crewmembers were in serious difficulty on today's mission.

The water, which was cloudy, had cleared considerably. Additional samples were sent in for analysis from sites #2, #6, and new communal site.

The Group participated in a raid over Germany this morning, invading the Ruhr. Returning ships reported heavy flak, weak fighter attack, and extremely cold weather. Temperature of −38° C indicated at briefing was said to have reached minus 44°. Sixteen crewmembers have frostbites of fingers, and/or toes, from 1st to 2nd degree. No severe or necessarily partial disability burns are thought to have occurred. One waste gunner froze the right side of his neck, sustaining a 2nd deg. burn. No other injuries occurred.

Three ships failed to return. Personnel involved follow:

532ⁿᵈ Bombardment Squadron (H)

B-17F #42-5847 — "Margie Mae"

Name	Rank	Position
Moon, Theodore L.	2ⁿᵈ Lt.	P
Hamer, James W.	2ⁿᵈ Lt.	CP
Pritz, Stephen J.	2ⁿᵈ Lt.	N
McNichol, Bernard J.	2ⁿᵈ Lt.	B
Ernharth, John F.	T/Sgt.	TTG
Fleming, Michael	S/Sgt.	RO
Wheeler, John L.	S/Sgt.	BTG
Alsheimer, Wilbur	S/Sgt.	WG
Wood, Howard F.	S/Sgt	WG
Mattfield, Paul A.	S/Sgt.	TG

534ᵗʰ Bombardment Squadron (H)

B-17F #42-29954 — "Devils Angel"

Name	Rank	Position
Wroblicka, William	1ˢᵗ Lt.	P
Neeley, Claude E.	2ⁿᵈ Lt.	CP
Harris, David E.	2ⁿᵈ Lt.	N
Schneider, Lester W.	2ⁿᵈ Lt.	B
Labushevicz, Joseph G.	S/Sgt.	TTG
Smith, Fred M.	S/Sgt.	RO
Jonson, Edwin M.	S/Sgt.	BTG
Kratzer, John L.	S/Sgt.	WG
Phelan, John C.	Sgt.	WG
Cecil, Walter R.	Sgt.	TG

535th. Bombardment Squadron (H)

B-17F #42-29950 — "Forget-me-not"

Name	Rank	Position
Evans, Fred G.	F/O	P
Robbins, Joseph K.	F/O	CP
Lander, John F.	2ⁿᵈ Lt.	N
Watkins, Clarence A.	2ⁿᵈ Lt.	B
Kern, Herbert R.	S/Sgt.	RO
Dodge, Charles G.	T/Sgt.	TTG
Messler, Walter V.	S/Sgt.	BTG
Miller, Charles C.	S/Sgt.	WG
Doll, Stuart A.	S/Sgt.	WG
Hackett, Kenneth L.	S/Sgt.	TG

13 August 1943 — The Wing Surgeon was called and advised of particulars regarding the diarrhea, which was causing so much trouble with combat crews. Explanation of efforts made and findings were reported. Request for any suggestions brought promise of help.

Captain Sutton, Eighth Air Force Medical Inspector, and Major R.R. Cleland, SC Hq. S.O.S., Chief Surgeon's office, arrived about 1500 hours. After talking over the entire situation, an inspection was made of the Consolidated and Combat Messes. It was the opinion of the consultants that several factors were involved. Firstly, the problem is probably one of food. This involves the use of leftovers of questionable condition, uncleanliness of the mess personnel and dirty clothes, improper disposal or wastes, and improper washing of dishes and utensils. Secondly, the water is not above suspicion, but not believed the prime factor. The following recommendations are being made:

a) Installation of filtration and chlorination systems.
b) Opening of additional mess to relieve congestion of Consolidated Mess.
c) Delivery of meat to base six times a week.
d) Screening of storage rooms in all messes.
e) Placing of water softener in Consolidated Mess in operation. Use of soda crystals and soap powder in washing dishes and utensils.
f) Ample, clean clothing for mess personnel.
g) Maintenance of high standard of personal cleanliness of mess personnel.
h) Proper use and/or disposal of wastes.
i) Feces exams for all food handlers.

14 August 1943 — About 1400 hours, Capt. Sutton and Major Cleland called per phone, stating that they had report of our last water sample, which was "Bad", but no comparison of previous reports was given. As an emergency measure, chlorination by addition of bleaching powder to the water tank was recommended. This was to be done by adding about 3 pounds per day on basis of 60,000-gallon tank, to be added in 3 operations throughout the day, ½ pound in each side at 0600, 1200 and 2000 hours. One pound was placed in each side of the tank at 1615 hours.

15 August 1943 — A chlorine testing set is not available at this Station; hence, no estimate of the chlorine content can be made. Several times during the day, samples of water were taken at various sites and the odor of chlorine was present. The quantity was not sufficient to produce noticeable alteration of taste.

The Group participated in an air raid this afternoon late, over an aircraft works outside or Brussels. Twenty-three planes took off, 2 aborted and 21 returned. Bombs were not dropped, due to poor visibility.

16 August 1943 — The Group participated in a raid over enemy territory bombing aircraft installation near Paris. Twenty planes took off, none aborted and 20 returned. Crewmembers reported a good pattern over the target area.

17 August 1943 — The Group participated in a raid over enemy territory this date going to the Kugel-Fischer ball-bearing factory, Schweinfurt—the deepest raid into enemy territory thus far. Flak was reported as light and fighter opposition extremely heavy. Twenty-six planes took off, one aborted, and eleven failed to return. One ship ditched in the English Channel and was subsequently rescued. Morale was pretty low this evening on return, particularly as soon as stories were compared and total losses realized.

Personnel in ditched ship were the following: Plane was a wreck, no injuries.

Approximate time in dinghy was one hour, fifteen minutes.

532nd Bombardment Squadron (H)

B-17F #42-29735 — "Rum Boogie", "Our Mom"

Darrow, George R.	F/O	P
Howcroft, John H.	2nd Lt.	CP
Waldman, Ralph J.	2nd Lt.	N
Rokosa, Phillip V.	2nd Lt.	B
Hartnett, Carl W.	T/Sgt.	E
Kaufman, Jack W.	T/Sgt.	RO
Jones, Clarence M.	S/Sgt.	G
Baker, James E.	S/Sgt.	G
Morrison, Richard G.	S/Sgt.	G
Seward, Paul V.	S/Sgt.	G

Personnel missing in action were as follows:

532nd Bombardment Squadron (H)

B-17F #42-29731 — "Moore-Fidite", "Ol' Swayback"

Jarvis, Leo (NMI)	1st Lt.	P
Mancinelli, Eugene E.	2nd Lt.	CP
Riley, Richard F.	1st Lt.	N
Lockhart, William D.	2nd Lt.	B
Seymore, Harold W.	T/Sgt.	E
Logan, Aychmonde R. (534th)	T/Sgt.	RO
Persinger, Charles L.	S/Sgt.	G
Stecher, Harry L.	S/Sgt.	G
Grossman, Herman E.	S/Sgt.	G
Roehl, Eugene E.	S/Sgt.	G

B-17F #42-30140 — "King Malfunction II"

Nelson, Robert F	1st Lt.	P
Painter, Jack B.	1st Lt.	P
Ragan, Everett B.	2nd Lt.	CP
Keays, William J., Jr.	2nd Lt.	N
Duke, Lloyd L.	2nd Lt.	B
Kowalski, Matthew B.	T/Sgt.	E
Balentine, William C.	S/Sgt.	RO
Kellogg, Allen P.	S/Sgt.	G
Genz, Raymond A.	S/Sgt.	G
Whitman, Norman G.	S/Sgt.	G
Mizell, James C.	S/Sgt.	G

533rd Bombardment Squadron

B-17F #42-3092 — "Strato Sam"

Hudson, James C.	F/O	P
Grant, William R.	2nd Lt.	CP
Delaney, Ronald T.	2nd Lt.	N
Robinson, Kenneth E.	2nd Lt.	B
Vaughn, Edward R.	T/Sgt.	E
Pinsky, David (NMI)	T/Sgt.	RO
Vaughn, John M.	S/Sgt.	G
Wakefield, James A.	S/Sgt.	G
Thueson, Ford W.	S/Sgt.	G
Doyle, George A.	S/Sgt.	G

B-17F #42-29983 — "Iris"

Atkison, Challen P.	1st Lt.	P
Dulberger, Murray E.	2nd Lt.	CP
Frieberger, Fred (NMI)	2nd Lt.	N
Marks, Julian N.	2nd Lt.	B
Hanna, Richard J.	T/Sgt.	E
Kasha, Stanley C.	T/Sgt.	RO
McGoldrick, James C.	S/Sgt.	G
Katsarelis, Peter A.	S/Sgt.	G
Goss, Hubert A.	S/Sgt.	G
Hyk, John (NMI)	S/Sgt.	G

534th Bombardment Squadron

B-17F #42-3227 — "No Name"

Forkner, Hamden L.	1st Lt.	P
Kelly, Joseph A.	2nd Lt.	CP
Hyatt, Robert E.	2nd Lt.	N
Vincent, Edwin L.	1st Lt.	B
Shipe, Paul F.	S/Sgt.	E
Shattuck, Chester E.	S/Sgt.	RO
Stease, Ralph E.	S/Sgt.	G
Sobelewski, Edward F.	S/Sgt.	G
Horton, Harry H.	S/Sgt.	G
Chew, Lin F.	S/Sgt.	G

B-17F #42-30028 — "Sweet Le Lani"

Wright, Neil H., Jr.	2nd Lt.	P
Rogers, Jack W.	2nd Lt.	CP
Haverkamp, Clifford M.	2nd Lt.	N
Stracetenko, John M.	2nd Lt.	B

Allen, Earl R.	T/Sgt.	E
Sewell, Walter F.	S/Sgt.	RO
Egliski, Paul J.	Sgt.	G
Bingenheimer, Ralph F.	S/Sgt.	G
Hill, James R.	S/Sgt.	G
St. Michael, Wilfred	Sgt.	G

B-17F #42-29978 — "Hells Angel"

King, Reinhardt M.	1st Lt.	P
Peeples, Henry C.	1st Lt.	CP
Mc Glynn, Edward S.	2nd Lt.	N
Petrille, Francis A.	1st Lt.	B
Floura, Cecil L.	S/Sgt.	E
Unger, Maynard W.	T/Sgt.	RO
Pollard, Albert A.	S/Sgt.	G
Dwyer, Robert E.	S/Sgt.	G
Mann, Julius D.	S/Sgt.	G
Lyons, Joseph E.	S/Sgt.	G

B-17F #42-30245 — "Lady Luck", "Lucky Lady II"

Simpson, Weldon L.	1st Lt.	P
Agler, Elden H.	2nd Lt.	CP
Nee, William H.	1st Lt.	N
Roraback, Douglas C.	2nd Lt.	B
Warwick, Russell L.	T/Sgt.	E
Edwards, Robert I.	S/Sgt.	RO
Beech, Frank M.	S/Sgt.	G
Bassinger, Robin L.	S/Sgt.	G
Gregory, Paul A.	Sgt.	G
Beasley, Chester J.	S/Sgt.	G

535th Bombardment Squadron (H)

B-17F #42-3225 — "Chug-a-Lug-Lulu"

Disbrow, Lorin C.	1st Lt.	P
Chapin, Allen J.	2nd Lt.	CP
Jones, David R.	2nd Lt.	N
Gaydos, George (NMI)	2nd Lt.	B
Bruzewski, Otto F.	T/Sgt.	E
Moore, Thomas H.	T/Sgt.	RO
Walters, Joseph J.	S/Sgt.	G
Kiniklis, William P.	S/Sgt.	G
Moulton, John H.	S/Sgt.	G
King, Ernest C.	S/Sgt.	G

B-17F #42-3220 — "Damfino"

Smith, Harry M.	1st Lt.	P
Hawkins, Samuel J.	2nd Lt.	CP
Noonan, John P.	2nd Lt.	N
Gwinn, Lloyd W.	2nd Lt.	B
Lischike, Judd 0.	S/Sgt.	E
Jupin, John (NMI)	Sgt.	G
Elsberry, John V.	S/Sgt.	G
Blake, Harold L.	S/Sgt.	G
Colborn, Robert L.	S/Sgt.	G
Sylvester, Tony A.	T/Sgt.	RO

18 August 1943 — F/O Darrow and crew returned to this Station after being rescued from their ditching in the Channel. All appeared to be in good shape and certainly were being plied with questions from every side.

Capt. Dosier, MC, Epidemiologist from Surgeon's office, arrived at the Station during the morning. He was conducted thru the Consolidated Mess by Lt. Col. Reed and arrived at the hospital just before noon. His appearance it seems was due to request from Chief Surgeon's office, SOS, for help with our diarrhea outbreak.

The entire past history, i.e., outbreaks, food and water problems, mess halls, food handlers, etc., was rehashed (no pun intended). The water tank and well area was inspected. The Combat Mess was gone over, and the following difficulties noted: (a) wiping silverware with dishcloth, (b) handling of food with hands when unnecessary, (c) dirty tables in kitchen and in meat room.

The Consolidated Mess was gone over thoroughly and was thought to be lacking in several aspects. Deficiencies noted: (a) dirty floors, (b) dirty tables in kitchen, mess halls and meat room, (c) washing of mess tables with chlorine solution instead of hot, soapy water, (d) cooks without shaves, (e) dirty and long fingernails in food handler in more than half those present, (f) delay in emptying of waste causing flies to congregate, (g) dirty clothes on mess personnel.

Capt. Dosier feels the problem is not one of water, but of mess hall trouble in which the factors mentioned in the preceding paragraph are involved. He does not explain, however, the discrepancy between the reports from 1st Medical Laboratory, which shows *Coli-Aerogenes*, and those from 121st Station Hospital, which show none.

No operational mission today as most crews are on pass.

19 August 1943 — The Group participated in a raid over enemy territory late this afternoon, presumably over Holland. Seven ships were sent out, one aborted, and one failed to return. There were no injuries.

The loss of this latest (mixed-crew) ship seemed to have a depressing effect on the combat crewmen, presumably because it was supposed to be an "easy one."

The line of reasoning, I presume, is to the effect that if losses can be sustained on the simple ones, what chance does anyone have?

The crewmembers lost were as follows:

533rd Bombardment Squadron (H)

B-17F #42-3101 — "No Name"

Mangarpan, Joseph L.	2nd Lt.	P (CP)
O'Loughlin, Edward T.	2nd Lt.	B
Chester, Russell (NMI)	T/Sgt.	RO
Sabourin, Eugene A.	S/Sgt.	TG

535th Bombardment Squadron (H) (Same ship)

Koenig, Orlando H.	1st Lt.	P
Spivey, Leonard L.	1st Lt.	N
Perkins, Leo I.	T/Sgt.	TTG
Buran, Walter J.	S/Sgt.	BTG
Everett, Arthur L.	S/Sgt.	WG
Jones, Wilbert G.	S/Sgt.	WG

HTH powder was increased to ¾# in each side of the tank three times a day on 18 August. No testing set is available and it could not be tasted or smelled in samples. The additional supply produced desired results.

20 August 1943 — Mission scheduled for today was scrubbed. Part of crews are on pass, rest, relatively inactive as far as duty is concerned. One crew shows signs of being a bit tired and down in the mouth, but with exception of the Bombardier, is in good condition. The Bombardier was present when his former Navigator was injured and died rather quickly on a previous mission. Since then, I have learned intimations have been made that had he been on the ball, the man's life might have been saved. I personally reassured man the day following the accident that such was not the case, but apparently, it has been a factor. The whole crew is leaving on 48 hour pass and interview will be made on their return and disposition made then.

The men of the combat crews are as a whole depressed over the events of the past few days, as are the rest of us. Colonel Nazzaro gave them a talk this morning in which he stressed the aims of the Air Force, together with the situation of the enemy existent at this time, and the necessity or pursuing the effort.

In addition, considerable information of informative and military statistical value was given in order that crewmembers more clearly appreciate the entire picture. In addition, it was pointed out that their associates, now in the hands of the enemy, would certainly not appreciate our inactivity, in as much as each effort, though small, shortens their restriction. This produced a line of thought just not heretofor encountered and started new thinking and rationalization. It is my belief that with this new thought and the necessity for continuing the push, we will have little trouble. Unquestionably, any loss will be a costly one to the Group at this time. It, however, is a means to an end. I believe they will feel duty bound to do what ever they are called on to do.

21 August 1943 — No mission scheduled for today as weather is unfavorable. Crews seem to be picking up a little.

Mess hall has been inspected daily, 3 times at meal times by a medical officer assigned to that mess hall. In general, the situation has improved. There is still a great deal of difficulty in properly operating the dishwasher, that is, maintenance of high temperature, sufficient soap, and inspection and rejection of dirty plates. Garbage is still not hauled away promptly in all cases and maggots were found in one can today. It seems to be a process of continual checking and rechecking.

Water sample sent to 1st Medical Lab collected 9 August 1943 and four days in transit was reported bacteriologically potable.

No new outbreaks of diarrhea have occurred since the eleventh. A few sporadic cases, three I believe, have occurred and each was thought to be due to dietary indiscretion.

24 August 1943 — A raid over enemy occupied territory was conducted this date, in which the Group furnished 7 ships. One aborted and 5 returned. The sixth ran short of gas and landed on the coast, re-gassed and returned. No injuries. Target: Airfield and repair installations at Ville Coublet, France.

There has been an improvement in the morale after all ships returned. Many of the men show evidence of being quite tired, although still eager. A lessening of enthusiasm is noticed. Arrangements were completed to have a pilot, who ditched in the Channel, sent to 5th General Hospital for Narcosis therapy. He has become increasingly nervous with loss of sleep since the experience. He was flown down during the afternoon. Three officers were to leave for Bournemouth, the A.R.C. Officers Club, for 3 days rest, tomorrow. Six enlisted crewmembers are going to Montsford Manor tomorrow.

Lt. Col. T. L. Badger, MC, Chief of Medical Section, 5th General Hospital, visited the Station presumably to meet Colonel Tracy. He was conducted over the base, saw a few patients, and seemed to enjoy the visit.

25 August 1943 — No mission has been scheduled today. Five new crews who have recently arrived here are being flown locally.

Col. E.J. Tracy, MC, Surgeon, VIIIth Bomber Command, was a guest of the Station today. He was accompanied by Dr. Bronk, a technical advisor on General Grant's staff, for flying equipment problems. The colonel and the doctor were conducted over the Station and inspected the WAAF Site Infirmary and Station Hospital. The visitors ate the noon meal at the Airmen's Mess.

Lt. Vernon Chadwick, VC, inspected the Consolidated and Airmen's Messes this morning just before noon. In the Consolidated Mess, the dishes were extremely dirty and had the appearance of being washed in water not sufficiently hot and an inadequate quantity of soap.

The garbage cans at the Airmen's Mess were clean, but three had considerable quantity of bread that was perfectly edible. This waste was called to the attention of the mess sergeant, who explained it by stating that unless the K.P.'s were watched closely, they would throw bread away.

26 August 1943 — Raid scheduled for this morning was scrubbed after planes were off the ground and headed for the assembly point. All planes returned to base. Colonel White, DC, E.T.O. Dental Surgeon, and Major Reuter, DC, Eighth Air Force Dental Surgeon, visited the Station. The hospital was looked over and Dental Clinic inspected and photographed under Colonel White's direction. These officers were impressed with the improvised set up necessitated by lack of equipment.

27 August 1943 — Raid scheduled over northeastern France this afternoon for a 1700 hr. take off. Ten planes were sent out, none aborted, and ten returned. Light fighter and flak attack reported. Morale was high upon return. I believe the morale is increasing gradually now, and new crews are helping.

I am convinced that operational fatigue would not have been a problem for some time to come, were it not for the intensive loss. Up to that point I am sure there was no higher morale and spirit in the Air Force. The Schweinfurt raid was so ghastly from the severity of fighter attack, most personnel surviving feel they are living on borrowed time. It is impossible for them to see how any heavy aircraft could possibly get thru such a dense fighter attack. As time goes on and the tension eased thru comparatively easy missions, the situation is getting better. If the Group could be built up to strength in men and ships, I am sure the most rapid recovery would be produced. A half empty dining room is a rather sinister reminder.

31 August 1943 — In a raid over northern France this date, the Group sent a small number of planes. All returned from the mission, and there were no injuries.

2 September 1943 — A late afternoon raid was scheduled over enemy occupied France. This was scrubbed before reaching the French coast, and all planes returned.

There is a considerable improvement in morale during the past week. Operational flights have been comparatively easy and no casualties or losses resulted. This has increased the feeling of confidence a great deal. Lt. Baltrusaitis and crew returned from 7-day leave. The officers traveled south to Bournemouth on the South English coast. Reports of rest and recreation in large quantities came from all officers, who heartily indorse this club. These men appear refreshed, and have profited by the leave.

3 September 1943 — The Group participated in a raid over enemy occupied France this date, leaving the Base about 0600 hours. The return was made shortly after 1100 hours. Twenty-two ships went out, and 18 returned. A QSM was received from one ship, and 2 additional landed on coastal airdromes for gasoline. One ship is unaccounted for. It is believed 10 chutes were seen leaving the ship.

The following are the ship and crewmembers involved:

533rd Bomb Squadron (H)

B-17F #42-29789 — "Big Time Operator"

Zum, Benjamin J.	2nd Lt.	P
Hoover, Charles H.	2nd Lt.	CP
Willis, John W., Jr.	2nd Lt.	N
Clark, Luther C.	2nd Lt.	B
Italiano, Robert W.	T/Sgt.	TTG
Myers, Edwin R.	T/Sgt.	RO
Terry, Floyd H.	S/Sgt.	BTG
Bang, Charles F.	S/Sgt.	LWG
Crocittio, Frank J.	S/Sgt.	RWG
Christofero, Ferdinand	S/Sgt.	TG

Two crewmembers were wounded. Both were in the nose of the same ship, into which a small caliber bullet penetrated the nose. The navigator was injured by penetration of multiple fragments of the bullet into the lateral surface, left leg. The bombardier suffered a perforating wound of medial aspect, left hand, medial border, between the 5th metacarpal and medial aspect.

5 September 1943 — There have been no raids since September 3rd. Twenty-one aircraft were sent to raid a factory in Stuttgart, Germany, a round trip total of 1350 miles. Two Aircraft aborted, and eleven returned to this base on schedule. The remaining eight had landed because of fuel shortage and two ships crash landed in southern England. No crews were lost. There were no casualties.

Major Garfield P. Schnabel was relieved of his duties as Station Surgeon today, per SO 211, par. 4, Hq. VIIIth Bomber Command, dd 2 September 1943. Major Ernest (NMI) Gaillard, Jr. arrived at this Station and assumed command of the Medical Detachment this date, per authority contained in par. 5, SO 211 Hq. VIIIth Bomber Command, dd 2 September 1943.

7 September 1943 — Seventeen aircraft took off for Brussels, Belgium, target Airdrome. Two ships aborted, and the remaining 15 aircraft returned safe to Base with no casualties. A meeting of Medical Officers was held in the afternoon and the general policies of the department were outlined.

The following assignments were made:

Captain Pease	Medical Inspector
Captain Ralston	Venereal Disease Control Officer
Captain Dwyer	Respiratory Disease Control Officer
Lieutenant Fick	Detachment Commander

The chief deficiencies that have been found are: A lack of proper base sanitation partially due to inadequate equipment, and secondly the lack of training of the enlisted Medical Dept., both military and professional.

9 September 1943 — Twenty-one Aircraft from this group took off for a target airdrome at Leille, France. Two ships aborted, and the remaining returned safely to Base. There were two men wounded, namely:

Abramo, Nicholas J. ASN 11088698 — S/Sgt. 533rd Bombardment Sqdn. — BTG DIAGNOSIS: 1. Wound, penetrating, severe, right foot, entrance on the plantar surface of the foot over the distal heads of the 3rd, 4th, & 5th metatarsals. The wound is 1¼" in length on the plantar surface and a pinpoint wound of the dorsal surface, 1" proximal to the metatarsal phalangeal joint. 2. Accidentally incurred while on an operational mission over enemy territory by flak, low velocity, about 0830 hours, 9 September. 1943 (The foreign body (flak) can be palpated in the wound on the dorsal surface of the foot). "H"

Dill, Marvin E. ASN O-739077 — 2nd Lt. — 533rd Bombardment Sqdn. — CP — DIAGNOSIS: 1. Wound, penetrating, mild, anterior, at the level of 4th rib, left, mild, clavicular, accidentally incurred by flak, low velocity while on an operational mission over enemy territory 0810 hours, 9 September 1943. 2. Abrasion, mild, face, one inch anterior to left ear, at temporal region, accidentally incurred as in #1. Removal of piece of flak 1/8" in length under Novocain anesthesia 1% 2 cc on 9 September 1943 @ 1200 hours.

One ship returned with sixty flak holes and a rudder cable shot away. No casualties aboard this ship — returned safely.

Captain Wymer was appointed Medical Liaison Equipment Officer and Captain Bland appointed Director of Training of Medical Detachment.

Major Shuler, 1st Wing Surgeon, visited this date and was especially concerned over passes for crewmembers and stated that the 381st was at the bottom of statistical list in number of leaves granted and he also remarked that crews completing 15 or more missions should automatically get a week of leave or a similar period at a rest home.

The Clerk of Works discussed water and sewage systems and a series of bacteriological reports on the potability of the water. The effluent from the sewage system is to be measured daily by this office and when sufficient data has accumulated, a report will be made to the RAF Section Officer.

Colonel Reed was informed of the stagnant creek that begins opposite Base Utilities and extending down to the sewage disposal system and stated that he would make corrections according to recommendation.

15 September 1943 — Nineteen aircraft took off at 1515 hours today for a raid on an Airdrome at Romilly-sur-Seine, France. Two of the Aircraft aborted. There were no ships lost. The mission was eventful in that it was the first time in the history of this group that the Aircraft carried external bombs. Two 1,000-pounders were carried on the outside and the total bomb load was 8,000 pounds — the heaviest load yet carried. The ships returned to the Airfield after dark and used the night lighting facilities for the first time. The destruction of the hangars at their target Airdrome was considered satisfactory. There were no wounded or killed. Three ships returned to England and landed safely at an RAF Airdrome in southern England, and the remainder returned safely to this base.

16 September 1943 — Twenty aircraft as part of the 121st Combat Wing had as a target a ship in the river at Nantes, France. The mission was considered unsuccessful. Two ships aborted and the remaining returned safely to this Airdrome. The wounded and their injuries are as follows:

Downey, Martin H. — 2nd Lt. — ASN O-741976 — CP —
DIAGNOSIS: Wound, lacerated, moderate severity, right forearm, involving posterio lateral surface, middle 1/3, 3½ inches long, and involving skin subcutaneous tissue, fascia, and muscle. Accidentally incurred by flak of low velocity while on operational mission over enemy territory about 1500 hours, this date. WIA (121st Station Hospital) (534th Sqdn.).

Milligan, Walter F. — T/Sgt. — ASN 31151221 — G —
DIAGNOSIS: 1. Wound, penetrating, severe, at outer aspect or middle third of rt. thigh, high velocity 20mm shell sustained over enemy occupied territory 16 September 1943. 2. Wound, penetrating, high velocity, at the lower back region at level of the crest of ilium, severe, sustained as above. 3. Wound, penetrating, multiple, moderate severity, low velocity, outer aspect of dorsum of rt. ankle sustained as above. (121st Station Hosp.) (533rd Sqdn.).

Horne, Emery M. — S/Sgt. — ASN 36235728 — G — 533rd Sqdn. —
DIAGNOSIS: 1. Abrasion, mild, middle and lateral surface or right thigh, 2 inches long, accidentally incurred by flak of low velocity while on operational mission. 2. Wound, lacerated, mild, right mid-lumbar region, accidentally incurred as in #1. "Duty"

Paterno, Vincent A. — S/Sgt. — ASN 32458421 — G — 533rd Sqdn. —
DIAGNOSIS: 1. Wound, perforating, severe, right shoulder, entrance at the upper and lateral border of scapula and exit at the anterior border of deltoid at upper 1/3 of humerus, accidentally incurred by MGB while on operational mission over enemy territory about 1630 hours, 16 September 1943. 2. Wounds, penetrating, mild, multiple, of right arm, accidentally incurred as in #1. (121st. Station Hospital)

The difficulties encountered in their evacuation were overcrowding at the ships during the evacuation aid lack of sufficient number or Medical Department soldiers to handle litters and give necessary aid, etc. We will attempt to "obliviate" this in the future by having four men assigned to each ambulance and each man will wear a Red Cross brassard for identification as medical personnel by the Military Police.

Visitors to the Medical Department included Lt. Colonel Hatcher, CO of the 121st Station Hospital, Braintree, Lt. Colonel Rogers, Chief of Surgical Service, and Lt. Howard, ANC, Chief of Nursing Service. They seemed very favorably impressed with the station and stated that they were more acutely aware of the function of a bomb group and in particular the Medical problems that confront us.

Lt. Clark, SC, Eastern base section, was here to inspect the sewage disposal system and a sample of the effluent was sent there.

Lt. Chadwick, VC, Station 169 made a sanitary inspection of the messes with Captain Pease, expressing satisfaction as to our sanitary condition. The medical department recommended basic changes in the field ration we are now receiving. It suggested that a higher protein and lower carbohydrate diet be supplied.

A dance at the Officers Club was held in the evening and we met for the first time Medical Officers and nurses from the Station Hospital at Acton.

17 September 1943 — There was a briefing of crews at 1000 hours and the mission was scrubbed at 1200 hours. The target was…and that's about it — it was.

Captain Arthur Briggs reported to Capt. Bland and stated that he did not wish to go on the mission. He further stated that he had had ideas of homicide and suicide.

Since the Schweinfurt raid on 17 August, Capt. Briggs states he has not slept well and feels that the odds are overwhelmingly against the individual in raids over German territory. He was interviewed by me, he was quite introspective and down cast, quiet, and stated that he had no desire what-so-ever to get near a B-17 and that he was not equal to going on this raid.

It is rather hard to decide whether it was feeling for personal safety or the weight of the responsibility of leading the Group into combat that was responsible for his attitude. It was pointed out to him that he was one of the leaders in the Group and that personnel looked to him for direction and guidance, and, further, that personal failure on his part would have a disastrous effect upon the Squadron and very likely upon the Group as a whole. He finally agreed somewhat reluctantly to go to the briefing.

The Group Surgeon spoke to Colonel Nazzaro and gave him the gist of the conversation outlined above and the Colonel put the issue of going on the mission squarely up to Captain Briggs, who agreed to go much easier than would have been anticipated. It is the feeling of myself and Captain Bland that another mission is indicated to restore confidence (Capt. Briggs has had 7 missions to date — 2 since Schweinfurt) and that following the mission a period of rest is indicated. It is also our feeling that unless this procedure is carried out, Captain Briggs will be lost to us as a combat flier. In the meantime, we are going to do our utmost to insure adequate sleep.

A meeting of the Medical Department enlisted men was held and the recommendation that four men would be assigned to ambulances to evacuate wounded returning from missions was made and that another table be placed in the treatment room for the care of casualties. Brassards will be worn by Ambulance personnel on the airdrome.

The other subjects discussed were the cleaning and pressing establishment, medical recreation room, medical department dance, and discipline. The medical department men are commended on the efficient manner of handling casualties on yesterday's raid.

19 September 1943 — Lt. Colonel Ralph L. Wicks, Flight Surgeon of the 65th Fighter Wing and Major W.P. Bunting, Group Surgeon of the 385th Bomb Group in Great Ashfield visited the Detachment.

20 September 1943 — The staff attended a medical meeting and a symposium on toxic hepatitis at 121st Station Hospital, Braintree. The chief things of interest were that the diseases that we have called infectious jaundice and the jaundice resulting from arsenic injection were felt to be the same disease entities. The disease is thought to be due to a virus.

It has been transmitted by nasal solutions, by respiratory droplet, and by saline emulsions from autopsied livers. Its incidence has increased in wartime and in periods of economic stress, and is felt to be due in part, at least, to a decrease in the protein content. The treatment that was advocated was the use of fairly large amounts of casein digest, which when given early seems to ameliorate the disease considerably. In the case of the arsenical hepatitis, it is felt that the amino acid radicals were used to detoxify the arsenic; consequently, high protein diet is indicated for the luetic patient.

22 September 1943 — Major Gaillard and Captain Bland attended a meeting of the E.T.O. Medical Society at the 67th General Hospital at Taunton. The topics discussed were on low back pain, fractures of the femur, line of duty, fetal circulation, knee joint derangements, dyspepsia, transfusion in the field, some 'cardiovascular concepts for military service, and last, the use of penicillin in the treatment of gonorrhea. We were somewhat disappointed in the professional side of the meeting. A number of medical officers were transported to and from the meeting by air, which we feel is a good liaison policy.

At 1915 hours, a plane was seen to explode in the air, northwest of this Station. Captain Pease and Lieut. Cohler with three ambulances left immediately for the site of the crashed plane, which was located at Poplar Farm about 8 miles northwest of the field.

The plane was an RAF Stirling, which had previously taken off for a combat mission from Hundon Plough Airdrome. The plane and its occupants were spread over an area of approximately 500 yards and parts of the burning plane hit a nearby farmhouse, causing a severe fire of the house. In the midst of the burning incendiary bombs and unexploded 1,000-pound bombs, the members of this station proceeded to evacuate the bodies of the RAF personnel of the plane. One member of the plane who was lying on a piece of fuselage was still alive, although unconscious, severely injured, and has an apparent skull fracture. He was immediately evacuated and taken by the RAF ambulance to an RAF hospital in Cambridge. His condition at present is unknown. Five other members of the crew, all dead, also turned over to the RAF personnel. The cause of the crash was not determined.

23 September 1943 — Eleven Aircraft from this group, flying as part of the combat wing, attacked shipping and docks at Nantes, France with good results. Of the twenty that took off for the mission, six were unable to find the rendezvous point, there were two abortions, and one aircraft went over the target with another group. All of the aircraft returned and there was only one wounded in action:

1st Lt. Frank Shimek — O-736034 — N — 532nd Bombardment Sqdn. — DIAGNOSIS: 1. Wound, penetrating, mild, lacerated at junction of middle and lower right leg. "Q"

26 September 1943 — Twenty aircraft from this command left the field at 1445 hours to attack aircraft factory north west of Paris, France. Two aircraft returned before crossing the channel. The remaining 18 returned with full bomb load because of poor visibility. The following men were wounded:
S/Sgt. Harold W. Harrington — 535th Bombardment Sqdn. — DIAGNOSIS: 1. Frostbite, mild, tips of right thumb, index, & middle fingers, 2. Reason: Filter valve on oxygen bottle froze on refilling, and was using bale out. On getting bottle back into turret, lead cord on heating unit became severed.

Channell, John S. — Sgt. — 535th Bombardment Sqdn. — DIAGNOSIS: 1. Frostbite, 2nd deg. chin, and both cheeks, malar region. 2. Reason: Oxygen mask froze to face.

S/Sgt. Hubert L. Greene — 533rd Bombardment Sqdn. — DIAGNOSIS: 1. Frostbite, slight, right upper cheek.

S/Sgt. Charles L. Carter — 534th Bombardment Sqdn. — DIAGNOSIS: 1. Frostbite, severe, lower left jaw.

S/Sgt. Alex Pszalgowski — 532nd Bombardment Sqdn. — DIAGNOSIS: 1. Frostbite, 2nd degree area, central right mandible, & 1st deg. right malar region.

The combat wing was led by Colonel Nazzaro and Lieutenant Colonel Dunlop today.

27 September 1943 — The target was Emden, Germany and the M.P.I. was the center of town near the shipping facilities. Nineteen aircraft from this command participated, with one abortion. Seventeen aircraft returned safely to the base on schedule and the eighteenth landed at Great Ashfield, Suffolk, and with wounded aboard. The ship was hit by many fighters just beyond the target area.

The two waist gunners stated that the aircraft, which hit them, came in level and between the fields of fire of the waist guns and the tail guns. The time of injury was approximately 1010 hours. Major Gaillard and Captain Bland went to Great Ashfield, and upon arrival, S/Sgt. James W. Dunn was in impending shock. His history is as follows:

Wounded 1010 hours, morphine gms. ½ at 1015 hours, morphine gms. ½ at 1025 hours. The wound was dressed and sulfanilamide laced in the wound by the other waist gunner, who himself was wounded. The ship landed at 1200 hours and at 1230 hours, plasma was started, and at 1515 hours, S/Sgt. Dunn had received 750 cc of plasma. It was felt that he was now safe to transport to the 12th Evacuation Hospital at Botesdale. Supporting treatment was continued at the hospital and an additional 500 cc of plasma was administered. The X-Ray revealed a large metal fragment behind the head of the right femur and a comminuted fracture of the right ischial tuberosity. Operation at 1830 hours by Major Willie Meyer.

The wound of the left thigh entered on the anterior surface about the junction of the middle and lower third and extended upward almost to the lower groin. A huge amount of tissue was devitalized. The scrotal portion of the spermatic cord and the left testicle were exposed and the shell, apparently continuing through the perineum, avulsed larger amounts of tissue, including the posterior 5 cm of the urethra, the urethral bulb, and the left lateral ¼ of the sphincter ani. A loop colostomy and & supra-pubic cystotomy were performed. The wound of the thigh was debrided. The left spermatic cord and testicle were removed, and an attempt was made to restore the urethra, but there was still a large deficit of tissue.

The anus and sphincter ani were widely opened at the site or damage. The fragment of shell and several pieces of bone were removed from the right ischium. The amount of destruction was tremendous. The wounds were sprinkled with 10 gms. of sulfanilamide powder, and dressed with Vaseline gauze and pressure dressings. In addition, 250 cc of plasma was administered and donors were typed for transfusion. His condition at the end of the operation was fair.

The other patient, Sgt. John J. Crawbuck, 534th Bombardment Squadron, was in the following condition:

The large wound, which was approximately 4 cm x 4 cm, was located between the anterior and superior spine and the trochanter of the right femur and was found to connect with the shell fragment that was located about 12 cm posteriorly in the right buttock. The tract was laid open, debrided, and packed open with sulfanilamide 5 grm. and Vaseline gauze.

The following named men were also wounded as a result of this mission:

2nd Lieut. Richard E. Rylands — 534th Bombardment Sqdn. —
DIAGNOSIS: 1. Abrasion mild, anterior, and lateral 1/3 of right leg. Caused by flak hitting ship and fragments of ship resulting in the abrasion.

Capt. Norman C. MacKay — 534th Bombardment Sqdn. —
DIAGNOSIS: 1. Abrasions, mild, lacerated on the left arm, middle 1/3 lateral surface and middle of left buttock. Caused by fragments from ship due to explosion of flak.

Sgt. Daniel A. Vina — 534th Bomb Sqdn. —
DIAGNOSIS: 1. Laceration of forehead, mild.

S/Sgt. Dean F. Sword — 534th Bomb Sqdn. —
DIAGNOSIS: 1. Frostbite, mod. severity of distal phalanx, 1st, 2nd, 3rd, toes of right and left foot.

Sgt. Mike S. Feller — 534th Bomb Sqdn. —
DIAGNOSIS: 1. Frostbite, distal phalanx, index finger, rt. hand, mild

Sgt. Joseph O. Long — 535th Bomb Sqdn. —
DIAGNOSIS: 1. Frostbite, tip of ring finger, right hand, 1st deg. Reason: None determined. Extreme cold. No equipment or personnel failure.

Sgt. Asa K. Burch — 534th Bomb Sqdn. —
DIAGNOSIS: 1. Frostbite, mild, face, right maxillary region. "D"

S/Sgt. George J. Tappero — 534th Sqdn. —
DIAGNOSIS: 1. Frostbite, mild, distal phalanx, 3rd finger, left hand.

2 October 1943 — Twenty aircraft from this base took off at 1345 hours for the second attack on Emden, Germany. Two aircraft aborted, the remaining eighteen went over the target, and returned safely home. There were no wounded or killed. For the second time, the Forts had a P-47 escort all the way. The mission was further remarkable in that Flak Suits were worn for the first time. An estimated 80% of the crewmembers wore the suits and experienced satisfaction with them. Others used them as anti-flak pads around the bottom of the airplane. The bombs were dropped on a pathfinder outfit through a 10,000-foot overcast.

Most of the Bombardiers and Navigators felt that time calculations the bombing was reasonably accurate. The air temperature at the bombing altitude, 22,000 feet, was –24° C. There were no frostbites.

Just before the flight, a tail gunner, S/Sgt. Clarence M. Jones, 534th Bombardment Squadron, became hysterical and refused to go on the mission. He had had six previous missions and his reactions seemed to be a profound emotional upset.

One thing that has impressed me is the impersonal attitude of the combat crews to their work. They seem to feel neither hate nor pity for the enemy. Their chief group reaction seems to be a healthy respect for the potentialities of aerial combat, and they direct their bombing and fighter attacks almost without emotion, and very much in the manner that a problem would be attacked in civil life.

4 October 1943 — Twenty-one aircraft took of at approximately 0700 hours for a mission. There were nine abortions, but 12 aircraft continued to the target, which was the center of the city of Frankfurt, Germany. Most of the aircraft aborted after being over the continent. The remaining aircraft completed the mission. We had no injured, but there were two cases of frostbite.

S/Sgt. William E. Abbott — 12154049 —533rd Bombardment Squadron received frostbite to the neck, 1st degree, and Sgt. Clyde C, Draa, 35301488 — 534th Bombardment Squadron received frostbite, mild to face, left side. He was put to duty, but Sgt. Abbott was admitted to Quarters.

From a group standpoint, bombing results were considered good.

At approximately 0600 hours, there was a head-on collision on the perimeter track at the south end of the north-south runway. M/Sgt. Victor A. Cottinger, 532nd Bomb Squadron, was driving a weapons carrier and Pvt. Robert Sabatina, 1142nd M.P. Company, was driving a command car. There were six men injured in the accident and were treated at sick quarters. Two men, M/Sgt. Cottinger, and Pvt. Harold M. Silvious, 553rd Bomb Squadron, were evacuated to 121st Station Hospital. S/Sgt. Robert (NMI) Miller, and Cpl. Armano I. Nicola, both in 553rd Bomb Squadron, were admitted to Station Sick Quarters. The other two men were returned to duty.

M/Sgt. Cottinger was sent to 121st Station Hospital, Braintree by ambulance after receiving first aid at Station Sick Quarters. About 1300 hours, he was flown by Fortress from this base, from Andrews Field to 49th Station Hospital, Diddington, Hunts. for surgical treatment by a neurosurgical team.

Two Medical Officers, Captain Milton H. Bland, and Captain George J. Pease, attended the Staff Meeting at 121st Station Hospital, Braintree, today.

8 October 1943 — A status board showing the combat crews and medical personnel has been obtained. It is black, covered with Plexiglas, and show's organization, position on crew, and number of the crew for each of the four squadrons. It also shows the organizations included in the medical department.

The new wing to the sick quarters was opened this date and is being used as an officer's ward.

Twenty-one aircraft from this station took off at 1200 hours — Target: Bremen, Germany. The ships returned at approximately 1730 hours. Seven aircraft were missing, and personnel included in these ships is as follows:

532nd Bombardment Squadron (H)

B-17F #42-29854 — "Old Flak Sack"

Sample, Arthur M.	1st Lt.	P
Cytarzynski, Edward A.	2nd Lt.	CP
Moore, Robert V.	S/Sgt	B
Ballou, Howard	Sgt.	TTG
Heintz, Warren G.	T/Sgt.	RO
Olson, Melvin J.	S/Sgt.	BTG
Grayson, William H.	S/Sgt.	RWG
Forbes, James R.	S/Sgt.	LWG
Johnston, George R	S/Sgt.	TG
*MacKay, Norman C.	Capt.	N

*This Capt. is in 534th Bomb Sqdn., but was flying position of Navigator on this crew.

B-17F #42-30009 — "Feather Merchant"

Pry, Jack S.	1st Lt.	P
Quinley, Cecil J.	2nd Lt.	CP
Burwell, Roger W.	2nd Lt.	N
Snyder, Theodore F.	2nd Lt.	B
LaPointe, Edward R.	T/Sgt.	TTG
Frautschi, Russell H.	T/Sgt.	RO
Smith, Irvin W.	S/Sgt.	BTG
Baird, Carl L.	S/Sgt.	BTG
Johnson, Alfred A.	S/Sgt.	LWG
Brandt, Martin D.	S/Sgt.	TG

533rd Bombardment Squadron (H)

B-17F #42-29765 — "Nip & Tuck"

Hartje, James W.	2nd Lt.	P
Jerome, Joseph C.	2nd Lt.	CP
Norton, Edgar O.	2nd Lt.	N
Chanault, Joseph P.	2nd Lt.	B
Kaseman, Eugene W.	S/Sgt.	TTG
LaPlace, Gerald G.	S/Sgt.	RO
Boykin, Clayton M.	S/Sgt.	BTG
Swackhamer, Edward A.	S/Sgt.	RWG
Czyz, Edward (NMI)	Sgt.	LWG
Sieber, Arthur T.	S/Sgt.	TG

534th Bombardment Squadron (H)

B-17F #42-30722 — "Bobby T"

Lishon, Dexter (NMI)	Capt.	P
Long, Carlton H.	2nd Lt.	CP
Gluck, Robert (NMI)	1st Lt.	N
Rokosa, Phillip V.	2nd Lt.	B
Johnson, Canute M.	T/Sgt.	TTG
Riddle, Lloyd C.	T/Sgt.	RO
Madison, Clarence D.	S/Sgt.	BTG
Stuart, George A.	S/Sgt.	RWG
Schnaltzer, John J.	S/Sgt.	LWG
Marques, William J.	S/Sgt.	TG

535th Bombardment Squadron (H)

B-17F #42-30864 — "No Name"

Ingenhutt, William W.	Major	SP
Cormany, William F., Jr.	1st Lt.	CP
Frost, Edwin D.	1st Lt.	N
Black, Robert C.	1st Lt.	B
Roeder, Robert R.	T/Sgt.	RWG
Miller, Earl F.	T/Sgt.	TTG
O'Hara, James J.	S/Sgt.	BTG
Smith, Richard W.	S/Sgt.	RWG
Dwyer, James J.	S/Sgt.	LWG
Weninger, Robert L.	S/Sgt.	TG

B-17F #42-29941 — "Tarfu & T.S. Too"

Manchester, Edwin R.	Capt.	P
Jukes, Elton D.	Capt.	CP
Smith, Marvin L.	1st Lt.	N
Moore, Keith D.	1st Lt.	B
Darrington, Lorenzo M.	T/Sgt.	RO
O'Donnel, James J.	T/Sgt.	TTG
Tucker, Arthur L.	S/Sgt.	BTG
McCook, Wade (NMI)	S/Sgt.	TG
Budzik, Anthony L.	S/Sgt.	RWG
Berk, Mathew, (NMI)	S/Sgt.	LWG

B-17F #42-3123 — "Ron-Chee"

Kemp, Leslie A.	1st Lt.	P
Heim, William C.	2nd Lt.	CP
Tomlin, Frank E.	2nd Lt.	N
Nelson, Thomas B.	2nd Lt.	B
Richards, Walter L.	S/Sgt.	RO
Jennette, Arthur F.	T/Sgt.	TTG
Gentry, Gilles E.	S/Sgt.	BTG
Osborn, Edward F.	S/Sgt.	TG

Duffy, Raymond V.	S/Sgt.	LWG
Stinsman, James	S/Sgt.	RWG

Of those ships returning, several were badly damaged and "Tinkertoy" ground-looped just off the runway. "Tinkertoy" had her nose shot out and the pilot, 1st Lieut. William J. Minerich had his head blown off by a 20mm cannon shell. There was hardly a square inch of the entire cockpit that was not covered with blood and brain tissue. One half of his face and a portion of his cervical vertebra were found just in front of the bomb bay. The decapitation was complete. The co-pilot, 2nd Lieut. Thomas D. Sellers is certainly deserving of any award that may be given him for his heroic work in bringing the ship back to the base. The Bombardier and Navigator, 2nd Lieut. Henry J. Palas (B) and 2nd Lieut. James E. Stickel (N), were also slightly wounded and frost bitten. The tail gunner on Lieut. Miller's crew, S/Sgt. Stephen J. Klinger, 32550635, 534th Bomb Squadron, was killed in action. His diagnosis is as follows:

1. Wound, perforating, midline of neck, about 2" in diameter involving the trachea and great vessels of the left side of neck. Incurred by low velocity bullet at approximately 1430 hours. 2. Compound fracture of upper 1/3 of forearm, wound of entrance about 1" in diameter. Incurred by low velocity missile, as in #1. KILLED IN ACTION.

After this mission, in visiting the many crews right after they hit the ground, the tense excitement of many was apparent and in many cases was borderline hysteria. An effort was made to massively sedate a large number of the crewmembers, and it seemed to work quite satisfactorily. This was the roughest mission experienced in some time and most of the personnel seemed to feel the losses keenly. At the briefing the morning of October 9th, most of those who had received the 6 grains of Sodium Amytal were in much better shape those who had not. However, there were 2 cases of dizziness and headache, which we attributed to the Sodium Amytal. The medical department ran into a little difficulty in the administering of this sedation, but we hope to be able to explain the value of the procedure to the satisfaction of the command.

The morale of the crews remains good. We are all looking forward to the day when we can have long-range fighter escort. There were 30 B-17's lost by the Eighth Air Force on this raid and an estimated 145 enemy fighters destroyed.

9 October 1943 — At 1200 hours, this date, 16 B-17's from this command took off with the target a Focke-Wulfe factory at Anklam, Germany. The target is thought to be destroyed. The greater part of the flight was over the North Sea and three aircraft failed to return to the base.

The missing in action are:

*532nd Bombardment Squadron (H)

Liming, Max E.	2nd Lt.	CP

Taormina, Anthony P.	2nd Lt.	N
Morgan, John B.	2nd Lt.	B
Teal, Gordon, (NMI)	T/Sgt.	TTG

533rd Bombardment Squadron (H)

B-17F #42-30012 — "No Name"

Hendricks, Landon C.	Major	P
Withers, Robert L.	Capt.	CP
Duggan William P.	2nd Lt.	TG
Turner, William T.	Capt.	N
English, Leo K.	Capt.	B
McNeil, Charles C.	T/Sgt.	TTG
Wildbridge, John M.	T/Sgt.	RO
Arbiter, Jerome	S/Sgt.	BTG
Howard, Lord A.	S/Sgt.	RWG
O'Hara, Ernest A.	S/Sgt.	LWG

*Story concerning these four men follows under this date.

533rd Bombardment Squadron (H)

B-17F #42-3180 — "Forget Me Not II"

Carqueville, Herbert	1st Lt.	P
Parsons, Robert R.	2nd Lt.	CP
Smith, Charles Hale	2nd Lt.	N
Cunningham, Thomas J.	1st Lt.	B
Geroulo, Vito J.	T/Sgt.	RO
Kaputska, John B.	T/Sgt.	TTG
Embardo, James J.	S/Sgt.	BTG
Greene, Elburn L.	S/Sgt.	LWG
Fox, Anthony F.	S/Sgt.	RWG
Horne, Emery M.	S/Sgt.	TG

534th Bombardment Squadron (H)

B-17F #42-29958 — "Battlin' Bombsprayer"

Loftin, James L.	1st Lt.	P
Cornell, Chester E.	2nd Lt.	CP
Beckerman, Hyman (NMI)	2nd Lt.	N
Czarny, Stanley J.	2nd Lt.	B
Kwoka, Leon J.	T/Sgt.	TTG
Silverberg, Charles G.	T/Sgt.	RO
Cyrek, Eugene E.	S/Sgt.	BTG
Huhn, Allen O.	S/Sgt.	WG
Nader, Joseph C.	T/Sgt.	WG
Alford, Allan T.	S/Sgt.	TG

Lieutenant Loftin's crew was seen to parachute over Denmark. Lieutenant Carqueville's left the formation somewhere in enemy territory. Major Hendricks was on his return trip over the North Sea, and apparently felt he was out of the fighter zone and left the formation. He was jumped by fighters and was seen to lose altitude rapidly, and estimates of four to six chutes were seen to leave the plane. Some crews reported the aircraft ditched and one crew reported the ship that the ship exploded just before it hit the water. However, it should be pointed out that the aircraft were flying at approximately 13,000 feet, and assuming that Major Hendrick's aircraft was in control, the distance between the formation and the ship as it reached sea level would be at least 20 - 30 miles, consequently, the accuracy of the observation may be questioned.

Just as the formation was reaching the Danish coast, a 20 mm cannon shell exploded in the cockpit of Lieut. Winter's ship and Lieut. Winters was temporarily stunned or blinded by the flash. When he came to, the Bombardier and Navigator had already left the ship, the co-pilot was jumping, and one of the crewmembers gave him a farewell salute jumped. (These are the four men listed in the previous page) The ship was in a steep gliding turn and there was a fire in the rear of the cockpit. Lieut. Winters righted the ship, put on the AFCE (Automatic Pilot) went back and put out the fire, and brought the ship safely back to England, landing at another base. He suffered a mild flash burn of the face. He was the only one in the forward part of the ship, and the courage, determination and skill that he displayed has been the basis for recommendation of a high military award.

In the last two days, this group has lost ten aircraft and many old crews and the effect has been demoralizing to the staff and to the combat crews. We all feel these losses very keenly and smiles and apparent cheerfulness are forced, and everyone is quite well aware of the others' feelings. The loss of the two squadron commanders, Major Ingenhutt and Major Hendricks, has especially affected us, both from the standpoint of morale and the standpoint of administration.
Four men received injuries on this raid:

2nd Lt. Donald R. Frieze, 532nd Squadron — received penetrating wound, external surface, left hand. "D"

Sgt. Clyde C. Drea, 534th Squadron — suffered two mild abrasions to forehead, and abrasions to index and fourth finger of left hand. "D"

Sgt. Michael S. Feller, 534th Squadron — received a mild burn, cervical region, behind angle of jaw, and contusion, mild over the middle of right clavicle. "D"

S/Sgt. Salvatore (NMI) Bozzette, 532nd Squadron — suffered wounds, penetrating, multiple, moderate severity, about 3 mm in diameter, 3 on right thigh, one on left thigh, 2 on forearm one on left cervical region, one on left lower chest, 1 left inguinal region, by fragments of exploding 20mm cannon. "Q"

10 October 1943 — Despite the punishment the Group had taken in the raids of October 7th, 8th, and 9th, eight aircraft were in commission on the 10th and took off at 1130 hours in an exceedingly heavy fog and haze and with the city

Münster, Germany as the destination. Lt. Colonel Dunlop and Lt. Colonel Terry were in the lead. The target was squarely hit. Six aircraft returned to this base safely and two aircraft landed elsewhere. There was one man wounded:

S/Sgt. Andrew C. Schnitzler, 35333448 — 534th Bombardment Squadron.
DIAGNOSIS: 1. Wound, multiple, mild of neck, posterior, WIA "H"

A number of the ships were badly shot up, and Lt. Clore's ship had two holes blown in the radio compartment and in taxing around the dispersal site, the radio operator and waist gunner had their heads stuck through the holes and were grinning like monkeys. They apparently had adequate reason to be happy.

There is an interesting story of anoxia, and from a medical viewpoint, it is doubtful that the narrative is correct. Vance, William F., 17042400 — T/Sgt. 24th mission, tube broke from O_2 bottle to turret when turret was cranked down when plane was airborne. Split at first. Tried to tape it without success. Tried to use bailout bottles. Passed out at enemy coast at 20,000 feet — out for 2 hours. Recovered at 20,000 feet on way back. Was at 25,000 and then down. Was out completely for a while. Later could hear pounding, but couldn't do anything about it. Eventually recovered enough to open turret after using fresh bailout bottle. Lay on floor in radio room. Landed at Wendling, went to hospital and got white pill, (EM gave it) and returned here (the sergeant showed no ill effects when he reported here–fishy). The mental attitude and morale of the crews is the lowest that has yet been observed.

13 October 1943 — Captain Briggs informed the commanding officer that he had no desire to continue flying. His case history, as written Captain Ralston and myself is attached. (see page entries after 03 November) Captain Briggs has been sent to the Central Medical Board as per directives pertaining to combat crew failures (see also note in diary, under entry for 17 September 1943, paragraph 2).

14 October 1943 — Crews were briefed at 0700 hours and the target was the ball-bearing works at Schweinfurt, Germany. The mention of the word "Schweinfurt" shocked the crews completely. It will be recalled that on 17 August 1943, this group lost so heavily on this same target. Also conspicuous by its omission was the estimated number of enemy fighters based along the route.

Upon checking with S-2 later, it was found that this omission was <u>intentional</u> and that the entire German fighter force of some 1100 fighter aircraft was based within 85 miles of the course. The implications are obvious. I went around to the crews to check our equipment, sandwiches, coffee, etc., the crews were scared, and it was obvious that many doubted they would return. We did get a break in that we didn't go over the target in our ordered sequence and the outfits that went on in the position we were supposed to occupy lost heavily. The radio this morning stated that 60 B-17's were lost on this operation.

There were three abortions in our group, and in our combat wing that went over the target, there were only 30 aircraft and a minimum of 40 is deemed almost mandatory. Someone must have held us by the hand.

Takeoff time was 1035 hours. The planes returned at 1730 hours. We were the only airdrome in the 1st division that was open and we expected to receive the entire division, but fortunately at the last minute, other airdromes opened and we received only a few ships from other bases. One ship failed to return. The wounded were as follows:

Missing in action:

533rd Bomb Squadron (H)

B-17F #42-29803 — "No Name" (MACR #1037 – Lt. Yorba's crew – not found in the body of this diary, however, unearthed later (see Reports & Endnotes)).

532nd Bombardment Squadron

Smith, Emmett E. — S/Sgt. —
DIAGNOSIS: 1. Wound, penetrating of thigh, right, junction of lower and middle third, anterior surface caused by exploding 20mm cannon shell. WIA "D"

533rd Bombardment Squadron (H)

Jones, Harmer L. — O-738851 — 2nd Lt.
DIAGNOSIS: 1. Wound, lacerated, nose, left side of bridge, severe. 2. Fracture, compound, comminuted, nose, severe. 3. Contusion, right infra orbital, mod. severe. WIA (flak) "H"

534th Bombardment Squadron (H)

Weaver, LeRoy C. — 17055170 — S/Sgt. —
DIAGNOSIS: 1. Contusion, moderate severity, left leg, distal one third, accidentally incurred by catching leg in ball turret of ship. 2. Abrasion, mild, left ankle, anterior surface, accidentally incurred as in #1.

535th Bombardment Squadron (H)

Dittus, Carl W. — O-736629 — 2nd Lt. —

DIAGNOSIS: 1. Wound, lacerated, 2" in length, moderate severity inner aspect, lower 1/3 forearm, left. Caused by 20mm cannon shell. WIA "D"

413th Bombardment Squadron (H), 96th Bomb Group

White, Alan V. — 32509907— S/Sgt. —
DIAGNOSIS: 1. Wound, penetrating, mild, posterior aspect, right thigh, midline 2½" above popliteal...caused by flak, low velocity.

Two ships ground-looped on their return. There were no injuries.

Lt. Yorba's crew went down in German territory after the target. Lt. Hutchins had extreme difficulty in bringing his ship back to England and finally landed down south several hours after the other ships had landed.

Berry, James L. — 35335115 — S/Sgt. —
DIAGNOSIS: 1. Wound, penetrating, scalp, frontal portion, 1" long, mod. severity, caused by flak.   2. Frostbite, mod. sev. 2nd. deg. involving all terminal phalanges, both feet and both small fingers. Caused by failure of heated suit.

Colonel Nazzaro was more visibly affected by this mission than by any that I have yet observed, and he stated last night that he was more tired than when he, himself, had flown long missions. He seems to embody the personal feeling for his men that is sometimes lacking in commanders, and yet does not hesitate to do what is necessary to accomplish the mission. He is a truly good man.

18 October 1943 — Eight planes took off about 0645 hours to Thurleigh, England for briefing and to make a composite group. Destination was Duran, Germany, but mission was scrubbed some while after takeoff. All planes returned safely. One enlisted man, S/Sgt. Edward J. Meyers, 535th Bomb Squadron (H), received a frostbite, right malar area, 2½" X 1¼" of moderate severity. No Lanolin was used. The staff visited the patients at 121st Station Hospital, Braintree. The staff meeting that was scheduled to be held did not materialize.

20 October 1943 — Eight planes took off about 0615 hours and were briefed at another base. They joined planes from another group to make up a composite group. The target was Duran, Germany. There was one abortion, and the other seven planes did not reach their target so returned with their bomb load. There were no losses, and one case of frostbite...namely:

Smith, Robert E. — Sgt. — 535th Bombardment Squadron
DIAGNOSIS: l. Frostbite, 4th & 5th fingers, right hand, mod. severity...Lanolin was used.

21 October 1943 — Fifteen planes took off this AM at 0545 hours. At 0617, Operations called that the mission had been scrubbed. All planes returned safely to the base.

3 November 1943 — For the past ten days, there has been very little aerial activity because of poor weather. The combat group is in good condition, but seen to be getting restless. However, there is nothing to warrant any apprehension. The monthly parties for the officers and enlisted men were held during the past week and were enjoyed by most and abused by the usual few. But, all in all, they were satisfactory, and I believe probably should be held more often.

Major Gaillard attended the Eighth Air Force Provisional Medical Field Service School at Hywickham from October 17th to the 23rd. The school was rather well conducted and the most interesting and instructive part was the outlining of the psychiatric evaluation and disposition of combat crew failures. The outline and disposition guide is attached (see Reports & Endnotes).

Captain Ralston attended the plaster school at 30th General Hospital. He had an interesting three days, but apparently didn't learn very much.

Captain Pease has departed for the American School Center, Chrivenham, Bucks., and in three weeks, we expect a full-fledged commando (better "watch it" from now on).

In the interests of self-preservation from a unit medical group standpoint, we have appointed a local medical board to review combat failures and other psychiatric cases before disposing of them. We feel that this will be interesting, informative, instructive, and to the best interests of the individual and the service. To date we have passed on three cases, namely, Lt. Lane, Lt. Baxter, and S/Sgt. Jones. We were reversed by the Central Medical Board on Lt. Lane, and upon reviewing our findings and their findings, we are inclined to maintain our original opinion.

There have been no missions flown in the past week. Twenty-two ships got off the ground on 30 October, but were called back before crossing the coast.

There have been about ten new crews assigned during the week.

HQ 381st BOMBARDMENT GROUP (H) AAF M-S-1
Office of the Surgeon
APO 634
U.S. Army

12 October 1943

C E R T I F I C A T E

1. In accordance with Hq. E.T.O. USA letter Ag 200, 6 MGA,
Subject: Awards and Decorations, dated 25 June 1943, the following is certified:

Sellers, Thomas D. — ASN O-678337 — 2nd Lieutenant — 535th
Bombardment Squadron (H) 381st Bombardment Group (H) AAF, was wounded in
action over enemy territory on 8 October 1943.

1. Wound, penetrating, left shoulder, moderate severity, involving
anterior, posterior and lateral surface of left. Accidentally incurred by the
explosion of a high velocity 20mm cannon shell in the cockpit of a B-17.

2. Wounds, penetrating multiple, mild, involving the left shoulder, lateral
surface of left arm and proximal 2/3 of the lateral surface of the of left
forearm and left side of neck, accidentally incurred as in #1.

3. Wound, penetrating, mild, anterior lateral of left thigh, accidentally
incurred as in #1.

 b. The wounds are classed as moderately severe.
 c. The wounds did not interfere greatly with performance of duty.
 d. The degree of pain was moderate.
 e. The fortitude displayed by this Officer could not be measured in
  terms of pain suffered or by the severity of his wounds, but rather
  in the horrible circumstances that surrounded him. The pilot had
  his head literally blown to bits by a 20mm cannon shell and upon
  inspection by the undersigned, there was hardly a square inch of
  cockpit that was not covered by blood and bits of brain tissue.
  The top and side glasses of the cockpit were broken and extreme
  cold windblast added to the hardship. The nose of the ship was
  shot out, which altered considerably the flying characteristics of
  the airplane.

It certainly must have been a trying ordeal to fly the aircraft under such unusual
conditions and especially when so covered with the blood and brains of a
headless friend.

     Ernest Gaillard, Jr.
     Major, MC Station Flight Surgeon

50

HQ 381st BOMBARDMENT GROUP (H) AAF M-R-2
Office of the Surgeon
APO 634
U.S. Army

13 October 1943

SUBJECT: Case History of Captain Arthur F. Briggs — Pilot —
ASN O-416993 — 532nd Bombardment Squadron, 381st
Bombardment Group (H) AAF

TO: President Central Medical Board, Station 101

Captain Arthur F. Briggs is referred to the Central Medical Board for observation and disposition following his request that he be relieved from flying duty.

Captain Briggs has been with the 381st Bombardment Group (H) since its formation in January 1943.

He has served as squadron operations officer, assistant Group operations officer, and Group plans and training officer.

To date, he has taken part in seven raids and one abortion. On one occasion, he crash-landed his aircraft in an English meadow, without any injuries to self or crew, when he was returning from a raid and three motors cut out at one time. It was considered at that time that he had displayed superb skill in successfully landing his ship.

He took part in the Schweinfurt raid on 17 August 1943 as co-pilot with the task-force leader. Eleven planes from this group failed to return and the fighter opposition was heavy. On the evening of this raid, Captain Briggs was involved in a fight with a ground personnel officer who spoke out of turn.

Later he went to London and reportedly was intoxicated for several days. Upon his return, he was quiet, depressed, and took little interest in operational affairs.

Captain Briggs has been on two raids since Schweinfurt. On 17 September 1943, Captain Briggs was scheduled to lead the Group. He reported to his Squadron Surgeon, stating that he did not want to go on the mission. He further stated that since the Schweinfurt raid he had not slept well and that he felt that the odds are overwhelmingly against survival of any man taking part in raids over German territory.

He further contended that the damage inflicted on the enemy is not proportional to the losses suffered by our Air Force.

He appeared to be quite introspective and downcast. Stated that he had no desire to go near a B-17 again and specifically that he did not wish to go on the raid.

It was pointed out to Captain Briggs that he was one of the senior Group officers and any failure on his part would have a disastrous effect on the Group as a whole.

The Commanding Officer, Colonel Nazzaro, gave Captain Briggs free choice as to whether he should go or not and the Captain decided to go. However, the mission was scrubbed.

Captain Briggs has aborted on one mission he started on recently. There is some question as to whether the cause of the abortion was adequate or not.

Captain Briggs was in the sick quarters several days, following, which he was sent to the Stanbridge Earls Rest Home 24 September 1943, for one week.

Captain Briggs today, 13 October 1943, requested that he be permanently grounded.

Diagnosis:

1. Psycho-neurosis, anxiety state, severe.

2. Operational fatigue, severe.

Ernest Gaillard, Jr.
Major, MC
Station Flight
Surgeon

(*Written by Ralston*)

HQ 381st BOMBARDMENT GROUP (H) AAF   M-S-2
Office of the Surgeon
APO 634
U.S. Army

14 October 1943

SUBJECT: Case History of Captain Arthur F. Briggs — Pilot —
          ASN O-416993 — Age 23 — 532nd Bombardment Squadron
          381st Bombardment Group (H) AAF

     TO: President Central Medical Board, Station 101

Captain Arthur F. Briggs is referred to the Central Medical Board for observation and disposition following his request of 13 October 1943 that he be permanently grounded.

This officer joined the 381st Bombardment Group (H) in January 1943 has served as squadron operations officer, assistant Group operations officer, Group plans and training officer and squadron commander.

He has taken part in seven raids. On one occasion, he crash landed his aircraft under very difficult circumstances without injury to himself or crew, and the skill that he displayed has been commented upon favourably upon by higher authority.

He took part in the Schweinfurt raid on 17 August 1943 as co-pilot with the task-force leader. The Schweinfurt mission is considered the worst mission this group has flown because of the extremely heavy fighter opposition and the fact that we lost eleven of our aircraft. Technically, Captain Briggs' ability has never been questioned. He is very much at home in an airplane and his flying ability is highly regarded by other pilots.

His past history is that of a normal boy and man. He took part in competitive athletics and his scholastic work was always satisfactory.

His difficulty seemed to begin after the Schweinfurt raid. He was involved in a fight with a ground officer the night of that mission, but was perfectly justified in it by the action he took. The following four days he remained more or less intoxicated in order to get some sleep. When the effects of the alcohol wore off, he would awaken and relive his terrifying experiences. He became progressively more morose, introspective, and less affable, and on 17 September 1943, he reported to the surgeon and stated he was all through. He had had ideas of homicide and suicide manifested by a compulsion to shoot a friend without reason. Apparently, ideas of homicide and suicide have occurred only on one occasion. He further stated that he had no chance of completing his combat tour, that he had no interest in his work, had difficulty concentrating on any given task, and had no desire to ever fly again.

It was pointed out to him that as a squadron commander many men looked to him for direction, guidance and example, and that failure on his part would have a disastrous effect upon his squadron and very likely upon the Group as a whole.

It was also explained to him that failure on his part might well be followed by court martial, disgrace at home, and a life of remorse. He apparently got a hold of himself, and agreed to fly the mission that he was scheduled for that day. Unfortunately, the mission was scrubbed.

Two days later, he was admitted to sick quarters and fairly heavily sedated for several days, and seemed to improve considerably. He was then sent to the rest home for seven days and returned looking and feeling considerably better. He apparently was doing quite well until the past week when this group flew missions on three consecutive days, lost two squadron commanders, a number of old crews, and a total of ten aircraft. He progressively has become more shut in and attempts to engage him in conversation have been futile. On 13 October 1943, he told the Group commander that he was through, and that he would rather face disgrace, court martial, etc., rather than fly again. He further stated that everyone on the field knew of his failure and he saw no reason to continue.

Comment: There is considerable difference in opinion in the medical department as to Captain Briggs' mental status. It is the opinion of the undersigned that he is an intelligent, capable individual and that he has reasoned that the hazard of combat flying is too great. He has voluntarily accepted the punishment and disgrace that might be facing him. It is further felt that his depression, retardation, introspection, and ideation is that of a normal mind that is facing a very serious personal problem. It is the opinion of some of the squadron surgeons that he represents a true anxiety neurosis.

Impression: Lack of moral fibre.[4]

> Ernest Gaillard, Jr.
> Major, MC
> Station Flight
> Surgeon

---

[4] Those who sometimes broke under the strain were rapidly (and rather arbitrarily) branded "LMF: Lack of Moral Fibre"; de-ranked, de-breveted (sometimes publicly), and whisked away to menial tasks. "Lack of moral fibre" or no, Capt. Briggs was eventually promoted to the rank of Major and finished his operational tour, flying (and leading) several more highly dangerous, "maximum effort" bombing missions over enemy territory with distinction. Major Briggs passed away at his home here in 1977 at the age of 57.

3 November 1943 (continued):

The following officers and enlisted men were sent to rest homes during the week.

TO: Eighth Air Force Officer's Rest Home — Stanbridge Earls.

533rd Bomb Squadron (H):

1st Lt. William J. McDaniel   2nd Lt. Ernest M. Klein
2nd Lt. Louis H. Gill

TO: Moulsford Manor — nr. Cholsey Castle, Berks. (AAF 511)

533rd Bomb Squadron (H):

T/Sgt. Louis S. Kalmar   S/Sgt. John S. Bunworth   S/Sgt. Howard A. Pope
S/Sgt. John O. Shepherd   S/Sgt. Robert K. Kay
S/Sgt. Charley O. Leazenby   S/Sgt. Walter E. Fields

1st Lt. Bernard E. Cohler has been appointed Respiratory and Disease Control Officer to fill the vacancy by Captain Dwyer being transferred.

Lieutenant Colonel Ralph G. LaRue inspected the medical detachment and was favorably impressed with the personnel and the physical equipment.

Major Gaillard was elected to the council of the Officers' Mess with specific duty in charge of entertainment.

The medical department, this date, inaugurated a new procedure in sanitary inspection. Four officers and four enlisted men descended upon the various sites, took them by storm, and left before the site realized they were being inspected. The only hitch in the machinery was Captain Wymer's volubility, which hindered the operations somewhat. In the future, he will either be gagged or left behind.

Changes in personnel have been:

DEPARTED: Captain Cornelius J. Dwyer. This officer has conducted himself quite well both medically and professionally in the two months that I have known him, and it is with reluctance that we lose his services.

ARRIVED: 1st Lieut. Leonard J. Lisnow — Dental Surgeon

Corporal William H. Jordan — Dental Technician

2nd Lieut. Grace P. Hawkes N732448 — Flight Nurse

2nd Lieut. Margaret M. Gudobba N730250 — Flight Nurse

T/3 Elmer S. Warzon —- T/3 William M. Van de Vender, both NCO's who are assigned to the above named flight nurses.

On Sunday, 1 November 1943, Doctor (Captain) Dunlop of the British home Guard was host to Major Gaillard and Captain Ralston at a Home Guard simulated warfare demonstration where they actually shot over the heads; had dynamite exploding, had simulated gas and smoke. It was a very realistic demonstration, and the Tommies that were observing said that it looked much worse from the observer's standpoint than from the soldier being indoctrinated. Captain Ralston and myself were quite content to observe.

04 November 1943 — The medical board was convened to determine the sanity and responsibility of the acts of Private James W. Williamson, 15323481, 1142nd M.P. Company. The board consisted of:

Major Ernest (NMI) Gaillard	O-330166 MC	President
Capt. Milton H. Bland	O-465678 MC	Member
Louis G. Ralston	O-479721 MC	Member
1st Lt. Joseph V. Fick	O-1543431 MAC	Recorder

with Lieutenant Colonel Michael H. Teitelbaum O-493784 MC neuro-psychiatric consultant. The board found the soldier to be mentally deficient, with the approximate age of 8 years. It was felt that he should be held accountable for his acts.

Major Gaillard and Captain Wymer were the guests of Doctor P. Dunlop at Steeple Bumstead this date as part of our "know the allies program". The meal was skimpy, but the refreshments were excellent.

Twenty-seven aircraft from this command took off at 0920 hours with the target the dock area of Wilhelmshaven, Germany. The flight was undercast throughout, and bombing was done by pathfinder. The three divisions attacked the target and those on the mission stated they could see the air solid with B-17's as far as 50 miles ahead and behind. The mission was also remarkable in that P-38's [5] accompanied the B-17's through the target area for the first time. The flak was light and inaccurate and caused no damage that was observed by our group. Bombing altitude was 25,000 feet. Temperature –28° Centigrade. The only casualty of the day was a Top Turret Gunner, S/Sgt. Shirley E. Goucher who suffered a fracture of the humerus when he fell out of the Top Turret. This was the only ship that aborted. All of the aircraft returned safely to this base, and the pick-up in morale of the crews was a pleasure to observe. It seemed to help everyone to know that the ships had gone over a heavily defended area like Wilhelmshaven and come back without a scratch.

---

[5] German pilots were so in wonderment and terror of the Lockheed P-38 Lightning and its maneuverability—and coupled with its raffish, twin-fuselage design—that they nicknamed it *Der Gabelschwanz Teufel*, or, the "Forked-Tail Devil".

5 November 1943 — Twenty-one ships from this command took off at 0920 hours with the target Gelsen Kirchen, Germany. It is located in Ruhr Valley. The target was bombed by pathfinder. Very little enemy fighter opposition was encountered, but the flak was very heavy and accurate. Ten chutes were seen to leave Lt. Hopp's ship just east of the Dutch coast. Six men left Lt. Butler's ship on the co-pilot's orders and Lt. Butler and 5 crewmembers landed at Great Malling. Lt. Brown suffered from exposure and multiple minor injuries, and Sgt. Osborne from a laceration of the dorsum of the left hand. When the order was given to prepare to bail out, the ship was at 28,000 feet. Lt. Brown, Bombardier, removed his oxygen mask and started to leave by the forward escape hatch. He apparently became anoxic, fell, and the ripcord was accidentally released. The chute bellowed out the hatch, wound around the ball turret, and pulled Lt. Brown's right leg out of the ship. The windblast tore off the right boot, but oddly enough, he suffered little frostbite. The duration of his unconsciousness is unknown, but it is estimated at 1½ to 2 hours.

Men missing in action are as follows:

533rd Bombardment Squadron (H)

Anderson, John K.	2nd Lt.	CP
Maloney, Wayne L.	T/Sgt.	RO
Lindsay, Kinley W.	T/Sgt.	TTG
Skrapits, John E.	S/Sgt.	RWG
McGinty, Francis R.	T/Sgt.	LWG
Smith, Charles F.	S/Sgt.	TG

535th Bombardment Squadron (H)

B-17F #42-30852 — "Hot Toddy", "Blowin' Bessie"

Hopp, Donald K.	1st Lt.	P
Carr, Walter C.	2nd Lt.	CP
Tyler, Marshall E.	2nd Lt.	N
Johnston, William J.	2nd Lt.	B
East, Roy W.	T/Sgt.	RO
Girvin, Alexander M.	T/Sgt.	TTG
Richard, Armond R.	S/Sgt.	BTG
True, Robert G.	S/Sgt.	LWG
Greer, Julius F.	S/Sgt.	RWG
Woodyatt, Richard E.	S/Sgt.	TG

This mission was remarkable in that the bombing altitude was 28,000 feet, and the outside air temperature was –40° C. The crews were individually instructed prior to takeoff on the prevention of frostbite, and we like to feel that our efforts were in part responsible for the fact that only one frostbite was received on this mission.

Major Gaillard attended a division officers meeting and according to his own statement, accomplished nothing.

6 November 1943 — Major Gaillard, Captain Ralston, Lt. Margaret Gudobba (Flight Nurse), and Captain William Thompson, MC, visitor from 121st Station hospital, went down to West Malling by air to pick up the two wounded described in yesterday's entry. Lt. Brown had a cast on his leg (hemorrhage and contusion of tibial collateral ligament) and had to be evacuated by ambulance and stretcher to the plane. The trip was uneventful.

7 November 1943 — Nineteen aircraft from this group took off at 0820 hours with the target the marshalling yards at Weswel, Germany. The bombing altitude was 26,000 feet and the outside temperature was –40° Centigrade. Bombing was done by pathfinder. The target was not seen. Six cases of frostbite were incurred during this mission and five of them were about the face and neck. The other was of the foot. No fighters were encountered, and flak was light and inaccurate. There were plenty of P-47's around and they gave excellent cover. All the ships returned to this base flying a beautiful formation.

The sense of relief that everyone feels when the ships come back, flying a good formation, and with none of them peeling off or shooting flares, is notable. It is a release to the anxious tension that we all feel when the ships are out on a mission. There were no wounded and the crews were in good shape.

11 November 1943 — Briefing this beautiful morning (for a change) was at 0620 hours; target Weswel, Germany, marshalling yards. Bombing altitude 28,000 feet, temperature –40° Centigrade, this group led by Captain Lord (see B-17 Formation Flight Pattern, p. 61). The total distance was 660 miles. Take-off time was at 1100 hours. The formation got within 2 miles of the Dutch coast. The clouds were up to 29,000 feet and rather than to take the top element or the formation to 32,000 feet, the air division commander decided to bring the ships back. There were two cases of anoxia, and one of them suffered frostbite in addition.

13 November 1943 — The crews were briefed quite early for a target in Germany. Bombing was to be done by pathfinder. The assembly point was to be over the field at 9,000 feet, so Col. Hall, Major Gaillard, Captain Wymer, Captain Delano, and an equipment sergeant took the tow-target ship up to watch the assembly at 9,000 feet. Poor guess! Cloud cover was up to 20,000 feet, went up without oxygen. There were three masks for the five of us, and at 17,500 feet, the Sergeant decided to pass out. Major Gaillard grabbed him by the backside and attempted to push him into the nose of the ship with Captain Wymer so that he could take care of him, but his parachute harness hung up. About that time, Captain Wymer was pushing him back up to the flight deck and Captain Wymer himself was getting cyanotic and certainly was not in the pink (no pun intended). Major Gaillard took a couple of whiffs off of Colonel Hall's oxygen mask, picked the Sergeant up behind the back of the neck, and brought Sergeant and mask together. When the Sgt. revived, he was sent down to the nose. The remainder of the stay at altitude was eventful in that Major Gaillard would watch Colonel

Hall's ears, and when they got good and blue, the mask would be given back to him. When they got pink, Major Gaillard would take it again. All in all, the whole trip was a monument to our own stupidity, but can as well be blamed on the airplane.

Our masks, with two exceptions, were demand masks and the ship was equipped with constant flow. It was rather cool, too. We were dressed for 9,000 feet, or zero weather, and it was –22° Centigrade at 20,000 feet.

Lieutenant Deering, Lt. Reese and crew got lost in trying to assemble and when the other ships were ordered back to the field, they continued on their merry way and took an unescorted tour of Europe. I imagine the continental populace was just about as surprised as our own wayward boys when they broke out of the clouds at 25,000 feet. After flying into some very bad weather and being used as a clay pigeon by all the flak installations enroute, our wayward boys returned home; no wounded or dead, but impressed by their experience. Said crew has now reverted to training status.

16 November 1943 — Twenty-one aircraft from this command took off at 0705 hours to bomb a Molybdenum plant at Knaben, Norway. Total distance 1060 miles, bombing altitude around 14,000 feet, temperature –32° C at that altitude. The weather was slightly stinko most of the way and they had to climb to 20,000 feet over the North Sea in order to avoid the clouds. Results of the bombing are not known at present. There were no wounded, but there were three cases of frostbite. The most severe was Sgt. Clarence T. Williams — 535th Bomb Squadron (H) who became inquisitive and stuck his head out of the left waist so he could see the bombs burst. He did — and he has a frozen face to prove it. The left zygomatic area and the left neck are involved. It does not appear to be too serious.

A rather unimportant event, but never the less interesting feature at the landing of the ships has been the hockey game between Major Gaillard and Captain Cohler. The crews at the interrogation were all in good spirits, all ships landed safely at the base, but Lt. Schultz and crew took a bit round-about way home.

26 November 1943 — Twenty-one aircraft from this group took off today with their target Bremen, Germany. Altitude flown was 25,000 feet, and temperature was –40° C. There were no aircraft lost, however there were 17 cases of frostbite, 2 cases of burns, and 3 cases of anoxia. One plane landed near Waterbury and evacuated Sgt. Homer, 534th Squadron, to the RAF Hospital, Waterbury. He suffered frostbite, face, severe.

1 December 1943 — Seventeen aircraft from this group took off today with their target Leverkusen, Germany. Bombing altitude was 26,000 feet, and air temperature –40° Centigrade. There were four aircraft lost on this raid. Four cases of frostbite, and 2 burns were suffered by personnel. One plane crash-landed in a field at Kent, and three officers were evacuated to an English Hospital, Rochester, Kent. 1st Lt. Harold H. Hytinen, 534th, Squadron, suffered pan fracture, skull and nose, and lacerations, face.

2nd Lt. William R. Cronin, 534th Squadron, suffered lacerations, face, fractured nose, sprain, left ankle, and fracture, olecranon, left ulna. 2nd Lt. Richard I. Maustead, 534th Squadron, suffered fracture, ribs, right.

These three officers have since been sent to the 38th Station Hospital, which is about 10 miles north of Southampton.

Men missing in action are as follows:

<u>532nd Bombardment Squadron (H)</u>

B-17F #42-29506 — "Full Boost!"

Duncan, Jason H.	2nd Lt.	P
Allchin, Harry, Jr.	2nd Lt.	CP
Huffman, Mac W.	2nd Lt.	N
Kessler, Robert G.	2nd Lt.	B
Doherty, Edward V.	S/Sgt.	RO
Wade, V. L.	S/Sgt.	TTG
Jeffers, Leon D.	S/Sgt.	BTG
Wall, M.A.	Sgt.	RWG
Starkey, Harold G.	Sgt.	LWG
Mattson, Roy F.	S/Sgt.	TG

<u>535th Bombardment Squadron (H)</u>

B-17F #42-31111 — "Four Aces, Pat Hand"

Noxon, Donald, E.	2nd Lt.	P
Giovannini, George E.	2nd Lt.	CP
Eichhorn, Edison	2nd Lt.	N
Utley, Walter A.	2nd Lt.	B
Phillips, Toby B., Jr.	T/Sgt.	TTG
Ludwigsen, Peter K.	T/Sgt.	BTG
Thompson, John F., Jr.	S/Sgt.	BTG
Mogush, Paul T.	S/Sgt.	RWG
Thompson, Harry M.	S/Sgt.	LWG
Channell, John S.	S/Sgt.	TG

Flight Surgeon

B-17 Formation Flight Pattern for 11 November 1943

BRIEFING   0620
STATIONS   0835
START ENG   0850
TAXI   0905
TAKE-OFF   0920
LEAVE FIELD   1007
ALTITUDE   8000'

LEAD — 532nd

LORD
HECKER
D | 9570

BECKMAN
E | 6076

HUTCHENS
F | 7760

BALTRUSAITIS
H | 9888

WOOD
C | 5725

ROBINSON
K | 9923

LOW – 535th

ALEXANDER
Q | 5878

RIDLEY
U | 0675

BAER
Q | 1067

RUTAN
D | 9751

HIGH– 534th

OHL
L | 7721

SCHOMBURG
I | 7754

HOPP
V | 0852

HAGARTY
B | 0732

HESS
N | 3540

MEYERS
O | 3177

NEIDERRITER
A | 5845

SILVERNALE
F | 9808

9999-Z SPARE
9832-H SPARE

7730-U SPARE

FOLLOW–533rd
LEAD

SHENK
S | 3215

BUTLER
Y | 9755

GLEICHAUF
X | 7719

HANSEN
W | 9761

CROZIER
O | 0014

CLORE
A | 9506

CROSSON
S | 1075

CAHOW
N | 3522

NOXON
T | 1047

61

1 December 1943 (continued)

B-17G #42-31097 — "Mission Belle"

Sunde, Harland V.	F/O	P
Sweeney, James W.	2nd Lt.	CP
Christensen, Roger G.	2nd Lt.	N
Tully O. D.	2nd Lt.	B
Carano, Claudio S.	Sgt.	RO
England, William P.	S/Sgt.	TTG
McCutchen, Doyle C.	Sgt.	BTG
Culver, Charles J.	Sgt.	RWG
Josephson, Carlton A.	Sgt.	LWG
Healy, John F.	Sgt.	TG

B-17G #42-3540 — "Bacta-th'-Sac", "Lucifer, Jr. II"

Hess, Warren C.	2nd Lt.	P
Smith, Charles L.	2nd Lt.	CP
Randle, David (NMI)	2nd Lt.	N
Wernersbach, Robert F.	2nd Lt.	B
Regan, John F.	T/Sgt.	RO
Gardella, Albert J.	T/Sgt.	TTG
Macklin, William M.	S/Sgt.	BTG
Ludwig, Allen G.	S/Sgt.	LWG
Burke, Phillip F.	S/Sgt.	RWG
Delp, Edgar G.	S/Sgt.	TG

4 December 1943 — During the past 2 weeks, things have gone along in a pretty humdrum manner and only three operational missions have been flown. The details of these missions have been described above.

On Sunday, 21 November 1943, Major Gaillard underwent spinal anesthesia and had his redundant intra and peri-anal tissue excised. The convalescence was uneventful ("like hell it was, but I fear the details would be boring; they certainly 'bored' me").

There has been a great increase in the respiratory disease incidence during the past two weeks, the rate having reached 1100 plus for the week of 21 November and 900 plus for the week of 28 November 1943. The disease seems to have an acute onset, with fever, general malaise, and muscular aches and pains. The course has been from 36 to 72 hours with some residual weakness. The rate is not considered excessive or alarming, however we are instituting what measures we can to prevent cross infection.

Captain Ralph M. Wymer is this week attending the Provisional Medical Field Service School at Pinetree. Captain George J. Pease returned on 26 November from the commando school at Chrivenham looking none the worse for his experience.

I lectured today to the new combat crews and found them a fairly receptive and intelligent group. During the course of their questioning, it was learned that their equipment levels of heated gloves and shoes, silk gloves, gauntlets, long-underwear and heavy socks were deficient. It seems rather futile to lecture to these groups about what they should have and then not be able to supply it. I also explained to them some of the mental mechanisms, the development of fear reaction, operational exhaustion, etc., and the amount of interest and intelligence they displayed was very encouraging. It probably will be interesting to explain mental "mechanixm" to a large group of combat crewmen and then see if there is any value in prophylaxis.

The weather the past two weeks has been dull and grey for the most part, and the mud is soft and juicy and everywhere present. However, this climate seems not too unlike North Carolina and Georgia at this time of year and I think that most people that complain are feeling sorry for themselves without adequate reason. In general, the disease incidence would compare favorably with that in the states.

The Saturday morning inspection was held as usual, and the organization seems to be maintaining its standards.

The monthly dance was held on 30 November, and it was the opinion of most that if the party had been any better behaved there would have been no point in having a party. The "Belle of the Ball" (Mignonne) was escorted by Major Gaillard, as usual.

Three rather decrepit, ancient meatballs from the E.V.S. Nursing staff were here to interrogate our wayward personnel on the source of their "Piccadilly flak". What an odd way for three nice old ladies to make a living.

Nine men were transferred out of the medical department into the Air Corps, and nine new men were sent to us from 1st Bomb Division.

Men transferred are as follows:

TRANSFERRED OUT:

532nd Bombardment Squadron (H)

Pfc. Robert H. Ball
Pvt. Francis R. Knight
Pvt. Raymond J. Lashure

533rd Bombardment Squadron (H)

Pvt. Anthony J. Goral

<u>534th Bombardment Squadron (H)</u>

S/Sgt. Homer B. Stamp
Pvt. Edward F. Lorenz

<u>535th Bombardment Squadron (H)</u>

Cpl. Harvey G. King
Pvt. Edward (NMI) Gonynor

<u>Hq. 381st Bomb Group (H)</u>

Cpl. Michael W. Spack

<u>TRANSFERRED IN</u>:

<u>Hq. 381st Bomb Group (H)</u>

T/5 Sammie C. Eads

<u>532nd Bombardment Squadron (H)</u>

Pfc. Benoit J. Caya
Pfc. Van Horne Smith
Pfc. Francis C. Cramer

<u>534th Bomb Squadron (H)</u>

S/Sgt. Harold J. Schloesser
Pfc. John F. Sweeney
Pfc. Harold E. Styers

<u>535th Bomb Squadron (H)</u>

Cpl. Geronimo A. Casaz
Pfc. Ralph A. Beaulieu

S/Sgt. Andrew H. Schnitzler was sent to the Central Medical Board during the past week from the 534th Bomb Squadron. He was sent with a diagnosis of:
1. Functional symptoms due to combat stress. 2. Nasopharyngitis, acute, sev.
3. Sprain, sacroiliac, left.

On 3 December 1943, we were notified that Cpl. Jack R. Flinn, 19099101, 533rd Bomb Squadron (H) had died at 121st Station Hospital. The following is a summary of Flinn's case, by Major Appleton, 121st Station Hospital:

"Cpl. Flinn admitted 19 November 1943 with urethral smear of positive gonococcus. Patient previously received 41 grains of sulfathiazole in ten days. Patient given 15 grains of sulfathiazole every 4 hours for 7 days and 15 grains four times a day for the next three days. Smear Positive on 30 November 1943. Sulfathiazole resistant. On December 1st, 1943 given 0.8 cc of Typhoid vaccine for fever therapy and supplemented with physio-therapy heat cradle.

Temperature rose to slightly above 106° F rectally for six hours, following, which he was comatose. 5,900 cc fluids and 500 cc of plasma given during next 24 hours. General condition of patient was fairly good at 7:00 A.M. on 3 Dec 1943, except unconsciousness. Urine output 360 cc for period following fever until his death.

"N.P.N. 59.6 — Urea 28.2 at 8:00 A.M. on 3 Dec 1943. Patient had suddenly a cardiac failure with death occurring suddenly at 10:30 A.M. on 3 Dec 1943. An autopsy is being performed."

5 December 1943 — About 0430 hours to 0600 hours there were 8 cases of acute gastro-intestinal upsets who reported to sick quarters and in all instances they had eaten mid-night chow at Consolidated Mess and all had had roast beef in common. Symptoms began from 0100 hours to 0300 hours and were characterized by repeated attacks of nausea and vomiting, frequent bowel movements, and abdominal cramps of varying severity. One patient was vomiting bright red blood and had such severe abdominal pain that it was necessary to give him a hypodermic of morphine and atropine to afford him relief. All were admitted to quarters and by noon were able to eat and felt practically normal, being discharged before the day was out.

Major Gaillard reported to the 8th Air Force Home at Stanbridge Earls to be medical officer in charge for a period of one week. He was flown down by a crew from this base, and was accompanied by Captain Louis C. Ralston.

About 1000 hours, an emergency call was received from the Police Station at Haverhill with information that there had been a truck turned over in a ditch and that there were about 3 to 5 soldiers injured fairy severely. Extra plasma and supplies, & blankets were placed in two ambulances, which were dispatched to the scene of the accident at the northern out-skirts of the city of Haverhill.

There was found a 2½-ton truck lying on its side in a deep drainage ditch just off the road. It was loaded with a group of Engineer band members who were on their way to play for an airfield dedication and dance. There were several fracture cases of the ankle, one clavicle, one with a possible concussion, and several with minor contusions, abrasions, and scratches. A British civilian doctor had been called and had rendered effective first aid treatment by the time of our arrival. We replaced the morphine and bandages he had used and thanked him for his services. Two ambulances were loaded with ten cases, four of them being stretcher. There were two others that we could not accommodate in our ambulances so were transported to Braintree, 121st Station Hospital, by an ambulance from the 49th Station Hospital, which arrived on the scene at this time. One of the patients they took was a stretcher case. In all, 12 cases were carried to the 121st Station Hospital where preparations had been made previously for a speedy handling of the injured.

8 December 1943 — Captain Cohler and Lieutenant Fick were witnesses at the General Court Martial Hearing for Private James W. Willison in the notorious Sudbury rape case.

The medical officers conducted lectures for six hours on first aid against chemical attack to base personnel.

9 December 1943 — The weather is still certainly bad, and there has been no flying for the past several days. Captain Ralston is still away, being grounded with aircraft, which carried Major Gaillard and party to the rest home.

The two nurses, Miss Margaret M. Gudobba, and Miss Grace Hawkes, and the two Sergeants assigned to them departed today for AAF Station 480, Grantham, Notts., per telephone orders as of 8 December from 50th Troop Carrier Wing. Transportation was furnished by command car and trailer. They departed from this station at 1330 hours.

11 December 1943 — Thirty aircraft from this command took off today with the target Emden, Germany. There were two abortions, and the other 28 planes returned safely to this station. No MIA or KIA.

At about 1915 hours, a red air raid alert was called over the Tannoy. The Jerries dropped flares and bombs on a near-by airdrome and did considerable damage to buildings as well as injuring several of the personnel. Lights were turned off at this base until late in the evening. This was one time that bombing in this vicinity was a little too close for comfort.

13 December 1943 — Twenty-eight aircraft from this command were briefed and sent to Bremen, Germany today. The mission proved to be very successful for our Group as we suffered no casualties or missing in action.

Due to fact that we had no lights or water on Friday evening, the regular weekly inspection was called off.

14 December 1943 — An inspection of combat crews living sites was made this date and there found to be in deplorable condition. They were dirty, crowded, inadequately blacked out, damp, inadequately heated, and seemed inadequate for the care of this type of personnel. The matter of stoves was taken up with the utility officer, Lt. Grey, and the Ground Executive, Colonel Reed, states that sixty American stoves were due shortly and would be used where necessary on combat sites. It is Colonel Reed's opinion that much of the grief of the combat crews is brought about by their laziness, lack of discipline, etc., and he feels disinclined to "baby" them, as he expressed it. The coke is distributed to the site daily in inadequate quantities and is appropriated by the first-come, first-served method; as a consequence, the combat crews have been chopping down trees in the surrounding territory, but the green wood will not burn and the barracks are still cold and damp. Many of them spend a great deal of their time as scavengers looking for fuel. Just the other night, a clear moonlight night, a 1st Lieutenant and 1st Pilot were seen running at full speed across a plowed field with a sack of coal over his shoulders (dubbed "midnight requisitioning"), and an Englishman close behind them. He made it, but the condition is obviously a rather sad one, and certainly does not contribute to the health and happiness of the troops.

Some of the officers have been sleeping in their flying clothing in order to keep warm. Colonel Reed states that everything that can be done has been done to obtain fuel and that it would serve no useful purpose for the medical department to write through command channels complaining of inadequate housing. Regardless of what measures are necessary (that is, to do the work for them, or see that they are severely disciplined to do it themselves), I feel it mandatory for the physical efficiency and morale that their lot be bettered.

Another thing that has come to my attention about the fuel shortage is that such notables as Captain Murray, the ex-professor of anatomy, and Captain Bland, Flight Surgeon of 535th Bomb Squadron, have been visiting the ash piles behind the enlisted men's barracks and are quite enthusiastic about the "big pieces" of coke that they have salvaged. Some ingenious members of the organization have found that a six pence can of shoe polish is a good substitute for kindling wood, and that the shoe impregnate that is supposed to protect against noxious gasses is also a highly inflammable item. Praise the Lord and pass the shoe polish! At last, we have found a useful use for this material we have been toting across the world with us for the past six months.

Thirty-three aircraft from this command took off at 0845 hours with the target Bremen, Germany. The bombing altitude was 26,000 feet, outside air temperature –40° Centigrade. The target was ten-tenths overcast and the group was in the third division that hit the target. The flak was quite intense, but apparently not too accurate for most of our group escaped serious damage. The target was, of course, not seen, but tremendous quantities of black smoke was seen to be welling up in the target area where the previous divisions had dropped their bombs. Some observers reported a few enemy fighters; others say that they were probably our own P-51's. All our ships are accounted for at this writing. There are no wounded.

20 December 1943 — Thirty-three aircraft from this command took off at 0815 hours with the target Bremen, Germany. Bombing altitude was 26,000 feet, and outside air temperature –42° C. The weather was beautifully clear eight-tenths of the way over and from six to eight tenths over the target area. Nine combat wings attacked the target. Our combat wing was third. The flak was the heaviest that we have encountered since Münster , Germany on October 10th. Four ships did not return and Colonel Leber and Lt. Clore landed at Mildenhall, an RAF base, and Lt. Petroski landed at Attlebridge. The top turret gunner, S/Sgt. Lee B. Gibson, 14181940, died of anoxia and details will follow.

Missing in action are as follows:

532nd Bombardment Squadron (H)

B-17F #42-3563 — "No Name"

Hollenkamp, Bernard F.	1st Lt.	P
Jones, George T.	2nd Lt.	CP
Clough, Herbert N.	F/O	N

Hazelton, Richard M.	2nd Lt.	B
Riemann, George C.	S/Sgt.	TTG
Soell, George W.	S/Sgt.	RO
Schulz, Elmo R.	Sgt.	BTG
Hutchens, Homer K.	Sgt.	RWG
Walker, Ira J.	Sgt.	LWG
Good, Harry L.	Sgt.	TG

534th Bombardment Squadron (H)

B-17F #42-5845 — "Whaletail II"

Canelake, Leo (NMI)	2nd Lt.	P
Johnson, Harry B.	F/O	CP
Boston, Jesse S.	2nd Lt.	N
Cisek, Max M.	2nd Lt.	B
McDonald, Paul F.	S/Sgt.	TTG
Hernandez, Tony T.	S/Sgt.	RO
Avrett, John V.	S/Sgt.	BTG
Brown, Richard W.	Sgt.	RWG
Phillips, Thomas W.	Sgt/	LWG
Belgrasch, Francis N.	Sgt.	TG

535th Bombardment Squadron (H)

B-17F #42-5846 — "Tinker Toy"

Lane, Dorman F.	2nd Lt.	P
Johnston, John B.	2nd Lt.	CP
Anderson, Everett S.	2nd Lt.	N
Mitchell, Richard M.	2nd Lt.	B
Peanoske, John (NMI)	S/Sgt.	TTG
Melchiorre, Alphonse A.	S/Sgt.	ROG
Cramer, Henry, Jr.	Sgt.	BTG
Fecho, Joseph	S/Sgt.	RWG
Hrapsky, William W.	Sgt.	LWG
McDonald, Frank H.	Sgt.	TG

B-17G #42-31075 — "The Rebel"

Crosson, Waldo B.	1st Lt.	P
Opitz, James R.	2nd Lt.	CP
Burke, Edward J.	2nd Lt.	N
Curran, John J.	2nd Lt.	B
Allen, John L.	T/Sgt.	TTG
McFarlane, Robert T.	T/Sgt.	ROG
Bulsock, Steve F.	S/Sgt.	BTG
Glawson, Jesse J.	S/Sgt.	RWG
Klima, Norman J.	S/Sgt.	LWG
Eloe, Robert N.	S/Sgt.	TG

Our ship, "Tinkertoy", was lost over the target area and the report is that it was rammed by two enemy ME 109's. It is surprising the effect that the loss of the "Tinkertoy" had upon the Group. The ship was in the Dianna Durbin film, *Hers to Hold*, and has been with the Group since its third phase of training. It has a long and interesting history and has been on many raids over enemy territory.

A number of people have been killed in this ship and the Group looked on it with mixed horror and affection. We all feel the loss a bit more keenly than would have been anticipated. The crews were affected by the raid and came back tired and quite sober in thought and action. However, I do not feel that the raid will have any permanent deleterious effect upon the crews. Captain Ralph M. Wymer went to Attlebridge to take the body of S/Sgt. Lee B. Gibson to the 2nd General Hospital at Oxford for autopsy.

21 December 1943 — Today, the first of a series of "Army Talks" were instigated by Major Gaillard. The reaction will depend upon whether or not they will continue. Any talks are supplied by E.T.O. USA Headquarters and the topic of this one was "Problems of Organized Peace"– a sanguine topic, indeed.

22 December 1943 — Briefing at 0730 hours this clear and beautiful morning with the target designation Osnabruck, Germany. Osnabruck's military importance is rail transportation between the industrial Ruhr and the Baltic seacoast. Twenty-four ships from this command took off at 0845 hours, bombing altitude 26,000 feet, temperature –46° Centigrade. The weather was clear in England and cloudy over the target area. Considerable fighter opposition was encountered and very little flak was seen. All the ships returned safely to this base. There were no killed or wounded. Frostbite continues to be one of our major problems and nine cases were received on the last two missions.

One thing that is causing quite a bit of concern amongst the combat personnel is the failure of the chin turret to operate above 20,000 feet.

Lt. Palas, bombardier, has been on five raids with the chin turret and on four of them the chin turret has not worked. He states it is rather a lonesome feeling to be sitting in the nose of a ship with inoperative machine guns.

A visitor of the day was, my brother, Lt. Warren K. Gaillard of the 447th Bomb Group.

23 December 1943 — Lt. Fick returned the box of paper cups to the supply depot and had them replaced with the microscope that he signed for originally. Another one like that and we will have to institute a report of survey on Lieut. Fick.

Of some humanitarian, if not medical interest, is the verbal persiflage that Major Gaillard is subjected to by his fellow officers regarding coming nuptials. He has been diagnosed, dissected, and even utterances have been put in the mouths of his unexpected progeny.

It seems to be the sadistic desire of most of his fellow officers to see that the pre-nuptial period is spent in alcoholic devulture to such an extent that the post-nuptial period will be spent in convalescence. It is probably a *res ipse loquitur* that Major Gaillard will do his utmost to look after his physical well-being. Captain Bland has received the unfortunate news that his wife is critically ill and we all hope that more favorable news will be received soon.

24 December 1943 — At 1045 hours this clear and crisp morning, 27 aircraft from this command took off to bomb rocket-gun installations in the Pas-de-Calais area. Bombing altitude was 21,000 feet and the outside air temperature was –42° Centigrade. The target was of especial interest because of the recent German threat to unload rockets on London. Fifteen hundred aircraft from the Eighth Air Force hit the target. The heavy bombardment aircraft were chosen for the mission because of the intense flak installations in the coastal areas. Bombing was done by individual squadrons and we are not yet sure of the results. Of especial interest to the author of these poor notes is the fact that this was his first combat mission and some of his reactions may be worthy of note. First, I was surprised at my experiencing no fear or apprehension at any time during the mission. The only reaction that I had was at the time we were receiving flak hits and I wondered just what in hell I was doing up there instead of back down on the ground where I belonged. There was a feeling of exhilaration and interest in what was going on around me, in watching the flak explode and seeing the puffs from the guns below. Another sound that was especially pleasant was the smooth functioning of all of our engines. They did not cough or spit once during the entire mission. The first burst of flak we heard prompted me to look out of the waist window whereupon I was unceremoniously grabbed by the tail and set down by one of the waist gunners. On the bombing run, I tried to get some pictures of "bombs away" and strike photos and was leaning out the window following the trailing bombs when the ship made a 30° turn to my side and almost tossed me out of the window. I clutched the air, airplane, and everything else and finally got back inside. All in all, my reaction was one of exhilaration and interest and I believe that I would enjoy aerial combat for a time at least, but, of course, my better judgment would prohibit such action. I flew the mission with Major Shackley and Lt. McDaniel in ship #721; name, "Sweet and Lovely".

27 December 1943 — Lieut. Fick, Sgt. Bassett, and Cpl. Johnson attended meeting in the conference room at 1st Division today. The meeting was intended to clear up problems that have been bothering the administrative personnel of late. MAC Officers and Chief Clerks from every station in the 1st Division were represented, and it was surprising and gratifying to learn that our detachment didn't have the only ignorant administrative staff. Also, we learned that our Squadron Surgeons were not the only offenders to the E.T.O. regulations. Several stations seemed to have more unruly surgeons than we have.

29 December 1943 — One ship lost due to mishap (no MACR available).

535th Bomb Squadron (H)

B-17F #42-30765 — "Chug-a-Lug", "Nip and Tuck"

30 December 1943 — Thirty-three aircraft from this command took off at 0800 hours with the target Ludwigshafen-Mannheim, Germany. Bombing altitude was 22,000 feet and outside air temperature –29° Centigrade. Bombing was done by pathfinder over ten-tenths cloud cover. There was very little flak and few fighters. All ships returned safely to this base and there was one anoxic death (see below). The group was composed of the normal group led by Colonel Nazzaro as our division commander and the composite group led by Major Halsey. The results of the bombing are not known.

Hickman, Curtis W. — S/Sgt. — Radio Operator — 17032667 — Age 23, 533rd Bomb Squadron, 381st Bomb Group (H) AAF. This individual when first seen by the medical department was dead. He was cyanotic, pupils were dilated, and he had froth at the mouth. There was a moderate amount of froth on the floor of the radio compartment. He is said to have been alive and talking over the interphone as the ship started its descent over the English Channel, which is approximately 1½ hours before he was seen by the department. Descent was at 400 feet a minute. The deceased was first noticed slumping over his chair by the ball turret operator as he was leaving the ball turret. The ball turret operator does not know if the deceased was breathing or not. Emergency oxygen and artificial respiration was begun immediately and continued until the ship returned some 45 - 50 minutes later. The oxygen mask was an A-14 demand unmodified, and when examined had two large pieces of ice in the two outlets. It is the opinion of the bombardier and the co-pilot that the ice was sufficient to obstruct exhalation. The fittings of the mask to the ship's system were checked and it was found that the male plug would catch in the female before being fully inserted, and that when inserted, it had to be separated with a pair of pliers with an estimated 25 - 30 pounds pull. The ball turret operator states that the hose was disconnected when the deceased was first seen. The last entry that was made in the radio operator's log was at 1235 hours, three hours before landing and about ten minutes after leaving the target. The ship was in no difficulty at the time and was not under enemy attack by flak or fighters. Upon further check, it was found that the male connection on the A-14 mask fit into other connections in the same ship in a normal manner. The body of S/Sgt. Hickman was taken to the 121st Station Hospital, Braintree for autopsy by Captain Louis G. Ralston.

1st Lieutenant Gleicauf, Paul B., 1st Lt. Richard J. Niederriter and Captain Harold L. Stralzer completed their operational tour this date.

31 December 1943 — Thirty-one aircraft from this command took off today with target a field near Bordeaux, France. It was quite a long hop and the ships that did not have Tokyo tanks were supplied with bomb-bay tanks. The field here seemed clear enough at the time of return, which was around 1600 hours, but for some reason or another, there were Division orders to land somewhere else in southern England. As a result, our aircraft were scattered all aver the southern end of the island and the weather did close in here about 1700. We were very much disappointed at not having the ships return because of the big party at the officer's club on New Year's Eve. We tried to fly down a couple cases of Scotch, but the ships were so scattered the idea was abandoned. Seven of the ships did return to this base.

The anticipated party went over with unusually good results and everyone, including this poor narrator, saw the old year out and the New Year in with a healthy golden glow. There were no untoward incidents and I think it was the best party to date, however, we were terribly disappointed in not having many of our crews here.

1 January 1944 — The medical department, including most of the enlisted men, are about the saddest bunch of soaks that I have ever seen. The reports had to get out just the same, however, being a Saturday as well as the first of the month.

One aircraft has been confirmed as missing in action from yesterday's raid. This is a 535th Bomb Squadron crew; its pilot being 2nd Lt. Earl B. Duarte. The crewmembers are listed as follows:

B-17G #42-39910 — "No Name"

Earl B. Duarte	2nd Lt.	P
Glen A. McCabe	2nd Lt.	CP
Cornelius A. Henitz, Jr.	2nd Lt.	N
Harry M. Grimball, Jr.	2nd Lt.	B
Russell N. Jevons	Sgt.	TTG
Joseph H. Balesh	Sgt.	RO
Howard B. Norris	Sgt.	BTG
James E. Martin	Sgt.	LWG
Albert H. Smith	Sgt.	RWG
Powell H. McDaniel	Sgt.	TG

4 January 1944 — The target Kiel, Germany, altitude 26,000 feet, outside air temperature –52° Centigrade. Bombing was done by pathfinder through a ten-tenths overcast. Lieutenant Clore and crew, most of whom were on their 25th mission, caught fire shortly after take off, salvoed their bombs, and crash landed, killing the entire crew. Five of the crewmembers were burned beyond recognition. The men on this crew are listed as follows:

532nd Bomb Squadron (H)

B-17G #42-31278 — "No Name"

Cecil M. Clore	1st Lt.	P
John W. Newell	2nd Lt.	CP
Ralph J. Waldman	1st Lt.	N
Marvin E. Dille	1st Lt.	B
Hamed M. Howard	S/Sgt.	BTG
Walter R. Trainer, Jr.	T/Sgt.	TTG
Salvatore (NMI) Bozzette	T/Sgt.	RO
Harold M. Robinson	S/Sgt.	LWG
Richard L. Streicher	S/Sgt.	RWG
Richard E. Ingmire	S/Sgt.	TG

The enemy opposition was accurate flak and no fighters. No ships were lost. Lt. Evan's ship dropped its bomb-bay gas tank along with the bombs over the target area and had to land short up near Norfolk. He was perilously low on gas and tried to come straight into the field without success, due to ice on the windshield. Attempting to go around, the ship crash-landed, struck a ditch, and did a 180° turn.

Two men on the ship, Lt. Kraut and Sgt. Julius E. Rivera, were killed as a result of the crash. Both men suffered skull fractures. Three enlisted men on the crew, S/Sgt. John H. Sasson, Sgt. Julius E. Vargo, and Sgt. Delbert D. Rasey, were injured. The extent of their injuries is not known at present.

Lieut. Larson became unconscious on the return from Kiel; lost consciousness when he failed to connect his high-pressure walk-around bottle to his A-8 mask promptly enough. He was revived by the crewmembers. Lt. Wilson had the stem of the bailout bottle in his mouth at 22,000 feet apparently with insufficient pressure and he became unconscious. He regained consciousness at 13,000 feet with the additional oxygen from another bailout bottle administered by another crewman. Another member of the same ship was anoxic, received frostbite of hands, face and feet, severe, and is now in the hospital. Additional data will be obtained.

5 January 1944 — Clear and cold as the very devil. Long underwear is only slight protection. Briefing at 0500 hours, target an airfield at Tours, France. Bombing altitude was 20,000 feet and outside air temperature –26° C. The target was bombed visually with good results. One ship was shot down by fighters using rockets. There were several fighter attacks described as mild, and no flak.

Missing in action are as follows:

532nd Bomb Squadron (H)

B-17F #42-30676 — "Baby Dumpling, Danny Dumpling"

Jack R. Zeman	2nd Lt.	P
Otis A. Montgomery	2nd Lt.	CP
Frank R. Bisagna	2nd Lt.	N
William C. Walker	2nd Lt.	B
John W. Sinquefield	S/Sgt.	TTG
Burton A. Givan	S/Sgt.	RO
Herve A. LeRoux	Sgt.	BTG
Francis B. Cater	Sgt.	RWG
Raymond F. Chevraux	Sgt.	LWG
George M. Day, Jr.	Sgt.	TG

There was a meeting at 1st Bomb Division for all surgeons, equipment surgeons, and equipment officers. Their biggest beef was the number of deaths from the lack of oxygen (8 from this division for one month), as against 22 in the Eighth Air Force in previous months.

This poor narrator's backside and brain became extremely weary and tired of the fat that was being chewed and felt as usual that very little was being accomplished.

Captain Charles L. York, from the 327th Station Hospital, APO 871, an old colleague, was a visitor at this station this date.

Captain Bland and two enlisted men flew to Station 120, Attlebridge, to pick up the bodies of Lt. Irving Kraut and Sgt. Julius Rivera. Four of the crewmembers came back with them and the other four are remaining in hospital.

7 January 1944 — Thirty aircraft, 29 from this command and 1 PFF, took off at 0745 hours with target Ludwigshaven, Germany. Bombing altitude 28,000 feet; temperature –38° C. Bombing was done by pathfinder method through a ten-tenths overcast. There were several fighter attacks, but most of them were described as light. Lieutenant Wilson's ship was seen to spiral down to the clouds far below and Lt. Potenza states that the ship exploded. This is unconfirmed. The flak encountered was moderate and not too accurate. There were four abortions, one due to personnel failure. The pilot, Lt. Bartlett, became ill at 15,000 feet and felt he was too weak to continue. There was no evidence of any fear reaction.

Missing in action are as follows:

534th Bombardment Squadron (H)

B-17F #42-3078 — "Winsome Winn"

Lt. Arden D. Wilson	2nd Lt.	P
Lt. Donald J. McDonald	2nd Lt.	CP
Joseph F. Connolly	2nd Lt.	N
Harry H. Ullom	2nd Lt.	B
John F. Embach	Sgt.	TTG
Peter (NMI) Kucher	Sgt.	ROG
Robert J. Geraghty	Sgt.	BTG
Walter H. Sussek	Sgt.	RWG
George E. Hawkins	S/Sgt.	LWG
Anthony E. Greco	Sgt.	TG

11 January 1944 — Thirty-three aircraft from this command took off at 0800 hours today with the target Oschersleben, Germany. Total distance 978 miles. Bombing altitude 20,000. Air temperature –32° Centigrade. Captain Briggs was in the lead ship. Major Gaillard took a ride in the weather ship and witnessed a beautiful sunrise over the overcast over the Channel. The weather over England was beautifully clear and full moonlight. The dispersal of the sun's rays by the overcast gave a multi-hued sky that had all of the colors of a pretty, burning fire, but without any motion. It was truly beautiful and worth arising at 0400 hours and missing breakfast, which I did. The assembly was normal, except for two wings flying a collision course and the resulting divergence broke up both of the formations temporarily. We also saw two B-24 wings. The weather began closing in about 1000 hours and about 1350 hours, the field was closed and it began to rain. The aircraft were diverted to Hardwick, Norfolk.

Eight aircraft were lost from this operation. The following is a list of the missing in action:

<u>532nd Bomb Squadron (H)</u>

B-17G #42-37962 — "Betty Lou"

Saur, Robert V.	2nd Lt.	P
Capobianco, Frank (NMI)	2nd Lt.	CP
Miller, Phil R.	2nd Lt.	N
Warren, Douglas M.	2nd Lt.	B
Davis, Robert E.	Sgt.	TTG
Brogden, John P.	Sgt.	RO
Prestwood, Harold F.	T/Sgt.	BTG
Keene, Bernard M.	Sgt.	RWG
Patterson, L.T. (IO)	Sgt.	LWG
Jones, James P.	Sgt.	TG

<u>533rd Bomb Squadron (H)</u>

B-17F #42-29999 — "Fertile Myrtle"

McEvoy, Matthew J.	2nd Lt.	P
Nikitin, Nicholas N.	2nd Lt.	CP
Lipsky, Henry I.	2nd Lt.	N
Ingram, William H.	F/O	B
Loehrer, Arthur T.	S/Sgt.	RO
Johnson, Fred W.	S/Sgt.	TTG
Wittwer, Weldon E.	Sgt.	BTG
Sexton, Mack, Jr.	Sgt.	LWG
Kracium, Eugene J.	Sgt.	RWG
Trueblood, Jack G.	Sgt.	TG

STATION SICK QUARTERS
AAF Station 167
APO 634

9 January 1944

SUBJECT: Late to Bed, Late to Rise.

   TO: Group Surgeon, 381st Bombardment Group (H).

1. In times of stress and strain such as we are facing at the present moment, men are not the servants of their conscious mind, but are subject to the call and the demands put upon them by their subconscious mind.

2. Consciously, man knows that work in the Army begins at 0800 hours daily depending upon the exigencies of the war problem at the moment, and ends at 1700 hours, theoretically.

3. Consciously, man intends to awaken in the darkness of the morning at 0700 hours so that he can be at his post by 0800 hours daily, however, occasionally at 0659 hours, man' s subconscious mind arises and presents itself to the conscious mind with a conflict: said conflict being a fight for what HAS to be done at 0700 hours, that is, duty calls, wake and rise, and what SHOULD be done at 0730 hours, that is, sleep, my pretty one, sleep.

4. Thus, as you see, the problem to be solved is whether the conscious or subconscious mind wins out in the end. Invariably, man's actions are based on his conscious thoughts, however, there comes a time in every man's life when the problem presented by the subconscious mind wins out — which is exactly what happened this dark, cold, dreary, Sunday morning in England.

                         BERNARD S. COHLER
                         Captain, MC
                         Flight Surgeon, 532nd Bomb Squadron (H)

              1st Ind.   *M-S-l*

Hq. 381st Bomb Group (H) AAF, Office of Surgeon, APO 634, U.S. Army, 9 January 1944.

TO: Surgeon, 532nd Bomb Squadron (H), 381st Bomb Group (H) AAF

1. *There is no problem to be solved. The theoretical considerations of conflict between the conscious and unconscious mind is of academic interest only and we in the work-a-day world must not rationalize our behaviour upon such euphemistic theories as propounded by Freud and his disciples, Jung and Adler.*

2. *Work still begins at 0800 hours. It is recommended that you fortify your conscious mind sufficiently to over come the desires of the subconscious.*

                         ERNEST GAILLARD, JR.
                         Major, MC
                         Station Surgeon

11 January 1944 (continued):

B-17G #42-3514 — "Doll Baby", "Dinah Might II"

Chason, Billy F.	1st Lt.	P
Mickelson, Henry B.	2nd Lt.	CP
Walker, Lawrence D.	2nd Lt.	N
Gentile, Americus J.	2nd Lt.	B
Wydra, Carl S.	Sgt.	RO
Vollbrecht, Robert F.	S/Sgt.	TTG
Martin, Raymond W.	Sgt.	BTG
Cobb, Thomas R.	S/Sgt.	RWG
Greenwood, Howard J.	Sgt.	LWG
Kudia, Steve A.	Sgt.	TG

B-17G #42-31417 — "Patches", "Big Time Operator II"

Klein, Ernest M.	1st Lt.	P
Chelf, Paul G.	2nd Lt.	CP
Counce, James (NMI)	S/Sgt.	N
Gill, Louis H.	1st Lt.	B
Soderstrom, Melvin A.	T/Sgt.	RO
Pope, Howard A.	T/Sgt.	TTG
Wright, Stanley A.	S/Sgt.	BTG
Miskin, John E.	S/Sgt.	RWG
Schuitema, Edward	S/Sgt.	LWG
Bunworth, John S.	S/Sgt.	TG

B-17G #42-37730 — "No Name"

Crozier, Gordon W.	1st Lt.	P
Van Ness, Sidney B.	2nd Lt.	CP
Hannon, George A.	2nd Lt.	N
Monaco, Albert F.	2nd Lt.	B
Balmore, George (NMI)	T/Sgt.	RO
Dideum, Clyde E.	S/Sgt.	TTG
Osborne, Robert J.	S/Sgt.	BTG
Easley, Cliff W.	S/Sgt.	RWG
Giddens, Gordon W.	S/Sgt.	LWG
Purnell, Walter R.	S/Sgt.	TG

B-17G #42-37719 — "Dinah Mite", "Hellcat"

Nasen, Donald E.	2nd Lt.	P
Byser, Joseph J.	2nd Lt.	CP
Anagnos, Athan (NMI)	2nd Lt.	N
Fiery, Charles D.	2nd Lt.	B
Lab, Ralph L.	Sgt.	RO
Harrah, Luster T.	S/Sgt.	TTG
Stonich, Paul W.	Sgt.	RWG
Beus, Raymond C.	Sgt.	BTG
Lantz, John R.	Sgt.	LWG
Whitney, George A.	Sgt.	TG

B-17F #42-5878 — "Yankee Eagle"

Perot, Wilfred R.	2nd Lt.	P
Jones, Dudley B.	2nd Lt.	CP
Weaver, Robert N.	2nd Lt.	N
Faulconer, Adelbert, Jr. (NMI)	2nd Lt.	B
Jerinowski, John S.	S/Sgt.	RO
Daniels, O.K. (IO)	Sgt.	TTG
Ball, Philip M.	Sgt.	BTG
Turk, Waiter H.	Sgt.	LWG
Bosley, Edwin B.	S/Sgt.	RWG
Graham, Thomas H.	Sgt.	TG

534th Bomb Squadron (H)

B-17F #42-3118 — "Green Hornet"

Larson, Austin G.	2nd Lt.	P
Wilson, Francis N.	2nd Lt.	CP
Neff, Horace R.	2nd Lt.	N
Regan, George T.	2nd Lt.	B
Nix, Edwin A.	S/Sgt.	TTG
Trainor, Michael J.	Sgt.	ROG
Copeland, Milton D.	Sgt.	BTG
Defenbaugh, Ross N.	Sgt.	RWG
Crawbuck, John (NMI)	S/Sgt.	LWG
Williams, Alex (NMI)	Sgt.	TG

This group was flying high and apparently the high squadron was flying poor formation. Enemy fighters flew around along side of the rank, picked the high squadron as the most likely target, and attacked in formation. Another reason for our heavy loss was that two of three divisions that were supposed to go into Germany were recalled because of weather.

A discussion with Captain Briggs revealed that he is adjusting quite well to the stress of combat. He states that his feeling is one of numbness toward eventualities rather than one of conflict between the pros and cons of the situation. He states that he is quite well, has no symptoms at all, and he feels capable of doing a job well. It was also agreed that in flying combat, there is not the sensation of personal danger that there is in intimate conflict, such as boxing. In flying high altitudes in the extreme cold, depending upon oxygen for livelihood, and depending upon mechanical communication, and seeing the earth so far below, gives the individual a sensation of being apart from it all, or living in a different world. The bursts of flak do not seem to have the same terrorizing effect that is experienced on the ground. It was further agreed that people are pretty much surprised when they do get hit. Captain Briggs always felt that if his ship was hit by flak, the first thing he would do would be to bail out.

On a recent mission, flak exploded directly under him, damaging the ship moderately, and his first reaction was to check the engine instruments. Surprisingly enough, the idea of bailing out did not enter his head at the time. He expressed the opinion that the battle on the ground between missions was much more hazardous to the mental processes than during the mission. That would seem to be borne out by our observations.

The local talent G.I. show, "Hey Joe", had its opening night last night and was a huge success. Most of the music and all of the script is original and Major Goodrum and associates are certainly to be commended.

17 January 1944 — A bachelor's party was given by Major Gaillard for a group of fellow officers at the Colonel's quarters this PM. Alcoholic beverages and food were served in great abundance. The bridegroom-to-be was the target of many famous and infamous remarks, all of which were taken in the spirit of fun. The party was greatly enjoyed by all present and adjourned about 2100 hours. The food was prepared by the Airmen's Mess, which consisted of delicious hamburgers, hot buns, French-fried potatoes, cake and appropriate sauces. The medical detachment kitchen personnel transported the food and dishes for the occasion.

Arrangements had been made with the medical department 121ˢᵗ Station Hospital to loan 2 medical officers to carry on the duties of the dispensary and quarters so that the medical officers at this station would be able to attend the nuptials of said Dorothy M. Nash and Major Ernest Gaillard, Jr. on the coming day. Captains King and Mosher arrived about 1730 hours and were billeted in sick quarters. The weather we hope will hold to its present inclement state and prevent a mission, so that all the medical officers may attend the wedding. The four bomb squadron surgeons tossed coins to decide, which two should remain in case the mission, which was scheduled would materialize. Captains Bland and Ralston lost the toss and will remain in case the mission goes on.

18 January 1944 — Today is the day. The morning broke cloudy and moderately hazy to the delight of Captains Ralston and Bland; the mission had been scrubbed about midnight.

About 0915 hours, the station ordnance officers' bus picked up the medical officers at sick quarters, and, in company with eight other officers from the base, proceeded to London, stopping at the Savoy Hotel. At the Savoy, several officers from other commands who were in London on the same mission joined our party and we proceeded to the Savoy Chapel where the main event of the day was to transpire. Promptly at high noon, the ceremony began in the rather picturesque chapel. The bridegroom and best man, Lieut. Gaillard, appeared at the chancel simultaneously with the clergyman. The bride was escorted by her father with her sister as bride's maid. They proceeded down the aisle to the accompaniment of Wagner's Wedding March. Major Gaillard's last few seconds of single blessedness were coming to a close close. At this late hour, no visible signs of a hasty retreat on the part of the bridegroom were evident. Vows were exchanged and the ceremony proceeded without an interruption from the interested gallery of officers. There was a battery of photographers including Captain Hawkins, base photo officer, to take pictures of the bride and groom on their departure from the chapel. The bride was the quintessence of English pulchritude attired in a beautiful aquamarine gown with accessories to match.

The groom was the epitome of tonsorial smartness in his best military garb, and as they posed for the photographers, they exemplified the pinnacle of Anglo-American unity resplendent in the glory of their first taste of marital bliss. As they proceeded down the aisle, one of the casual officers in the audience remarked to a fellow officer, "Note the blushing bride", whereupon he replied, "No, that is the first flush of V..." After the battery of photographers had been satisfied, there was a hasty retreat to the Gondolier's Suite of the Hotel where the reception was held amidst the clink of glasses, toasts to the bride and groom, and resounding cheers of friends and family, and well wishes of the bride and groom. *Hors d' oeuvres* and buffet lunch were served to lessen the effects of the champagne, wines and liquors served. The climax came with the cutting of the cake by the bride and groom. The participants hope and feel they were successful in launching the happy couple on a long journey in the realm of matrimonial bliss.

21 January 1944 — Thirty-six aircraft from this command were dispatched to the coastal area of France across the Channel to bomb "rocket gun" emplacements. All ships returned safely. Two squadrons released their bombs and two squadrons returned without bombing. There were no casualties from the mission.

22 January 1944 — Twelve aircraft from this command were sent on air-sea rescue patrol this morning. All ships returned about 1800 hours with no casualties.

29 January 1944 – Thirty-nine aircraft from this command took off in darkness at 0730 hours — Target — Frankfurt, Germany. Pathfinder bombing at 21,000 feet. Temperature at bombing altitude –34° C. The mission was delayed in take-off by collapse of a portion of the perimeter track resulting in blocking of following aircraft. Eventually, all aircraft were airborne. The assembly was not carried out as planned, and groups, wings and divisions were dispersed and just simply intermingled. Flak was moderate and fighters did not bother our group greatly, but they hit the following wing hard. The escort was P-51, P-47 and P-38 and was good.

Two aircraft are missing:

534th Bombardment Squadron (H)

B-17G #42-38045 — "No Name"

Mohnacky, Robert W.	2nd Lt.	P
Flood, Joe (NMI)	2nd Lt.	CP
Light, James A.	2nd Lt.	B
Yake, William J.	2nd Lt.	N
Gentch, Dale (NMI)	S/Sgt.	TTG
Hagen, Elmer F.	S/Sgt.	ROG
Berg, Robert J.	Sgt.	BTG
Grugan, Joseph W.	Sgt.	RWG
Meyer, Russell A.	Sgt.	LWG
Schenck, Peter (NMI)	S/Sgt.	TG

B-17G #42-37884 — "No Name"

Mickow, Lawrence H.	1st Lt.	P
Hennessey, William H.	2nd Lt.	CP
Wendell, Roy E., Jr.	2nd Lt.	N
Maguire, Hugh E.	2nd Lt.	B
Pierson, Glendon B.	S/Sgt.	TTG
Chandler, Julian R.	S/Sgt.	ROG
Ayers, George (NMI)	S/Sgt.	BTG
Dwyer, Jack E.	Sgt.	RWG
Nersinger, Raymond G.	Sgt.	LWG
Fabianski, Joseph E.	Sgt.	TG

There were nine abortions — one due to personnel failure: S/Sgt. Thomas G. Lawrence ASN 39456024 — RWG. This gunner began to note pains in the abdomen on ascending to altitude. When the plane was at 21,000 feet, the pains were so severe that he could not bear them longer, and were doubling him up. The other waist gunner called the co-pilot as the patient was unable to do so. He states that he was unable to belch or pass any flatus per rectum. After about ten minutes at this altitude, it was necessary to descend in order to get relief. The pilot made a rather rapid descent, and, on reaching lower altitude, exact altitude unknown to patient, he was able to belch and pass flatus per rectum and obtain marked relief. His crew states that he passes great quantities of gas frequently. There was no vomiting or diarrhea, and when patient returned to the ground, he was perfectly comfortable and felt quite normal, happily farting, hiccoughing, and belching his way all over this station. When examined at Station Sick quarters immediately after landing, there were no abnormal findings. He was returned to operational status.

There was one man wounded by 30-calibre machine gun bullet in the right chest. The flak suit was responsible for preventing death or serious injury.

DIAGNOSIS and statement by enlisted man, Sgt. Raymond M. Castellane, ASN 12156922, RWG, 534th Bombardment Squadron (H): 1. Wound, lacerated, superficial, ½" X 3", over eighth rib, posterior, axillary line, right. 2. Contusion, of chest wall, posterior line, over eighth rib, this man was admitted to Station Sick Quarters.

Statement: "In no fewer words can I say, 'I'll live by my flak suit!'; a Frankfurt mission convinced me of that.

"We passed over the target, encountering but light flak. Our ship was left stranded, on turning off the target, which was a perfect target for 'Jerry'. 'Jerry' thought so, too, for here they came — six of them one right after another, attacking us from the tail. I was firing at them from my right waist position, as they peeled off. Three of the 'Jerries' (ME-109's) made their attack! 'Number four is coming in', said the tail gunner. I could see pieces of the vertical stabilizer fly off. Then a hole was made, near the escape hatch. For a moment, I hadn't realized that the bullet not only penetrated the ship's skin, but mine as well. I felt my side, it was burning. I called the pilot and asked if we were free from fighter attacks. Someone answered with a loud 'no!' That didn't make me feel any too good.

"My side began to burn more, so I finally called the pilot and told him that I had been hit. He instructed the radioman to come to my aid, which he did. I was taken to the radio room where medical aid was given to me by the radio operator. I asked the radio operator if the wound was bad. He told me that it was only a fairly deep graze. As I lay in the radio room, I wondered if it was the medal of St. Christopher that kept the bullet from penetrating the chest wall. At this time, the radio operator pointed to my flak suit, and there was a hole, made by a 30-calibre bullet, and at the approximate position of my abdomen.

"I'm getting the Purple Heart for my wound. If it weren't for the flak suit, I'd be getting the Purple Heart posthumously. The bullet, a 30-calibre, went through the suit, knocking one of the pieces out. The bullet careened off another piece, penetrating my A-3 jacket, heated suit, shirt, underwear, and then creased my skin. I was lucky that it didn't hit any of the electric wires in my heated suit. To sum it all up you can say, 'flak suit saves gunner from serious injury'.

"Fellows — <u>wear</u> that flak suit. I can't write anything that may impress you more, so I'll say again, 'flak suit, I love you'".

Statement by Flight Surgeon: "There is little doubt that the flak suit saved this soldier from death or serious injury".

The morale of the crews seems quite good, but the increased number of new crews, losses, and graduates makes it increasingly difficult to know the men personally.

Inspection of the medical detachment this date revealed most things in their usual good condition.

The 533rd Bomb Squadron party was held at the Post Theatre and was enjoyed by all.

There were no missions in the period skipped in the diary. There were several briefings and one mission that was called back after flying over enemy territory. The only other unusual thing was that on 18 January 1944 — the only day in the year there were no doctors from the station here — the semiannual inspection was made.

30 January 1944 — As dawn was breaking this beautiful day, thirty-one aircraft from this command took off for the target of Brunswick, Germany. Bombing altitude 20,000 feet by pathfinder method. Fighter escort of P-51 Mustangs, P-38 Lightnings, and P-47 Thunderbolts. The target was overcast 10/10.

Three aircraft are missing:

533rd Bombardment Squadron (H)

B-17F #42-31047 — "Little Duchess", "Wolverine"

Deering, Robert P.	2nd Lt.	P
Williams, Robert P.	2nd Lt.	CP
Barer, David (NMI)	2nd Lt.	N
Crabtree, Paul O.	2nd Lt.	B
Horne, Wardell H.	S/Sgt.	TTG
Richards, Andrew H.	S/Sgt.	RO
Husvar, Floyd L.	Sgt.	BTG
Scott, Wallace K.	Sgt.	RWG
Jackson, Lloyd H.	Sgt.	LWG
Sanford, Loren L.	Sgt.	TG

B-17F #42-29761 — "Martha the II"

Steele, Henry D.	2nd Lt.	P
Settle, James R.	2nd Lt.	CP
Anderson, Robert F.	2nd Lt.	N
Flores, Leopold L.	2nd Lt.	B
Beach, Perry E.	S/Sgt.	TTG
Eason, Wilbert E.	Sgt.	ROG
Lee, Harry F.	Sgt.	BTG
Hlynsky, Peter (NMI)	Sgt.	RWG
Holtz, Harold A.	Sgt.	LWG
Welch, Paul O.	Sgt.	TG

535ᵗʰ Bombardment Squadron (H)

B-17F #42-30029 — "Chaps Flying Circus"

Baer, Carl O.	1ˢᵗ Lt.	P
Remple, Robert C.	2ⁿᵈ Lt.	CP
VanHise, Malcolm J.	1ˢᵗ Lt.	N
Palas, Henry G.	2ⁿᵈ Lt.	B
Vogelbaugh, Robert R.	T/Sgt.	TTG
Moore, John F.	T/Sgt.	ROG
Phillipuk, Phillip (NMI)	S/Sgt.	BTG
Meyers, Edward J.	S/Sgt.	TG
Tully, John T.	S/Sgt.	LWG
Rigat, James (NMI)	S/Sgt.	RWG

Lt. Baer and crew are thought to be in dinghies in the North Sea and air-sea rescue has been dispatched. He was flying ship #029 "Chap's Flying Circus". The fate of the other ships is not known.

There were several fighter attacks that were not persistent and the flak was described as mild. The group was led by Major Fitzgerald and Captain Becker. There were no wounded or injured. Two ships aborted because of mechanical oxygen trouble.

3 February 1944 — Briefing was held at 0500 hours this morning and the target announced was Wilhelmshaven, Germany. The bombing altitude announced as 25,000 feet, but actual bombing was done at 28,500 feet. The increased altitude was due to the heavy condensation trails, which even at the increased altitude, impaired visibility markedly and prevented good formation flying. The target area was overcast 10/10 and bombing was done by pathfinder. Outside temperature was −43° C and there were five mild cases of frostbite. One placed in Sick Quarters. No ships were lost and the flak and fighters were almost negligible. Thirty-three aircraft from this command took part in the raid. Captain Briggs led the Group and reported what he believed to be a **German** B-17 flying alone over Germany, out of range.

Today a medical board, consisting of:

Major Ernest Gaillard, Jr.	O-330166	President
Capt. Louis G. Ralston	O-479721	Member
Capt. George J. Pease	O-1690307	Member
Capt. Bernard E. Cohler	O-382023	Recorder

convened to determine the mental status of Pvt. George L. Jackson, 17087658, 532ⁿᵈ Bombardment Squadron. Case history filed. He was found to be a constitutional inadequate. Recommendation was made that he be held accountable for his acts and that he be discharged from the service.

Photos
&
Images

DIARY OF MEDICAL DETACHMENT

Book One

STATION—181

Major Ernest Gaillard, Jr., USAAF MC, Flight Surgeon, 242nd Medical Dispensary (Dad)

Mignonne Nash Gaillard, *née* Dorothy Mignonne Nash (Mom)

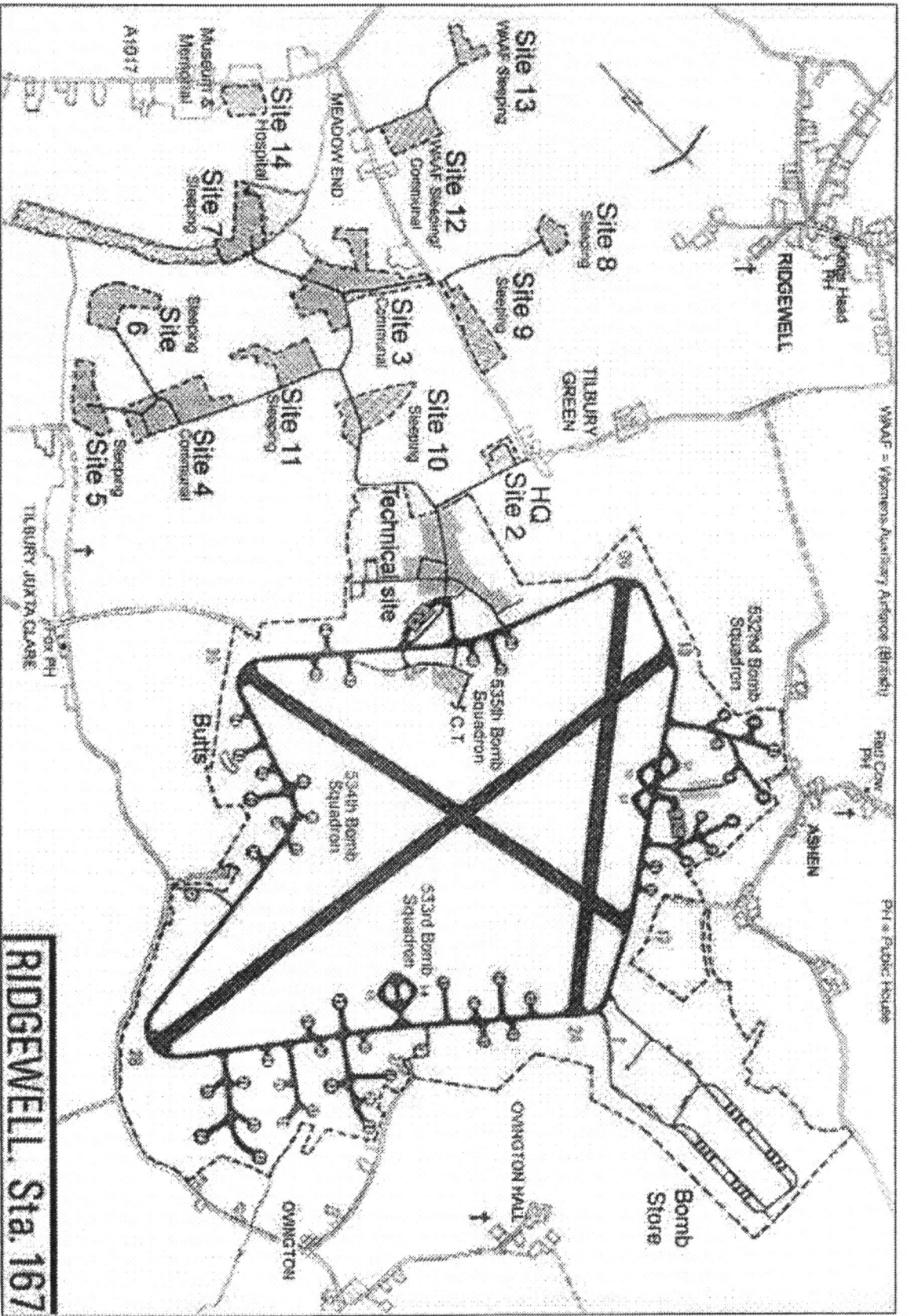

Overhead Map of Station 167, Ridgewell, Essex, England (Courtesy of Ridgewell Airfield Commemorative Association, "381st.com")

RIDGEWELL, Sta. 167

Site 13
WAAF Sleeping

Site 14
Hospital

Site 7
Sleeping

Museum & Memorial

A1017

MEADOW END

Site 12
WAAF Sleeping/
Communal

Site 8
Sleeping

Site 9
Sleeping

Site 3
Communal

Site 6
Sleeping

Site 11
Sleeping

Site 4
Communal

Site 5
Sleeping

Site 10
Sleeping

TILBURY JUXTA CLARE

Fox PH

Butts

TILBURY GREEN

HQ
Site 2

Technical site

C.T.

535th Bomb Squadron

532nd Bomb Squadron

534th Bomb Squadron

533rd Bomb Squadron

RIDGEWELL

Wagon Head

WAAF = Women's Auxiliary Airforce (British)

PH = Public House

Red Cow PH

ASHEN

Bomb Store

OVINGTON HALL

OVINGTON

The English Page, clockwise from top left: my uncle, Lt. (later Cdr.) Denis John Holmes, Royal Navy, Fleet Air Arm; the *HMS Indefatigable (sic)*, the flattop that carried the torpedo bombers; Cdr. Holmes and his support crew in front of his Swordfish Torpedo Bomber deployed to Ceylon against General Hideki Tojo (Denis is in the Navy dress whites, lower right); the *Fairey* Swordfish TSR II (the "Stringbag"), the terror of the Third Reich over the Eastern Atlantic. This one airplane (and with some help from a few others just like it—note the tail hook) harassed and eventually sank the most formidable battleship ever known to modern man: the *Bismarck*. Reich Admiral Karl Doenitz didn't appreciate him much either.

Ridgewell Station 167

Left to right from top left: flight line preparing for battle (going for that "luncheon in München"); flight control tower from about 500 feet; this bicycling navigator is late, but doesn't really appear to care; 381st BG ambulance assigned to the 532nd BS; Dad in front of one of his ambulances off base; Col. Nazzaro, middle, and 381st Bomb Group Surgeons, Majors G.P. Schnabel & E. Gaillard, Jr., M.D.'s

English stained–glass window icon memorializing the US Army Air Forces in WW II
(Village Church, Northampton)

Dad (right front) with Ridgewell Station 167 top brass (photo dated 05 March 1944)

Bombardment Squadron Insigniae, 381st Bomb Group

532nd Bombardment Squadron

533rd Bombardment Squadron

534th Bombardment Squadron

535th Bombardment Squadron

Post Nuptials, left to right from top left: wedding reception in the Gondolier Room at the Savoy, London; Mom and Dad at their home, Tagley Cottage, Ridgewell; Mom, Dad & members of the Medical Detachment; ever the equestrian; Tagley Cottage

Later Years: Mom and Dad after having finally achieved a most important life's goal—winning the Kentucky Derby

4 February 1944 — Briefing at 0515 this frigid morning with take-off at 0845 hours. Thirty-three aircraft from this command took off with the target designated as two areas in the city of Frankfurt, Germany. Bombing was by pathfinder over 10/10 overcast. Bombing was at 20,000 feet — temperature –35° C. The briefing route avoided most flak areas, but route taken went over the heart of the Ruhr Valley both going in and coming out. All ships returned to this base. There was no enemy fighter opposition and friendly fighters escorted the whole distance. P-47's, P-38's and P-51's were used. There were no killed or wounded. Lt. Festrop's co-pilot hit the landing gear switch instead of the flap switch and the ship collapsed on runway 28. Lt. Kuhl had engines #3 & #4 knocked out by flak over Germany, and, displaying great courage and tenacity, brought the ship back to land at this base 3½ hours after the formation. The landing gear would not come down and a beautiful crash-landing was made. Most of us had given the ship up for lost.

The body of 1st Lieut. Carl O. Baer, ASN O-735735, was found washed ashore at Great Yarmouth, Norfolk last night. When he ditched on 30 January, he was in good spirits and wise-cracking on the radio. He will be buried at the U. S. Military Cemetery at Cambridge.

5 February 1944 — Twenty-eight aircraft from this command took off at 0745 hours with the target designated as an airfield at Avord, in South France, just west of Bourges. The air division was led by Lt. Colonel Hall. Bombing was at 18,000 feet and the hits were right on the nose in excellent visibility. No flak or fighters were encountered.

There were no wounded, no missing in action, and no aircraft were damaged. A perfect mission. The only event of the day was on landing when one ship could not get the ball turret guns out of the down position and had to grind them off on landing. We have had briefings seven out of the last ten mornings and five missions flown. The crews are in good shape.

6 February 1944 — Thirty-three aircraft from this command took off for Nancy, France with the target an airdrome. The weather was overcast and the ships returned without dropping bombs. Lt. Putek and crew were near the target when there was an explosion near the T.T., which set off flares and a severe blaze ensued.

The ship landed at Dunkeswell near Taunton. The ship had many 20mm and flak holes, the nose was shot out, the ball turret shot up, and partically burned, the cockpit windows shattered and rolled back, and the wings and fuselage riddled with bullets. Three officers bailed out over France and the following were injured and hospitalized at the 67th General Hospital, Taunton.

Men missing in action:

535ᵗʰ Bomb Squadron (H)

B-17G #42-40025 — "Touch-the-Button-Nell"

2ⁿᵈ Lt. Alfred T. Coffman	O-751986	CP
2ⁿᵈ Lt. Conrad M. Blalock	O-809511	N
2ⁿᵈ Lt. Harvey L. Christensen	O-741470	B

Wounded in Action:

535ᵗʰ Bomb Squadron

S/Sgt. Lifford E. French   ASN 34335103   TTG
DIAGNOSIS: 1. Burn, 2ⁿᵈ degree, face. "H"

Sgt. Herbert J. Burgasser   ASN 32731258   BTG
DIAGNOSIS: 1. Multiple lacerations of face, left, mod. severity.   2. Wound, penetrating of left eye, mod. sev. #1 & #2 caused by flak, low velocity. "H"
Major Gaillard and Captain Bland visited the wounded on 8 February 1944 at 67ᵗʰ General Hospital, Taunton.

10 February 1944 — The ships were dispatched and recalled on February 9ᵗʰ. A practice mission was flown today.   For the past two weeks, the medical department has been having quite a lot of psychiatric activity.   There has been a Section VIII Board on Private George L. Jackson, 532ⁿᵈ Bomb Squadron; a case of hysterical amnesia, 2ⁿᵈ Lt. Ashley L. Hamory, 534ᵗʰ Bomb Squadron; and a psychosis of unclassified type, Private Hugh Sutton, 534ᵗʰ Bomb Squadron. Several consultations have been held on patients found not to be psychotic.

11 February 1944 — Thirty-three aircraft from this command took off in darkness at 0715 hours after a 0415 briefing. The sack sure is hard to leave that early (0330 hours). Target: Frankfurt, Germany. Bombing altitude 25,000 feet by pathfinder method over thick, ten-tenths overcast.   The estimated outside temperature is –45° Centigrade at bombing altitude. Fighter escort is P-47 in and out with P-38's and P-51's over the target.   The Group is leading the air division with Colonel Leber in command. There are two pathfinder aircraft. The target was bombed by visual bombing and the results are thought to be good.   There were three men wounded and are as follows:

S/Sgt. Richard G. Morrison, BTG, 532ⁿᵈ Bomb Squadron.
DIAGNOSIS: 1. Wound, perforating, left ankle, entrance above and posterior to internal malleolus, exit posterior and proximal to lateral malleolus, mod. severe. Caused by 30 cal. bullet, high-velocity.

1ˢᵗ Lt. George A. Hoffman, 535ᵗʰ Bomb Squadron, received: 1. Abrasion, minor, ½" medial to left nipple. WIA

S/Sgt. Charles L. Carter, TTG, 534ᵗʰ Bomb Squadron, suffered: 1. Burn, 2ⁿᵈ deg, lt. heel. WIA

Contrary to expectancy, there were only three cases or frostbite—and one was on the cheek of a previously bitten right waist gunner.

Missing in Action:

532nd Bomb Squadron (H)

B-17G #42-31099 — "Tenabove"

Laux, Robert V.	2nd Lt.	P
Harrer, Donald G.	2nd Lt.	CP
Wright, Phlemon T.	2nd Lt.	N
Doyle, Judson F.	2nd Lt.	B
Bolton, John E.	S/Sgt.	TTG
Helfgott, Abe A.	Sgt.	RO
Hamilton, Richard C.	Sgt.	BTG
Cutino, Rudolph (NMI)	Sgt.	RWG
Glennan, Thomas J.	Sgt.	LWG
Barr, Henry R.	Sgt.	TG

The men do not seem unusually tired after this mission and did not run into any strong enemy opposition.

19 February 1944 — The weather has been stinko for the past eight days and no operational missions have been flown.

On Monday, February 14th, a dinner meeting was held for the commanding officers and the surgeons in the Group, and an attempt was made to present the psychiatric problems and the their dispositions that confront the Eighth Air Force. All were kind enough to listen attentively, but the memory of the hamburgers seems to remain a bit longer than the pearls of wisdom that were given by this poor narrator. The chief topic of the week among the medical officers has been when who was going on pass. I think I will settle the question in the near future and go on pass myself.

We had several accidents during the week. The first, Corporal John Vodden, R.A.S.C. (Royal Army Service Corps), who suffered a compound fracture of the right tibia and fibula, and lacerations about the face, when he continued to travel after his motor cycle had stopped. His commanding officer, Major Lloyd, gave me an "achtung" salute as he entered, and Yours Truly thought he was being addressed by the G.I. Joe of the Army until the Major identified himself. He turned out to be quite a cocoa guzzler and I believe only pride kept him from polishing off his third cup in as many minutes. Cpl. Vodden was sent to the 121st Station Hospital, Braintree.

Later in the afternoon one of our own G.I.'s, Cpl. Irving T. Boorman, 533rd Squadron, was cutting wood and attempted to bisect his foot along with the log. He was given plasma before evacuation on account he was in shock.

To top Captain Bland's rather interesting tour of duty, he was called to see two soldiers that a jeep had inadvertently taken off the base without permission and said jeep had piled into the truck that was returning with the local band. The two injured men were:

Pvt. Clarence J. Caswell, 334th Squadron.
DIAGNOSIS: 1. Wounds, lacerated, cheek and supraorbital region, left, moderate severity and mild, respectively. 2. Wound, lacerated, face, leg, middle third, left, mod. sev.

Sgt. Johnny T. Mills, 535th Squadron.
DIAGNOSIS: 1. Abrasions, end contusions of forelegs, mod. sev. 2. Shock, post-traumatic, mild.

Poor Captain Bland finally got to bed at 4:00 A.M., and the bed clothes rising and falling about four feet with each respiration gave articulate evidence that said Captain Bland was completely pooped upon retiring. He was able to sit up and take nourishment about noon the following day.

20 February 1944 — Today was the busiest day of the war as far as the number of ships dispatched was concerned. Two groups, a total of 47 aircraft, attacked the targets (two) in Germany. One target was Leipzig, and the other was Auscherleven. The effort was directed at German fighter production. One aircraft is missing. A top turret gunner, T/Sgt. Edward J. Senk, 533rd Bomb Squadron, was killed apparently by a .50 calibre machine gun bullet while over friendly territory. A tail gunner, S/Sgt. Johnnie U. Gibson, 532nd Squadron, received a compound fracture of the right forearm with extensive tissue destruction from an enemy .30 cal. bullet. He was evacuated to the 121st Station Hospital. Another gunner was wounded mildly in the face by flak, S/Sgt. Richard L. Walters, 532nd Squadron. He was returned to full duty. One case of frostbite occurred.

Missing in action are as follows:

532nd Bombardment Squadron (H)

B-17G #42-3562 — "No Name"

Cogswell, Kirch J.	1st Lt.	P
Borrego, William (NMI)	2nd Lt.	CP
Meehan, William R.	2nd Lt.	N
Espinosa, Lorenzo (NMI)	2nd Lt.	B
Leccese, Raymond J.	S/Sgt.	TTG
Urban, Frank 0.	S/Sgt.	ROG
Durnin, Joseph L.	Sgt.	BTG
Duncan, Charles E.	Sgt.	RWG
Kangas, John Y.	Sgt.	LWG
Miller, Wilfred L.	Sgt.	TG

Everything, Even Allied AA, Hit Nell

By Ray Ingham

Stars and Stripes Unit
Correspondent

A FORTRESS BASE, Feb. 9—It was shades of "Snuffy Smith", the Congressional Medal of Honor winner, when S/Sgt. Lifford E. French of Athens, Ala., came down in the co-pilot's seat of the B-17 "Touch-the-Button-Nell" last week.

About the only thing that didn't attack 1/Lt. Henry Putek's Fort on the raid was the supporting U.S. fighter planes. Old Nell was hit by a mess of flak, by two kinds of German fighters, and finally by English ack-ack.

The trip seemed like a milk-run most of the way. Near the target there was a terrific explosion between the bomb bay and the top turret, just over the fuel pump. The turret was badly damaged, both cockpit windows were blown out, and the windshield in front of Putek was shattered. French, burned by the explosion, immediately went to work with the extinguisher on flames licking into the cockpit and crackling only two feet from Nell's lethal load.

Putek told the men to bail out at will, and the bombardier, navigator, and co-pilot went overboard. He did not know that his own chute was almost burned off his back. French, getting the fire under control, took over as co-pilot.

Putek salvoed his bomb load in a vacant field and took Nell down to about 4,000 feet, just below the overcast, and headed in the direction he hoped home was in, for he had no instruments to guide him.

Down on the deck every German flak battery seemed to open up. The plexiglass nose was shot away, a large hole was ripped in the wing, and hot flak tore through the self-sealing cover of the wing tanks.

With the top-turret guns out and no one to man the nose guns after the navigator and bombardier had bailed out, the ship was blind for head-on attacks by fighters Luckily, the first attacks came from the rear where Sgt. George Vinovich of East Liverpool, Ohio, was doing the best he could with only one of his two guns working. Both Vinovich and S/Sgt. Herbert Burgasser of Buffalo, N.Y., ball-turret man, destroyed attacking German planes before 20mm. shells from German fighters silenced both gun positions.

The tail-gunner's one good gun was knocked out by a German fighter and at about the same time the rest of the crew heard a burst of 20mm. shells splatter up against Burgasser's ball turret. In the next minute, Burgasser staggered out of the turret.

"I could hear four or five 20mm. shells smashing into the turret", said the right waist gunner Sgt. Vincent R. Shortell, of Kingston, N.Y. "I never want to hear that sound again".

The third and last attacking fighter destroyed by Nell's crew was shot down by S/Sgt. James W. Bomar of Talpa, Tex., radio gunner, whose equipment, as well as signal flares, were destroyed by flak.

Up front French and the pilot, Putek, were struggling to keep the plane in the air. "We nearly broke the plane in two with evasive action", Putek said. Despite the low altitude both French and Putek left their oxygen masks on because with the wind blasting through the broken windshield they couldn't catch a breath.

In the waist, Sgt. Thomas G. Lawrence, of Lewiston, Idaho, stayed at one of the three functioning guns in the ship while the others treated the wounded did what they could to keep the ship in the air.

The worst blow came when "Touch-the-Button-Nell" approached the English coast. In the cockpit French was doing everything he could for Putek. He was navigator, engineer, co-pilot. With binoculars he sighted the coast and started looking for a place to set down.

As they approached the land, ack-ack batteries fired a challenge round across Nell's bow. For a few minutes Putek and French feared their guesswork navigation had led them back to enemy territory. They made a complete circle and looked more carefully. There was no doubt the countryside was English.

With radio equipment shot out and flares destroyed, there was no way they could indicate to the British ack-ack crews the plane was American. Finally French spotted a field and Putek brought Nell down with five men who could walk away from the plane and two who asked to be helped.

20 February 1944 (continued):

The officer's dance of the month was held this evening, most of the time during a red alert, which no one knew anything about—or wouldn't have cared if they did know—and the party was one of the most successful we have had. Lieut. Colonel W. K. Martin and Major George S. Robinson were guests.

21 February 1944 — Briefing at 0530 hours this clear but cold, frosty morning. Most of us were a bit under the weather as a result of the previous evening's activities and it was with a shaking hand and an aching head that most of us attended the briefing. Thirty-three aircraft from this command took off with 12 500 lb. bombs — bombing altitude 22,900 feet — outside air temperature –36° C, target: Ascher, Germany, which was not the primary target. The results were excellent. All the ships returned from this mission. Lieut. Mackintosh's ship was hit in the nose and the Bombardier, 2nd Lt. William F. Piekarski, O-736603, and the Navigator, 2nd Lt. Allen E. Bergreen, O-685370, bailed out (535th Squadron). The co-pilot went down and put the fire out and the ship was brought safely back to this base. One EM, T/Sgt. John D. Sinclair, 533rd Bomb Squadron, was injured by mild fragment wounds in both feet. This was his 25th mission. The fighter support was good on the way in and fair on the way out. Fighter attack was intense for some combat wings, but slight for this one.

22 February 1944 — Briefing at 0530 hours and thirty-two aircraft took off with their primary target and aircraft factory at Oscherlaven, Germany. Due to weather conditions, the rendezvous was again messed up and all but thirteen of the aircraft returned to the base after being unable to assemble, or join the group. The returning crews reported intense fighter opposition. Two crews landed short at another base and only five returned to the home base. Six crews were lost during the aerial combat. T/Sgt. Fred T. Berg was flying as top turret gunner in the lead ship and received a severe cold injury of the hands, which was the result of having to crank up the bomb bay doors without gloves. This was his 25th mission.

Missing in Action:

532nd Bomb Squadron (H)

B-17G #42-31443 — "Friday the 13th"

Flaherty, Francis J.	1st Lt.	P
Hoffer, John I.	2nd Lt.	CP
Austin, Russell D.	F/O	N
Farrell, William R.	2nd Lt.	B
Bright, Notra J.	T/Sgt.	TTG
Roe, John P.	T/Sgt.	ROG
Larson, Burling (NMI)	S/Sgt.	BTG
Krzyzak, Henry R.	S/Sgt.	RWG
Burkowski, Gasimer L.	S/Sgt.	LWG
Butler, Arthur N.	S/Sgt.	TG

533rd Bomb Squadron (H)

B-17G #42-97474 — "Homing Pigeon"

Fridgen, Francis N.	1st Lt.	P
Waller, David E.	2nd Lt.	CP
Ehmann, Paul J.	2nd Lt.	N
Palmer, Philip (NMI)	2nd Lt.	B
Brennen, Robert (NMI)	T/Sgt.	TTG
Reilly, William J.	T/Sgt.	ROG
Bartle, Garrett M.	S/Sgt.	BTG
Abernathy, Walter H.	S/Sgt.	LWG
Gaby, Oliver G.	S/Sgt.	RWG
Slayton, Lowell E.	S/Sgt.	TG

B-17G #42-39946 — "No Name"

Rolling, Hal E.	1st Lt.	P
Bull, Raymond A.	2nd Lt.	CP
Jackson, Johns R., Jr.	2nd Lt.	N
Soled, Milton (NMI)	2nd Lt.	B
Jemiolo, John (NMI)	S/Sgt.	ROG
Thompson, Asbury M., Jr.	S/Sgt.	TTG
Ruark, William L.	Sgt.	BTG
Martin, Othel L.	Sgt.	LWG
Day, George W.	Sgt.	RWG
Eggert, Robert D.	Sgt.	TG

535th Bomb Squadron (H)

B-17G #42-39895 — "Bermondsay Battler"

Smith, Lee W.	1st Lt.	P
Evans, Rowland H.	2nd Lt.	CP
Meier, Leonard P.	2nd Lt.	N
Kaufman, Harold W.	2nd Lt.	B
Kemper, Harold C.	T/Sgt.	TTG
Zappala, John W.	T/Sgt.	ROG
Larson, Lester P.	S/Sgt.	BTG
Solway, Reginald C.	Sgt.	RWG
Manning, Andrew F.	S/Sgt.	LWG
Eden, Lawrence V.	S/Sgt.	TG

B-17G #42-31696 — "No Name"

Hustedt, Henry (NMI)	2nd Lt.	P
Mauzy, Keith S.	2nd Lt.	CP
Hert, Oral H.	2nd Lt.	N

Inglis, Stanley B.	2nd Lt.	B
Tell, Arthur R.	Sgt.	TTG
Rodriquez, Abelardo L.	S/Sgt.	ROG
Russo, Rocco F.	Sgt.	BTG
Kuracina, Vito R.	Sgt.	RWG
Hanna, Leslie J.	Sgt.	LWG
Pingel, Robert C.	Sgt.	TG

B-17G #42-31533 — "No Name"

Downey, Charles H.	2nd Lt.	P
Herdlicka, Donald E.	2nd Lt.	CP
Hicks, John D.	2nd Lt.	N
Evans, James C.	2nd Lt.	B
Chauvin, Miller P.	S/Sgt.	TTG
Matheson, Earl E.	S/Sgt.	ROG
Schiek, Earl B.	Sgt.	BTG
Phillips, Norman E.	S/Sgt.	RWG
Carini, Adolph V.	S/Sgt.	LWG
Sorbino, Joseph G.	S/Sgt.	TG

24 February 1944 — Briefing was at 0530 hours. Take off at 0830 hours. Thirty-two planes took off, six aborted and three crews got back from the field early enough to make a second take off and join the group at the rendezvous point. The target was the ball bearing factory at Schweinfurt, Germany. This is the third trip to this target made by this group and it fell to the honor of Major Shackley to lead the combat wing. Incidentally, this is Major Shackley's third trip to Schweinfurt. The weather over the continent was ideal and the crews all reported unusually satisfactory bombing results. The primary target had been hit previous to our bomb run. Fighter cover was reported as being the best yet and no doubt is the reason for all of our aircraft returning, though some had received battle damage of a major nature.

Sgt. William F. Seifermann, 32779730, 532nd Bomb Squadron (H) on Lt. McCrory's crew received a wound from a piece of flak, which came in the left window of the tail assembly and apparently struck him at the right side of the base of the neck posteriorly and then came out through the left sterno-cleidal muscle just above the point of its insertion. He had received very excellent first aid care by the members of the crew and particularly the radio operator, Sgt. Dick, is to be commended for keeping oxygen going to him constantly until their return to this field. Captain Ralston met the plane on the runway and immediately began preparations to administer blood plasma to the stricken gunner who was in the radio room on the floor. There was no radial pulse obtained, pallor, and he was in extreme shock. He was conscious and attempted to mutter something at intervals, but his mutterings were unintelligible. He had not received morphine and several members of the crew stated he asked not to be given morphine at the time of the injury. He could not move any of his extremities. Captain Ralston started plasma in each arm and 3 units (750 cc) were given in the plane.

His condition had improved slightly and it was felt by the three medical officers that were present that it was safe to remove him from the plane by Neil-Robertson litter to the station sick quarters. He was brought to sick quarters about 1800 hours after a 4th unit of plasma and there was a noticeable improvement in his condition. The radial pulse was present and blood pressure was about 70/40. He received Holy Sacrament by the chaplain. About 1/6 of a grain of morphine was given and a 5th unit of plasma was started. About 1700 hours, he was transported by ambulance to the 121st Station Hospital, Braintree with the plasma running. He was accompanied by Captain Cohler and six or eight potential blood donors were taken to the hospital in a separate ambulance. He arrived at the hospital and according to Captain Cohler he was only slightly weaker than when he left sick quarters. X-Ray at the hospital revealed a compound, comminuted fracture of the 5th and 6th cervical vertebrae. (This gunner died at the 121st Station Hospital on 27 February 1944 as a result of his injuries — complete section of the cervical cord).

25 February 1944 — Briefing at 0545 hours this morning. Thirty-two aircraft from this command took off at 0845 hours; target the main assembly building for Messerschmitt fighters and an adjoining school for training purposes at Augsburg, Germany. The returning crews reported the weather as being excellent with visibility unlimited, and a good concentration of bombs in the target area. Flak at the target area was moderately heavy, but fairly accurate.

Two aircraft failed to return to the field. Lieut. Kels in the 533rd Bomb Squadron landed at an airdrome near the coast, while Lieut. Henderson, 532nd Bomb Squadron, was seen to go out of formation, apparently, under control of the plane and some crews reported seeing his plane burning on the ground later. There were no battle casualties, and only the one plane was lost. This mission was the longest flown by this group, total distance being 1,380 miles. The first planes to land touched down at 1730 hours.

Missing in action:

532nd Bomb Squadron (H)

B-17G #42-37786 — "No Name"

Henderson, Donald G.	2nd Lt.	P
Fournier, Jack H.	2nd Lt.	CP
Wonning, Earl H.	2nd Lt.	N
DeRose, Nicholas J.	2nd Lt.	B
Ramos, Raoul B.	T/Sgt.	TTG
Burgess, Boyd E.	T/Sgt.	ROG
Korkuc, Anthony J.	S/Sgt.	BTG
Bartolo, Anthony J.	S/Sgt.	RWG
Hunnicutt, Thomas R.	S/Sgt.	LWG
Schilling, Dale E.	S/Sgt.	TG

2 March 1944 — Thirty-six aircraft from this command took off at 0830 hours with the designated target Frankfurt, Germany. Bombing altitude was 25,000 feet; outside air temperature –45° C. The weather was clear over England, but there was a six- to eight-tenths cloudiness over the target. Bombing was done by pathfinder, and the bomb run was thought to be good. Major Briggs led the 1st group and Captain Wood led the 2nd group. One ship was lost, Lieut. Shultz and crew, and were knocked down by flak near the target. Eight chutes were seen to leave the ship while the ship was still under control. No enemy fighters were encountered. The remainder of the ships returned safely to the base. There were no killed or wounded, and only two cases of mild burns and one frostbite reported in. Sgt. Gordon on Lt. Fastrup's crew, 532nd Bomb Squadron reported in with a very severe case of bilateral aero-titis and was admitted to sick quarters.

Missing in Action:

533rd Bomb Squadron (H)

B-17G #42-39891 — "No Name"

Shultz, Eugene (NMI)	1st Lt.	P
Plemmons, Howard M.	2nd Lt.	CP
Neeves, Arthur E., Jr.	2nd Lt.	N
Hearn, William D.	2nd Lt.	B
Mehaffey, Hubert G.	T/Sgt.	RO
Kulivinski, John W.	T/Sgt.	TTG
Trapnell, Robert M.	S/Sgt.	BTG
Farr, John T.	S/Sgt.	RWG
Abramo, Nicholas J.	S/Sgt.	LWG
Smith, Charles F.	S/Sgt.	TG

Today, the author of these poor notes was a professional witness at a Courts Martial where they asked him a lot of silly questions such as, "Do you keep records in your hospital?" and "What are the stages of drunkedness?"*(sic)*, to which this old sage replied that he didn't know the classification of drunkedness in stages and asked for enlightenment. I don't believe I contributed much either pro or con. Lieut. Carl Dittus was on trial and was fined $100.00 a month for twelve months—and just for hitting Lieutenant Keating. Combat pay only works in the air over enemy territory.

4 March 1944 — Yesterday and today, 36 and 33 aircraft, respectively, were briefed to attack a ball bearing factory 18 miles east of Berlin, Germany. Yesterday, the air division commander scrubbed the mission when just inside the enemy coast. The approach was over the North and Baltic Seas. The mission was scrubbed because of weather. Lieutenant Rogers and crew are missing in action.

Missing in action (3 March 1944):

534th Bomb Squadron (H)

B-17G #42-37986 — "No Name"

Rogers, Robert H.	2nd Lt.	P
Mills, Edgar J.	2nd Lt.	CP
McGrath, Francis R.	2nd Lt.	N
Taylor, Harold E.	2nd Lt.	B
Meyer, Russell E.	S/Sgt.	TTG
Moses, John (NMI)	S/Sgt.	RO
Casey, Elbert R.	S/Sgt.	BTG
Jernigan, Cecil L. Jr.	Sgt.	RWG
Pouch, Phillip L.	S/Sgt.	LWG
Taylor, Warren G.	Sgt.	TG

The remaining aircraft returned to this base and there no wounded and only two cases of frostbite.

Today the same mission was briefed with the approach over the continent instead of over the sea. On take-off, Lieut. Kuhl's ship caught fire in the #3 engine. It was finally brought under control. Nine other aircraft aborted; one by personnel failure. Sgt. Theodore A. Setela, 32803279, TG, 532nd Bomb Squadron (H), became airsick and his pilot had to return.

This EM has been airsick seven or eight times previously while training in the phases and his pilot, Lieut. Rickerson, had tried to replace him without success. A recommendation has been sent to the CO of his squadron requesting that he be permanently grounded and removed from flying status.

The formation was briefed for 21,000 feet, but, due to haze, the formation climbed to 25,000 feet and eventually ran into weather so bad they had to return. A target of opportunity was bombed by pathfinder and was identified as Cologne, Germany. They encountered intense flak over the target area. Lieutenant Keyes and crew failed to return to the base.

Missing in action: (4 March 1944)

532nd Bomb Squadron (H)

B-17F #42-30151 — "Spare Parts"

Keyes, David D.	2nd Lt.	P
Seal, Richard C.	2nd Lt.	CP
Lynch, Ralph W.	2nd Lt.	N
Hughes, John C.	2nd Lt.	B
Van Voorhis, Charles C.	Sgt.	TTG
Fair, Jon L.	Sgt.	ROG
Simone, Theodore R.	Sgt.	BTG
Hullett, Dail E.	Sgt.	RWG
Levandoski, Henry H.	Sgt.	LWG
Davis, Charles E.	Sgt.	TG

On yesterday's mission, Lieut. Hytinen had the unusual experience of climbing up through the clouds, and, when he broke out, he was still leading the formation all right, but the rest of the formation were FW 190's. No other aircraft were in sight. Nobody shot at nobody, and some of the fighters just peeled off to hit the group below. I guess "Jerry" must have felt sorry for him.

Because of the large number of personnel abortions (non-medical), a meeting of all flying personnel was held in two sessions; one for officers and one for enlisted men, at which time the Group policy regarding groundings and abortions was outlined by command. The policy is to be more severe and only in exceptional cases will individuals be grounded immediately before missions, and any pilot that aborts without adequate cause will be handled by disciplinary action according to the merits of the case.

6 March 1944 — Thirty aircraft from this command took off at 0800 hours this morning. Target: Erkner, Germany, a ball bearing factory 16 miles southeast of Berlin. Captain Wood led this group and we furnished the high squadron in the composite. The bombing altitude was 21,000 feet, outside air temperature –50° Centigrade, undercast of two- to four-tenths, and observed bombing results were said to be good.

Many enemy fighters were encountered: FW 190's, JU 88's, and ME 109's. The flak was heavy over the target and over Osnabruck, Germany on the way in. Lieut. Coyle and Lieut. Haushalter were seen to leave the formation with an engine on fire somewhere near the I.P. Lieut. Fastrup also lost an engine, but I don't know just where. Lieut. Cahill lost an engine over Osnabruck on the way in, dropped his bombs to keep up with the formation, but was unable to, left the formation, and finally had to ditch just off North Foreland, which is at the south east end of the Thames estuary. The crew is said to be intact and uninjured and they are at the RAF Hospital at Manston. Captain Cohler and Captain Frick are on their way to pick them up now. There is considerable damage to most of the aircraft that returned, but most of the damage is not major. The crewmembers seemed quite happy to see Ridgewell again, but are convinced that the back of the *Luftwaffe* is not broken.

Only one man was wounded, Sergeant Emery Y. Naha, 535th Bomb Squadron, TG.
DIAGNOSIS: I. Wound, penetrating, mild, infra-scapular region, right, at posterior axillary line. Caused by explosion of 20mm cannon shell near ship.

Aircraft ditched in Thames estuary:

532nd Bomb Squadron (H)

B-17G #42-37983 — "No Name"

Missing in Action:

<u>532nd Bomb Squadron (H)</u>

B-17G #42-31448 — "Half-Breed"

Fastrup, Milton A.	2nd Lt.	P
Mann, Edward C.	2nd Lt.	CP
King, Martin P.	2nd Lt.	N
Atkinson, Howard C.	S/Sgt.	B
Glauer, Raymond R.	T/Sgt.	TTG
Estle, Elmer E.	Sgt.	RO
Snyder, John	S/Sgt.	BTG
Shorten, Christopher J.	S/Sgt.	RWG
Provonsha, William W.	S/Sgt.	LWG
Dynan, George J.	Sgt.	TG

Missing in action:

<u>533rd Bomb Squadron (H)</u>

B-17F #42-3215 — "Linda Mary"

Coyle, Richard W.	2nd Lt.	P
Wiermen, John B.	2nd Lt.	CP
Hasseltine, Robert E.	2nd Lt.	N
Baker, Robert J.	2nd Lt.	B
Seabaugh, Albert C., Jr.	S/Sgt.	TTG
Smith, Peter W.	S/Sgt.	ROG
Mendoza, Daniel (NMI)	Sgt.	BTG
Legg, Raymond F.	S/Sgt.	RWG
Mueller, John E.	Sgt.	LWG
Shultz, Louis C.	Sgt.	TG

Missing in action:

<u>534th Bomb Squadron (H)</u>

B-17G #42-31553 — "Myer's Flaw"

Haushalter, Edward E.	1st Lt.	P
Hensley, Herman M.	2nd Lt.	CP
Schuit, Richard R.	2nd Lt.	N
Herrick, John W.	2nd Lt.	B
Lee, Harry E.	S/Sgt.	TTG
Nisbet, Richard H.	S/Sgt.	RO
Creevy, Edward J.	Sgt.	BTG
Langston, Everett V.	Sgt.	LWG
Alfaro, Ralph A.	Sgt.	RWG
Jones, Eldon P.	Sgt.	TG

There has been a recent increase in the respiratory disease incidence and it has just about reached the peak in November. We know of no cause for it other than insufficient fuel and we have submitted a certificate to the quartermaster stating we felt that additional fuel was necessary. This certificate was submitted a month ago and no action has been taken yet.

After take-off this morning, this poor scribe took himself to bed and was awakened with difficulty some five hours later. To be awake and alert instead of tired and dopey from lack of sleep is indeed a good feeling, and, if possible, I intend to log more sack time in the near future.

8 March 1944 — Our target was again Erkner, Germany, a suburb 16 miles to the southeast of Berlin. Colonel Kunkle and Captain Hecker led the formation, and the target was attacked by twenty-one aircraft from this command. One ship aborted. Lieut. Pirtle was seen to abort well inside enemy territory and this is the last news we have had of him. Bombing altitude was 25,000 feet; outside air temperature was –40° Centigrade. The weather was beautifully clear and visibility was up to 100 miles, and many of the large German cities could be seen enroute. The city of Berlin was plainly visible and landmarks were easily identified. The target area, a ball-bearing factory, was hit by the formations that preceded us, and Captain Hester, the lead Bombardier, led the bombs right on the target. The fighter escort met at the scheduled time and place and not one enemy fighter was seen by this group.

Flak was only moderate in the target area and the outer guns of Berlin's defences were almost at ineffective range. There were no wounded or killed. The crews were tired after the long mission, 0845 hours to 1730 hours, but were mildly euphoric over their good fortune, by destroying their objective, and not encountering any enemy attack of any significance. It has been quite a while since the medical department has had any real work to do on the return of a mission and I hope that our good fortune continues.

Missing in action:

532nd Bombardment Squadron (H)

B-17G #42-38O29 — "No Name"

Pirtle, Thomas A.	2nd Lt.	P
Schlintz, Paul M.	2nd Lt.	CP
Stern, Milton V.	2nd Lt.	N
Cooper, Harry F.	2nd Lt.	B
Cassody, George W.	Sgt.	TTG
Burrows, Robert W.	S/Sgt.	RO
Kinney, William C.	Sgt.	BTG
Warren, James W.	S/Sgt.	RWG
Estep, James E., Jr.	Sgt.	LWG
Bull, William L.	Sgt.	TG

Sergeant Michael G. Babines, Jr., ASN 33281199, 534th Bomb Squadron, 381st Bomb Group (H), was fatally injured at 1930 Hours today. He was in the flight deck of an airplane and three engines had been started. Number four engine

Flight Surgeon

caught fire and this soldier hastily got out of the escape hatch and ran into the number-two propellor. He was brought to Station Sick Quarters by ambulance, and was immediately taken to 121st Station Hospital, Braintree where he died at 0300 hours, 8 March 1944.

His final diagnosis is as follows:

a. Concussion, cerebral, severe.
b. Fracture, skull, multiple, severe.
c. Contusion, rt. hand, rt. arm, rt. parietal area of skull, severe.
d. Deceased.

His remains are to be interred at the American Military Cemetery, Cambridge, England.

9 March 1944 — It sure gets early quick these days. Seven out of the last eight mornings this poor scribe has arisen at 5 AM or before. Thirty-one ships from this command took off with the target again in the suburbs of Berlin, a bomber assembly plant and airdrome at an outlying district.

Take-off was at 0800 hours and the briefed weather was at 500-1000 feet over England with the top at 4000 and scattered clouds over the target area about six- to eight-tenths cover. The mission returned to this base without loss and without having seen a single enemy fighter. The target was completely overcast and bombing was done by pathfinder method. The target could not be located, so the Group bombed Berlin instead. Bombing was done at an altitude of 25,000 feet. On the return trip, due to an error in navigation, the Group flew over Hanover, Germany and flak was encountered. One man was wounded, Sgt. William D. Ingram, RWG, 535th Bomb Squadron (H), and was evacuated to the 121st Station Hospital. He received a flak wound in the right thigh. Lieut. Hoffman completed his operational tour this date.

16 March 1944 — Thirty-three aircraft from this command took off for a 1,300-mile round trip with an airdrome just 20 miles west of Munich as the target. Bombing was done at 21,000 feet through a ten-tenths overcast by pathfinder method. All ships returned safely to this base. There was one man injured, T/Sgt. John T. Eylens, TTG, 533rd Bomb Squadron. He suffered a burn, 2nd deg. of rt. thenar eminence and a burn 1st deg., rt. hand. This was caused by trying to put out a fire in the cockpit of Lt. Duncan's ship. The right waist gunner, T/Sgt. William J. Yanzek, jumped out over enemy territory when the fire started and has been confirmed as MIA.

The liquor ration was issued to combat crews at the briefing block just before they were interrogated. Most of them seemed to like the idea, but I am not convinced that it has the real value, nor am I convinced of the idea of having the medical department associated with a bottle of whiskey. At the present time, we are doing about as much catering as we are medical work, and at every mission we dole out carbohydrates, coffee, cookies—and now whiskey.

For the past three days, Major Stokes and Captain Weishart attached to the Eighth Air Force, were visitors here on the station.

99

Captain Cohler is attending school in London on War Surgery.

18 March 1944 — Thirty-three aircraft from this command took off at about 0800 hours with the target the Dornier aircraft factory and airfield at Oberpfoffenhoffen, Germany, which is just southwest of Munich. Bombing was at 22,500 feet; visibility good and direct hits on the objectives were observed. Flak was light in the target area and only one group of enemy fighters was seen and these were quickly scattered by friendly fighters. The temperature at bombing altitude was at –41° Centigrade. All ships returned safely to this base. There were no injured or killed.

Lieut. Robert Miller, 534th Bomb Squadron, completed his operational tour and buzzed the tower on three engines.

19 March 1944 — The monthly officers' dance was held this date and this poor scribe having been saddled with the job of entertainment chairman did his utmost to entertain and straighten out a very unfunny comedy of errors. Transportation, chorus girls, food, lodgings, towels, whiskey, money, visitors, uninvited guests, inebriates, broken glass, spilled ice cream, vomit, etc., etc., all added to their collective merriment and my misery. Most of my energies in the coming month are going to be directed to relieve myself of the responsibility. The delegation of duties has already begun. It is the opinion of many of the members that this is the best party we have had to date.

20 March 1944 — Thirty aircraft from this command took off with the target designated as Frankfurt, Germany. The Group was led by Major Briggs and Lieut. Silvernale. The Group was scattered over the target due to poor weather. Six ships failed to return to this base. Lieut. McIntosh and crew have not been heard from and when last contacted, they were over the Atlantic, south of England, and had been given orders to ditch. Air-sea rescue and fighters were on the way. Lieut.'s. Urban, Williams and Schromberg landed at Exeter. Lieut. Wilson at Predannack and Lt. Honohan landed at Harrow Beer. No significant enemy opposition was encountered either by flak or fighters. It is the opinion of the pilots that flew the mission that the higher headquarters were in error in sending them on this mission.

Missing in Action:

535th Bomb Squadron (H)

B-17G #42-31381 — "Jaynee B"

McIntosh, George B.	1st Lt.	P
Fowler, Robert J.	2nd Lt.	CP
Rabay, Nicholas R.	1st Lt.	N
Dittus, Carl W.	2nd Lt.	B
Dever, Harry F.	T/Sgt.	TTG
Rose, Russell M.	T/Sgt.	ROG
Carson, Garland C.	S/Sgt.	BTG

Matcham, Robert S.	S/Sgt.	RWG
Copp, Eugene F.	S/Sgt.	LWG
Craig, Clyde V.	S/Sgt.	TG

Mr. Lawrence Smith of Cambridge, Massachusetts, a war correspondent serving under the Surgeon General with the duty of depicting war medicine pictorially is visiting at this station. He was sent to this base by Col. Wright of the Air Division who seemed to think we had a bit more "atmosphere" than most (you can construe this last remark in your own light).

Captain Milton H. Bland went on his leave to Scotland today, and Captain Bernard E. Cohler returned from his trip to London.

22 March 1944 — Thirty aircraft from this command took of at 0730 hours with the target designated as Berlin, Germany. Bombing altitude was 25,000 and the outside air temperature was –31° Centigrade. Major Osce V. Jones led this group. The target was ten-tenths overcast and the secondary target (in Berlin) was bombed by pathfinder method. All the aircraft returned safely to this air base about 1630 hours, which was one long flight. Enemy fighters were seen, but none attacked. Flak was light and inaccurate.

Last night during an air raid, two German planes were shot down and there were two parachutists in the vicinity. Station Defense and the Home Guard were called out and had a hell of a good time catching them. Unfortunately, the culprits were apprehended by the Home Guard rather than by our own stalwarts.

2nd Lt. Clifford W. Collum, Bombardier, 533rd Bombardment Squadron (H) walked into a propellor of an aircraft prior to the mission and was killed instantly. His diagnosis is as follows:

a. Fracture, compound, comminuted, skull, left frontal and parietal regions with complete evisceration of brain. Accidentally incurred about 0615 hours at AAF Station 167 when struck by a prop of a B-I7.
b. Wound, lacerated, severe, left deltoid region, extending down to the head of the humerus, measuring 4" in length. Incurred as in #1.
c. Fracture, compound, comminuted, severe head and neck of left humerus. Incurred as in #1.
d. Deceased.

The remains were taken to the American Military Cemetery, Cambridge, England.

Captain Odell L. Dannenbrink, O-1690299, M.C. arrived at this Station today and is assigned to the 7th Station Complement Squadron per par 32, SO 78, Hq. Eighth Air Force Replacement Depot, APO 635, AAF Station 594, dated 18 March 1944.

23 March 1944 — Thirty-three aircraft took off at 0645 hours after a briefing at 0345 hours this A.M. Target was an airfield southeast of the Ruhr. Bombing altitude was 20,000 feet, and the outside air temperature was –31° Centigrade. The Group was led by Colonel Kunkel with Major Halsey as deputy and the 381st led the combat wing. The target was completely overcast and the city of Hamm was attacked through broken cloud cover and bombed successfully. All aircraft returned safely to this base at 1315 hours.

24 March 1944 — Twenty-two aircraft from this command took off at 0545 hours after a briefing at 0245 hours. The designated target was Schweinfurt, Germany, the ball bearing factory that has been hit by this group before. Bombing altitude was 20,000 feet and the weather was lousy from the word go. Crews were briefed for three cloud layers, but ran into bad weather all the way and had had heavy dense clouds at flight altitude in the bombing area. One bombardier reported that two 532nd Squadron ships collided in mid-air. One exploded and the other left the formation damaged. The crews are listed as missing in action below.

On take-off, the third ship, which was flown by Lieut. Haynes, hit the ground about four miles from this airdrome at Bailey Hill, Birdbrook, nr. Haverhill, Essex, England, and exploded in the air. Seven identifiable bodies have been recovered and parts of the other three bodies have been found.

532nd Bombardment Squadron (H)

B-17G #42-38102 — "No Name" CJO (Ship destroyed in mid-air explosion)

Unidentified Bodies:

Stahlecker, Harry J.	2nd Lt.	B
Sauld, Edward N.	S/Sgt.	TTG
Ham, Kenneth M.	Sgt.	RWG

Identified Bodies:

Haynes, Kenneth T., Jr.   2nd Lt.   P
DIAGNOSIS: 1. Avulsion, complete, top half of head. Remainder of body hardly identifiable as to structure.

Bemis, Ralph (NMI), Jr.   2nd Lt.   CP
DIAGNOSIS: 1. Body disintegrated.

Cusson, Edmond P.   2nd Lt.   N
DIAGNOSIS: 1. Decapitation, complete. 2. Evisceration of thoracic and abdominal cavities. 3. Amputation of both legs below the knee.

Loparco, Harry C.   S/Sgt.   RO
DIAGNOSIS: 1. Decapitation, complete. 2. Complete avulsion of lower one-half of body. 3. Fracture, compound, both arms.

Herrera, Zeke P.   Sgt.   BTG
DIAGNOSIS: 1. Fracture, compound, comminuted, skull. 2. Partial avulsion of right foot. 3. Fracture, compound, lower 1/3, left fibula.

Mahaffey, Donald B.   Sgt.   LWG
DIAGNOSIS: 1. Fracture, compound, comminuted, skull, with complete evisceration of brain. 2. Fracture, compound, 1st and 2nd metacarpals, left hand. 3. Fracture, compound, leg, left with partial avulsion.

Plows, Arthur M.   Sgt.   TG
DIAGNOSIS: 1. Fracture, compound comminuted, skull, with complete evisceration of brain. 2. Avulsion partial, hand, left. 3. Wound, penetrating, chest, right.

The crash was strewn over an area of about seven hundred yards with engines and props at almost unbelievable distances from the scene of the explosion.

Missing in action:

532nd Bomb Squadron (H)

B-17G #42-40008 — "Bar Fly"

Thompson, Thomas P.	1st Lt.	P
Bowen, George A.	2nd Lt.	CP
Brozoska, Walter (NMI)	2nd Lt.	N
Neville, Edward J.	2nd Lt.	B
Poquette, Howard R.	T/Sgt.	RO
Holub, Libor J.	T/Sgt.	TTG
Hickey, Paul A.	S/Sgt.	BTG
Bollinger, Hubert S.	S/Sgt.	RWG
Draa, Clyde C.	S/Sgt.	LWG
Cavalieri, Rivaldo (NMI)	S/Sgt.	TG

B-17G #42-31490 — "No Name"

Rickerson, John A.	2nd Lt.	P
Wilson, Donald M.	2nd Lt.	CP
Oneshak, Walter (NMI)	F/O	N
Hammer, Edward J.	2nd Lt.	B
Wilbur, Gerard B.	Sgt.	TTG
Williams, Durwood I.	Sgt.	RO
Lujan, Alfredo (NMI)	Sgt.	BTG
Phelps, John R.	Sgt.	RWG
Sanzone, Paul B.	Sgt.	LWG
Lamore, Thomas L.	S/Sgt.	TG

2nd Lt. Buscbaum, Michael W., Bombardier, was wounded by flak, which came through the nose and his diagnosis is: 1. Fracture, simple, 2nd phalanx, 4th finger, rt. hand. 2. Wound, contused, minor, of dorsum of 4th & 5th fingers, rt. hand. 3. Wound, lacerated, minor, at base of nose in midline.

The ships returned about 1300 hours and landed in haze with visibility down to about one mile.

26 March 1944 — Captain George J. Pease returned from a month at the 303rd Station Hospital yesterday. Captain Cohler accompanied the bodies of the victims of the aircraft accident on 24 March 1944 to the U. S. Military Cemetery, Cambridge.

After a 0345 briefing of a target in Germany, which was scrubbed just before take off, twenty-three ships of this command took off at 1300 hours for targets in the Pas-de- Calais area with visual bombing to be done by the individual squadrons at an altitude of 20,000 feet. The mission was uneventful; especially the small of flak, and all of the aircraft returned to this base. There was a tie-up on take off when a ship went through the perimeter track and blocked six aircraft, so take off was slightly delayed.

Lieut. David A. McCarthy, Navigator, and Lieut. Connors C. Myers completed their operational tour of 25 missions.

27 March 1944 — Twenty-nine aircraft from this command took off at about 1000 hours following a briefing at 0345 with scheduled takeoff at 0645 hours. The target was an airdrome at St. Jean d' Angely, France, which is in the south of France and not too far from the Spanish border. The weather here was fog and haze up to about 4,000' and beautifully clear over the continent and up to the target area. The bombs were away on the target and Capt. Hester, the lead bombardier, states that the hangar (the M.P.I.) opened up like a flower and a breeze carried the smoke away in time for the composite group to blast it again. Bombing altitude was 22,500 feet. No one was wounded or killed and all the ships returned to this base. There was no enemy fighter opposition. Flak was light and inaccurate and the fighter support superb. The crews described it as the perfect mission, however, all the crews were rather tired following the long haul and the return to this base was around 1730 hours, which makes a total of 16 hours to 18 hours of very hard work.

28 March 1944 — Briefing at 0530 hours and the scheduled take off at 0830 hours; actual take off 1030 hours because of haze. The target today was an airport north of Reims, France. Bombing altitude was around 18,000 feet and the enemy coast was crossed at 20,000 feet. Here again, the bombing was by visual method and quite successful. Fighter support was very good. Flak over the target area was light, but accurate. Lieut. Liddle caught some flak in one of his engines and they caught fire over the south of England. All the crew bailed out and the ship was put on A.F.C.E. and headed toward Germany, but, unfortunately, crashed in England. All the crewmembers were safe and uninjured.

Lieut. Henry brought his ship back to the field, and from the control tower with the aid of field glasses, a large through-and-through hole was seen just back of the waist windows where a direct flak hit had killed two waist gunners, S/Sgt. James F. Norcom, ASN 33325382, LWG, and Sgt. Richard (NMI) Toler, ASN 35636311, RWG, 534th Sqdn., and, presumably, the tail gunner, S/Sgt. Frank J. Kurtz, ASN 32707711. The rudder and elevator controls were shot out and Lieut. Henry was flying the ship on A.F.C.E.

Five crewmembers bailed out over the field, and, after driving over plowed fields, through woods, over ruts and ditches, I finally rounded up four of them, but missed the man who was wounded. He, Carl A. Mongrue, ASN 18151927, RO, had been picked up by the British and had received treatment at station sick quarters by the time I arrived. 1st Lt. Daniel C. Henry, Pilot, and 2nd Lt. Robert W. Crisler, Co-Pilot, headed the ship out to sea and jumped about ten miles this side of the coast. Both returned safely to this base. The crew was heavily sedated and we are going to send them to the rest home. The remaining crewmembers, 2nd Lt. Fred (NMI) Beardsworth, Navigator, and 2nd Lt. Rudolph J. Jasiak, Bombardier, T/Sgt. Sebastian (NMI) Quaresma, TTG, and S/Sgt. Kyle B. Wheatley, BTG are uninjured.

S/Sgt. Mongrue's diagnosis is as follows, and he was sent to the 121st Station Hospital.

DIAGNOSIS: 1. Wound, penetrating, mild, 3½" distal to the olecranon on the posterior portion of the forearm.

Aircraft lost in crash:

534th Bomb Squadron (H)

B-17G #42-37754 — "Whodat – The Dingbat!"

Captain Dannenbrink was transferred to the Group at Bassingbourne after a long stay of three to four days.

Lt. Colonel Shuller was a visitor of the station this date.

Also, and of personal interest, if not medical interest, was this poor scribe's unheralded and ignominious fall from one of the genus *equus*—the first since the summer of 1942. She was a thoroughbred mare (my sister-in-law, Ellen Nash's horse "Cola") who had not been ridden for a number of months, and, while going at a full trot, I was urging her forward when her front legs collapsed and I did a full somersault remaining in the air an interminable length of time, and finally landed smack on my back. Dazed and undaunted, I remounted and rode her home.

Captain Bland returned from his trip to Scotland today.

29 March 1944 — Briefing was at 0700 hours this morning. Thirty-three aircraft were dispatched to Brunswick, Germany with an aircraft assembly and component factory as target with an airdrome as primary target.

The 381st was leading the combat wing and Major Halsey was deputy leader. PFF ships were flying with the lead group as the weather was unsettled and there was very little likelihood of visual bombing. On return to home base, the planes were about an hour late arriving and the weather was closing in rapidly, visibility being less than one mile when the first ships landed, and by the time the last one landed, it was much less with slight drizzle of rain. Only twenty aircraft returned to the home base, the other thirteen landing at various RAF and USAAF bases. The following crews are still at the bases listed below during this writing, (30 March 1944). Lieut. Renick, Ratton Common; Lieut. Meyers, Bassingbourne; Lieut. Hesse, Milden Hall; Lieut. Bradner, Chedburgh; Lieut. Moore, Snedington Heath; Lieut. Urban, Lebenham. No aircraft were lost and the crews reported intense fighter attacks in the target area. Major Halsey's ship received direct hits from 20mm cannon shells, which knocked him out of formation and he was escorted back by numerous friendly fighters. Ship #721, 533rd Bomb Squadron, got a direct hit in the waist and both waist gunners, Sgt. Fred (NMI) Lawson, 35668835, and Sgt. Rutherford B. Clark, 35648533, received multiple, minor wounds from the fragments of the exploding 20mm cannon shell. The radio operator on Lieut. McElhare's crew, Sgt. Phillip M. Smith, received a mild, penetrating wound, posterior aspect, thigh, left, as a result of an exploding 20mm cannon shell.

Squadron Leader Brown arrived at this station to acquaint himself with our methods of handling Operations, medical care, etc. Captain Ralston went to the RAF Station, Gransden Lodge, for seven days for the same purpose.

Captain Wymer went to the Eighth Air Force EM Rest Home, Lymington, Hampshire as medical officer in charge for a period of seven days.

31 March 1944 — 1st Lt. Wayne G. Schomburg and Captain Paul H. Stull, Jr. and four Enlisted men, T/Sgt. Charles L. Carter, T/Sgt. Donald B. Carr, T/Sgt. Melvin F. Wilson, and Pfc. Albert (NMI) McClain, 534th Bombardment Squadron (H), were instantly killed when the aircraft they were flying stalled on approach and hit the ground at about a 45° angle. It is generally assumed, but without proof, that Captain Stull, an engineering officer, was attempting to land the airplane. His interest in flying has long been known to me and I know he obtained as much unofficial stick time as possible. Capt. Stull and T/Sgt. Carr were identified by dog tags, Lieut. Schomburg by an unburned V-Mail letter in his pocket and by his wallet, T/Sgt. Wilson by dental identification, T/Sgt. Carter by dental examination, and Pfc. McClain by exclusion. The bodies were taken to the U.S. Military Cemetery, Cambridge, England.

Aircraft lost in crash:

534th Bomb Squadron (H)

B-17F #42-29751 — "Miss Abortion", "Stuff"

8 April 1944 — Twenty-nine aircraft from this command took off in haze at 1045 hours after an 0545 hour briefing for Oldenburg, Germany, an airfield being the target. Bombing altitude was 20,000 feet, temperature –23° C. The 91st Combat Wing led and considerable flak was encountered over the target and in the Wilhelmshaven area. All aircraft returned to this base and the only event of the day was the crash landing of Lieut. Bond and crew because the landing gear would not come down. There were no casualties and the crew was sedated after the incident.

9 April 1944 — Easter Sunday and the longest mission of the war was scheduled for us with the target in Poland. The flight was to last 11 hours and 28 minutes and everybody would have been completely exhausted for the big party we planned for this evening. When a short way over the North Sea, the mission was scrubbed because of weather. The party will probably go on OK now. This morning on take off, Lt. Soeder, 535th Bomb Squadron, nosed up at the end at the runway. There were no injuries.

10 April 1944 — Approximately thirty aircraft from this command took off at 0830 hours this morning with aircraft attacking an airdrome in Brussels, Belgium. The bombing altitude was 22,500 feet and first reports indicate the bombing was good. All crews returned safely to this base. There were no casualties. The monthly party was held Easter, yesterday, and seemed to be enjoyed by all.

11 April 1944 — Thirty-five aircraft took off from this command at 0715 hours and 0745 hours for targets south east of Berlin. Factories at Cottsburg and Sorau, Germany were the objectives. Total distance was 1,450 miles and the planes were in the air 10 hours and 20 minutes, which is indeed a long and tail-wearying haul. The undercast was complete when the enemy coast was reached and was six-tenths from there on out. Bombing was done visually and results were good. One aircraft is missing, Lieut. Hesse and crew, having lost two engines near the target area. They were seen to go down in control. The (remaining) aircraft returned to this base about 1800 hours and the crews did not seem unduly fatigued. Hooch was served.

Missing in action:

534th Bomb Squadron (H)

B-17G #42-31497 — "Round Trip"

Hesse, Robert W.	2nd Lt.	P
Gatewood, Robert W.	2nd Lt.	CP
Noga, Theodore F.	2nd Lt.	N
Bach, Leo S.	2nd Lt.	B
Hallenbeck, Brua A., Jr.	Sgt.	TTG
Sexton, Frank C.	S/Sgt.	RO
Blanch, Bernard J.	S/Sgt.	BTG
Nelson, Alvin L.	Sgt.	WG
Puryear, Roy A.	Sgt.	TG

Major and Mrs. Gaillard entertained Captains Wymer and Ralston and Mr. Lawrence Smith, war correspondent, at their country home last evening, also Major Kidd.

13 April 1944 — Thirty-three aircraft from this command took off at 1000 hour with the target for the fourth time in the history of this group the ball-bearing factory at Schweinfurt, Germany. The 381st Group was led by Major Halsey and the composite group by Captain Franek. Bombing Altitude was 20,000 feet and outside air temperature was –27° Centigrade. The weather was hazy on take-off, but good on return, and the cloud cover over the target area was six- to eight-tenths. Considerable fighter opposition was encountered by the wing ahead of ours on the way into the target. About 60 ME-109's took out 7 Forts in that formation in one pass. Lieut. Mullane lost one engine over the target and one shortly afterward and lagged behind the formation losing about 500 feet a minute. It is thought he had a windmilling propeller. Lieut. Sherwood, co-pilot, has been one of our problem children since he was assigned to this group. He came to the E.T.O. about 18 – 20 months ago and was grounded shortly thereafter for a possible fear reaction, and at the end of his first 14 months, had completed only one operational mission, I believe. We have nursed him along through many complaints, both real and imaginary, and recently, it looked as though he was finally becoming a man, adjusting himself to his lot in life fairly well.

He had only two or three more missions to complete. Lieut. O'Phelan, the Navigator, has also been one of our problem children and we have had to nurse him through upper respiratory infections and numerous minor complaints. Despite the fact that it solves the problem for us, we would rather not have individuals disposed of in this way.

Missing in action:

535th Bomb Squadron (H)

B-17G #42-31357 — "Our Desire"

Mullane, James F.	2nd Lt.	P
Sherwood, Thomas P.	1st Lt.	CP
O'Phelan, Patrick D.	2nd Lt.	N
Kirby, John J.	2nd Lt.	B
Stahlke, Edward A.	T/Sgt.	TTG
Kettlety, Robert E.	T/Sgt.	RO
Tarezynski, Thaddeus J.	S/Sgt.	BTG
Sparrow, Lewis F.	S/Sgt.	WG
Traxler, Frank G.	S/Sgt.	TG

Lawrence B. Smith, artist war correspondent, departed this station yesterday after a three weeks' stay. He was a nice type of individual and apparently well liked.

Captain Ralph M. Wymer is scheduled to go to the RAF field at Wratting Common about twelve miles northwest of here for a period of one week beginning tomorrow.

18 April 1944 — Thirty-three aircraft from this command took off at 1000 hours with the primary target designated as an airfield at Orienburg, Germany, which is just sixteen miles northwest of Berlin. The secondary target was the Fredrickstrausse railway station. Bombing altitude was designated at 25,000 feet and actual bombing altitude was 22,500 feet. The weather was perfect and when in the target area, their lateral visibility became stinky, but the ground could be seen. The primary target was bombed successfully. Lieutenant Soeder and crew went down in the target area in control and apparently had lost two engines. The remainder of the ships landed safely at this base about 1900 hours. There were no killed or wounded. Temperature was –32° C and there was one frostbite of the chin.

Missing in action:

535th Bomb Squadron (H)

B-17G #42-37733 — "Patches 'n Prayers"

Soeder, Harlan D.	1st Lt.	P
Mulhall, Phillip E.	2nd Lt.	CP
Becker, Jerome D.	F/O	N
Grote, George C.	2nd Lt.	B
Sedoryk, Harry C.	S/Sgt.	TTG
Boland, John J.	S/Sgt.	RO
Marushack, Frank J.	S/Sgt.	BTG
Hawkinson, Alan D.	S/Sgt.	WG
Bailes, Milton G.	S/Sgt.	TG

19 April 1944 — Briefing at the unholy hour of 0345 A.M. with takeoff at 0645 hours. The target an airfield at Oschwege, Germany. The Group made a 360° at the target and the high squadron, the 534th, caught it from both flak and fighters. Lieut. Bond and Lieut. Rayburn did not return and are presumably lost over enemy territory. The wounded that returned here were:

2nd Lt. Edward L. Hampton, O-808832, 534th Bomb Squadron.
DIAGNOSIS: 1. Wound, penetrating, rt. ankle, lateral aspect, wound entrance above and medial exit below and lateral to lateral malleolus, mod. sev. Caused by 20mm fragments. "H"

2nd Lt. Lee R. Hagen, O-809592, 534th Bomb Squadron.
DIAGNOSIS: 1. Fracture, skull, compound, comminuted. Caused by piece of 20mm penetrating skull ½" above rt. orbital ridge. 2. Wound, penetrating, mod. sev., rt. cheek nr. opening of parotid duct. 3. Wounds, multiple, penetrating, rt. hand & forearm, mod. sev. "H"

HEADQUARTERS
AAF Station 167
Office of the Surgeon
APO 557

M-R-2

9 April 1944

SUBJECT: Informal report, following detached service of one week at RAF Station.

TO: Surgeon, 1st Bombardment Division, APO 557, U.S. Army

I spent seven days at Gransden Lodge Air Base. This station is RAF, but the operational pathfinder squadron is RCAF

There were approximately one thousand personnel on the field and one medical officer and myself to take care of these. As a result, I took an active part in the medical set-up and in addition was given every opportunity to visit throughout the base and to fly with the air crews (Lancaster planes).

My impressions were essentially as follows:

    a. The air crews appeared to be under about the same stress as our crews and the air crew personnel appeared to be of about the same quality.

    b. The RAF system of passes and leaves is much superior to our own and the men seemed to look forward to their regular leaves with great anticipation.

    c. The American Medical equipment and supply is superior to that supplied to the RAF

    d. It is my impression that it would be advantageous to continue to exchange medical officers and, in addition, other officers as communication officers, squadron commanders, etc.

LOUIS G. RALSTON
Captain, MC

19 April 1944 (continued):

S/Sgt. William P. Palmisano, 17122477, 534th Sqdn.
DIAGNOSIS: 1. Wound, penetrating, right chest, sev., with hemothorax, posterior axillary line, at level of 7th rib. 2. Wounds, penetrating, multiple, mod. sev., rt. shoulder. #1 & #2 caused by 20mm fragments.

Lieut. Martyniak landed at Framingham with his ship on fire and one EM dead, S/Sgt. Gerald A. Goodman, 39199675, 534th Sq.
DIAGNOSIS: 1. KIA, penetrating wound through forehead, caused by 20mm shell.

He (the pilot) and F/O Murray were wounded also. Their diagnoses are as follows:

Martyniak, John A., 2nd Lt., O-754288, 534th Sqdn.
DIAGNOSIS: 1. WIA, GSW, penetrating wound over middle third, inner aspect, left tibia.

Murray, Arthur J., F/O, T-123581, 534th Sq.
DIAGNOSIS: 1. WIA, GSW, multiple, penetrating wounds of left forearm and hand; penetrating wound of lt. cervical region and forehead, caused by 20mm.

Both of the above officers were sent to 65th General Hospital. The remaining aircraft returned safely to this base.

Missing in action:

534th Bomb Squadron (H)

B-17G #42-38004 — "Ol' Man Tucker"

Rayburn, Robert W.	1st Lt.	P
Craft, Maynard V.	2nd Lt.	CP
Morse, Loren C.	2nd Lt.	N
Simons, Ralph G.	2nd Lt.	B
Purser, William R.	S/Sgt.	TTG
Peterson, Donald C.	S/Sgt.	ROG
Bristow, John L.	S/Sgt.	BTG
Main, De Forest E.	S/Sgt.	WG
Gerber, Gerald (NMI)	S/Sgt.	TG

B-17F #42-3525 — "No Name"

Bond, Leslie A.	2nd Lt.	P
Mason, Wilbur M.	2nd Lt.	CP
Brumback, Charles E.	2nd Lt.	N
Hilton, Gerald O.	2nd Lt.	B
Clyman, Neal V.	S/Sgt.	TTG
Jones, William E., Jr.	S/Sgt.	ROG

Caserta, Anthony J.	S/Sgt.	BTG
Derrington, A.C. (IO)	Sgt.	WG
Batchelder, Robert K.	Sgt.	TG

We finally had the inspection that the base has been preparing for for the last two weeks at the expense of the war effort, and the inspecting Generals were Lieutenant Generals James E. Doolittle, Carl A. Spaatz, J. C. Lee, and Lt. Gen. J. F. McNarney. Major General Kemper of Fighter Command; and Brigadier General Robert S. Williams, Brigadier General Bartlett Beaman, and one other one I did not know were along with Colonels and Lieutenant Colonels by the dozen. In addition, all of the Heavy Bomb Group commanding officers were present to meet the Generals. The Assistant Secretary of War, Mr. McCloy, was present and apparently out-ranked all the Generals. They inspected our humble institution and Lieut. Gen. Lee was kind enough to say it was the best dispensary of this type he had ever seen, and a Colonel, the chief engineer of this base section, was of the same opinion. Tea was served at the lounge of the officer's club and, fortunately, they did not stay too long.

The 121st Station Hospital was successfully bombed by the Germans on 18 April, yesterday, and nine wards were demolished, two of which were completely flattened.

There was one broken leg and a few minor injuries, despite the fact that many of the wards were full of patients. The work of evacuation, re-registration and rearrangement was carried out expeditiously by all hospital personnel and the officers have commented that the thing that impressed them the most was the eagerness and willingness all personnel to help, including patients.

20 April 1944 — Briefing at 1400 hours and take-off at 1600 hours for the rocket gun installations—or whatever they are—in the vicinity of Cocove, France just across the Channel. Thirty-five aircraft were dispatched. These missions are almost always considered milk runs, but the flak is most always intense and accurate. The ships returned from this mission with full bomb load because of poor visibility in the target area. Lt. Jones and Lt. Weezowicz landed without brakes without any damage or injury. Lieut. Zapinski landed with two injured aboard, the radio operator and co-pilot, and #4 prop. is gone. The injured were:

2nd Lt. Othmer G. Widosh, O-759780, 532nd Squadron.
DIAGNOSIS: 1. Wound, perforating, arm, left, sub-deltoid area, caused by flak.

S/Sgt. George (NMI) Pastre, 39554149, 532nd Squadron.
DIAGNOSIS: 1. Wound, perforating ½" below left shoulder, caused by flak.

2nd Lt. Robert (NMI) Van Buskirk, O-743872, 532nd Squadron.
DIAGNOSIS: 1. Abrasion, mild, lower third outer aspect, left thigh, due to flak.

2nd Lt. James M. Hopkins, O-675774, 534th Squadron.
DIAGNOSIS: 1. Wound, penetrating, mild, pin-point size, middle third aspect, rt. leg, caused by .50 calibre bullet.[6]

Lt. Widosh and S/Sgt. Pastre were sent to 136th Station Hospital. Lieut's. VanBuskirk and Hopkins were returned to full flying duty. All the ships returned to this base.

21 April 1944 — Briefing at 1000 hours this morning with the designated target an airfield deep into Germany.

Luncheon this noon with stars of the stage and screen and high military figures and other dignitaries who were here to christen the ship "Stage Door Canteen". The dignitaries included Major General Anderson, Chief of Eighth Air Force Operations, Air Chief Marshall Harris, the high mogul of the British Air Force, Mary Churchill, daughter of the Prime Minister, Vivian Leigh, Lawrence Olivier, Alfred Lunt and, regrettably, not Lynne Fontaine.

The ship was christened by Mary Churchill and she had to take a couple of heavy left swings to break the Coca-Cola bottle on the chin turret guns. Colonel Leber (our commanding officer) was inadvertently christened on the second swing along with the ship. Cameras were very much in evidence and the most interesting scenes shot were pictures of people taking pictures. The christening party watched the take-off at 1345 in weather that was becoming increasingly poor and the mission was scrubbed at about 1500 hours.

Comment: If we don't quit having inspections and so many dignified visitors, I am going to wear out my Sunday pants.

22 April 1944 — Twenty-nine aircraft from this command took off at 1615 hours with the designated target a huge marshalling yard in the vicinity of Hamm, Germany. The importance of this target, which connects the Ruhr with Eastern Germany was realized when the task force sent over to destroy it consisted of fifteen combat wings. Bombing altitude was 22,000 feet and outside air temperature was –30° Centigrade. No enemy fighters were encountered and the flak was light. The ships landed at this base at 2200 hours, which was after dark and this was the first time they have landed in quite some time at night. Just as the lead squadron was peeling off, we had an air raid warning and, shortly after, we were notified that a German ship had been shot down 20 miles from the airdrome. No ships were lost, and no one was killed or wounded. Lieut. Carroll landed at Manston because they had a couple of engines shot out.

---

[6] Note: It was from our very own .50 calibre machine guns (the M-2, "Ma Deuce") that we eventually developed and incorporated into the American lexicon the colloquial term, "the whole nine yards" — to give absolute maximum effort when trying to win or achieve something. B-17 Flying Fortress defensive aircraft machine guns utilized ammunition belts that were nine yards long.

Five-and-one-half hours after the ships landed, there was another briefing, so most of the crews averaged about two hours sleep. Fortunately, the mission was scrubbed right after pilots' meeting.

25 April 1944 — Thirty-one aircraft from this command took off at 0615 hours with the designated target an airdrome at Metz, France, which is northeast of Paris. Bombing altitude was 20,000 feet, and, although there were no strike photos taken, the bombing results were said to be good. One ship, Lieut. Claytor and crew, are missing. He was last seen about 15 miles inside France on two engines and the ship was smoking. It is thought that he landed in France. He was under escort and no report has been made of ditching. The remainder of the ships returned safely to this base.

Missing in action:

535th Bomb Squadron (H)

B-17F #42-3511 — "No Name"

Claytor, Andrew G.	2nd Lt.	P
Rice, Roy J., Jr.	2nd Lt.	CP
Chisholm, Robert H.	2nd Lt.	N
Middleton, Charles D.	S/Sgt.	B
Sango, Nicholas A.	S/Sgt.	TTG
Williams, Walter R.	S/Sgt.	RO
Souder, David W.	Sgt.	BTG
Connable, Joseph M.	Sgt.	WG
Vitkus, Raymond D.	Sgt.	TG

Major Gaillard and Captain Wymer went to Nuthampstead to lecture to the 398th Bomb Group on first aid. The Group seemed ready, willing, and able—and was ready for combat.

26 April 1944 — Briefing at the unholy hour of 0215 A.M. Take-off at 0515 with designated target an airdrome four miles north of Brunswick, Germany. Thirty-one aircraft from this group were dispatched. The 381st led the combat wing with Colonel Leber leading and Lieutenant Colonel Fitzgerald leading, the composite of which we comprised two squadrons. The target was overcast and was bombed by pathfinder method. All aircraft returned safely to this base. Two men received flak injuries:

2nd Lt. Joseph R. Scott, O-811510, Navigator, 535th Bomb Squadron
DIAGNOSIS: 1. Wound, penetrating, scapular region, lateral, right, mod. sev, 3cm x 5cm, who was sent to 136th Station Hospital; and

T/Sgt. Arthur P. Andrzejewski, 16124049, 535th Bomb Squadron.
DIAGNOSIS: 1. Wound, penetrating, mild, mid scapular region, left, who was returned to full flying duty.

There was not <u>one</u> aircraft lost on this mission in the entire Eighth Air Force and Five Hundred Heavy Bombers (U.S.) were dispatched.

27 April 1944 — This is the one-hundredth mission for the 381st Bombardment Group (H). It does indeed seem a long cry from the first raid on June 22, 1943 when the Group raided Antwerp, Belgium.

The early raids in France are characterized by small B-17 formations and intense hostile fighter attacks, and little, if any, fighter support. It certainly seems as though the Eighth Air Force has accomplished a tremendous amount now that it can raid most any point in Germany with impunity and without the losses being too severe. The increasing number of crews, friendly fighter support through a mission, and the huge formations that are now being sent over Germany, has lessened the mental strain on the crewmembers and we do not see as many instances of clinically manifested fear as we did formerly. The trend is favorable. Twenty aircraft were dispatched today with the secret weapon installations on the coast of France as the target for the one hundredth mission of this group.

The Group was led by Major Jones and the composite group leader was Captain Armstead. Bombing altitude was 20,000 feet and the target was on Cherbourg Peninsula right in the center of a heavy flak area. The weather was good, the ships made one pass at the target without dropping their bombs, and returned to the base. There were five ships with feathered props and many of the ships had been hit by flak. There were no wounded or killed.

24 April 1944 — (omitted previously) Twenty-nine aircraft from this command and 2 PFF ships attacked an airdrome in the Munich area, by name, Erding, Germany. There were no losses, killed or wounded.

28 April 1944 — Twenty-seven ships from this command took off at 0815 hours this morning with the designated target an airdrome at St. Avord, France. St. Avord is just about due south of Paris. Bombing altitude was 14,000 feet. Major Jones was leading the Group. He received a direct hit by 20mm flak in his #2 engine. The engine twisted, caught fire, and fell out of the nacelle. The ship pulled up and careened off to the left and went down through the low squadron and was seen to break up. The most accurate reports would indicate that the tail gunner got out, but his chute fouled on the tail and he was carried down with the ship. It is believed three other chutes came out.

**Office of the Surgeon
351ˢᵗ Bombardment Group (H)
APO 557**

20 April 1944

SUBJECT: Statements Concerning Use of Steel Helmet on Combat Missions.
    TO: The Surgeon, 1ˢᵗ Bombardment Division, APO 557

The following are Statements to accompany the photograph[7] of the steel helmet worn by 2ⁿᵈ Lt. Honor G. Windes, O-684589, Co-Pilot:

I would like to tell all flying personnel that although I did not advocate a regulation steel helmet much before I was hit by a 20mm shell fragment, I am certainly a firm believer in them now and will always wear one on missions.

I had been wearing my helmet up until the time we dropped our bombs over a target in Germany, but took it off as we started for home. We had several fighter attacks, but they were not persistent so I did not put my helmet on again until we noticed an increased amount of flak bursts near Denmark. I had not had it on more than 2 minutes when approximately eight fighters hit us. I was suddenly dazed by a tremendous explosion, and when my head cleared and the smoke cleared away, I took the helmet off and found a huge hole in it and a great deal of blood on it. The pilot was hit in the leg by the same shell and for a few seconds we had our hands full. We finally got the ship home OK. Our crew, at least, will always wear their helmets during the entire mission.

/s/ HONOR G. WINDES /t/ HONOR G. WINDES 2ⁿᵈ Lt. AC

---

[7] I made a photo exception in the case of this particular WIA, not because of its disturbing nature, but, rather, because of the simply unbelievable miracle that it depicts; and in footnoted comments to this letter, the Medical Corps agreed (see Reports & Endnotes). Maybe there's something to today's helmet laws after all—especially if you're going to get hit in the head by an exploding, 20mm cannon shell.

28 April 1944 (continued):

Missing in action:

535th Bomb Squadron (H)

B-17G #42-38061 — "Georgia Rebel II"

Henslin, Harold F.	1st Lt.	P
Jones, Osce V.	Major	CP
Guertin, Arthur L.	2nd Lt.	N
Arning, Eugene (NMI)	1st Lt.	B
Karr, Jo R.	T/Sgt.	TTG
Padgett, J. W. (IO)	T/Sgt.	RO
McLaughlin, George B.	S/Sgt.	BTG
Williams, Clarence T.	S/Sgt.	RWG
Blackmon, William B.	Sgt.	LWG
Sell, Edward H.	S/Sgt.	TG

The loss of Major Jones is keenly felt by the Group. On a previous raid to the southeastern coast of Norway on 24 July 1943, Major Jones was forced to land in Sweden. He spent a number of months there and returned to this group on operational status. He was operations officer of the 535th Bomb Squadron.

Major Gaillard gave a lecture to new combat crews of the 398th Bomb Group (H) at Nuthampstead.

29 April 1944 — The Group this date attacked the city of Berlin, Germany with Colonel Kunkle leading. Bombing was by pathfinder method. Major Halsey was the leader of the "B" group. Bombing altitude was 25,000 feet. The flak was intense to moderate and bombing results were, of course, not observed. Twenty-nine aircraft from this group and two PFF's were dispatched. We had no losses, none killed, and a few minor injuries, i.e., three slight cases of burns, one frostbite, one knee abrasion, and one case of anoxia.

Lieut. Zapinski landed late because of engine trouble. Lt. Gnatzig landed elsewhere after an awful long haul on two engines. In the over all picture, sixty-three heavy bombers were lost on this operation. We were very fortunate not losing any.

30 April 1944 — This date, thirteen ships from this group attacked an airfield at Lyons, France with briefing at 0330. The bombing altitude was 20,000 feet. The weather was beautiful and results were good. There were no killed or wounded and our ships landed safely at this base.

1 May 1944 — Briefing at 1145 hours with take-off at 1415 hours. Twenty-five aircraft from this command took off with the target the rail yards and station at Troyes, France. The weather was beautiful and bombing results were said to be good. All aircraft returned at 2045 to this base. There were no injuries or deaths.

6 May 1944 — Thirty-seven aircraft from this command took off at 0530 hours after a briefing at 0230 hours with the target designated as the rocket gun installations at Cherbourg, France. The bombing altitude was 25,000. The target was nine-tenths overcast and the bombs were not dropped. The flak was intense. All the ships landed at this base except Lieut. Wardnicki who landed safely at Bigen Hill. While we were standing in the control tower, a P-51 was seen to crash from an estimated 3,000 feet (he was only at about 300 feet when I first saw him) and burst into flames. We were on the scene about five to ten minutes later and picked up the pilot, Lieut. R. G. Boyce, O-758928, who was decapitated, eviscerated, had his right leg amputated and had a compound fracture of the left leg. Division was notified and he was found to be from Debden, Essex and a member of the Fourth Fighter Group.

Lieut. Joseph F. Grace on Lt. Yates crew was wounded and has the following diagnosis: 1. Wound, low velocity missile, 2" x ¾", avulsive type through skin and subcutaneous layers to muscle and deep fascia right leg, lateral aspect, three inches above lateral malleolus. 2nd Lt. John J. Monahan, O-748213, received minor abrasions of the forehead due to plexiglass set in motion by low velocity flak.

7 May 1944 — Twenty-nine aircraft from this command led by Lt. Colonel Hall took off at 0530 hours and bombed Berlin by pathfinder method from 26,000 feet. Flak was moderate, but not too accurate. A few enemy fighters were seen. There were no wounded or killed and all ships returned safely to this base. There were five cases of anoxia: one due to resistance by other anoxic individuals, two by disconnection of the mask from the ship's system, and two by freezing of the A-14 mask.

The monthly officers' dance was held and approximately seventy show girls from London were guests. The party progressed with only a mild amount of trauma and most everyone felt it was one of our better dances.

8 May 1944 — Briefing at 0300, take-off at 0545 with the target designated as Berlin. Bombing was at 26,000 feet by pathfinder method. All ships returned safely and there were no killed or wounded. One case of frostbite was reported and the individual was admitted to quarters. Combat crewmembers reported seeing enemy "flying wings" that did not attempt to engage them.

Because of the influx of new crews, the missions do not seem to be causing any undue strain on personnel and we have not had any psychiatric casualties that have required disposition for some time.

Major Gaillard went to Nuthampstead Friday, 5 May 1944, to lecture to new combat crews.

9 May 1944 — Thirty-one aircraft from this command took off at 0545 hours with designated target an airdrome at St. Dizier, France. The Group was led by Colonel Leber with deputy leader Lt. Colonel Shackley.

The weather was beautiful and bombing was done from 20,000 feet. The bomb run was good, but bombing results were not obtained. There were no killed or wounded and there were no abortions or ships that received battle damage.

11 May 1944 — The first target was Bettembourg in Luxembourg and the second target was Theonville. Bombing altitudes were 20,000 and 20,500 feet, respectively. Thirty-one aircraft were dispatched from this group. The bombing was done by pathfinder method. There were no wounded or killed. Fifty enemy aircraft were sighted, but did not attack. All ships returned safely to this base.

12 May 1944 — The Group dispatched eighteen ships today and the formation was led by Major Halsey. The target was designated as Lutzkendorf. Bombing altitude was 24,500 feet by pathfinder method. Enemy fighter opposition was nil. All ships returned safely to this base. There were no killed or wounded.

13 May 1944 — Again we had a dual target with the targets Stralsund and Stettin, Germany. Bombing altitudes were 23,300 and 23,500 feet, respectively. The Group was led by Lt. Colonel Kunkel. Enemy opposition was nil. Bombing was done by pathfinder. All ships returned safely to this base with no wounded or killed aboard. As a commentary on the Group as a whole, it seems to me that many individuals, both officers and enlisted men, are becoming a bit stale and have less interest and drive than heretofore.

The war has lost its novelty for most of us and has taken on more drudgery than heretofore. Several officers have complained of being tired, fed up, irritable, and just plain sick of the routine, day-after-day work with no break. The answer will probably be one of two things: with awakened interest by the opening of the long awaited and delayed second front, or the number of passes and leaves will have to be increased if efficiency is to be maintained. It would also seem advisable to have a rotation policy for the return to the zone of interior, because if individuals have a real hope or returning in the reasonably near future, their outlook seems to be improved considerably.

19 May 1944 — Thirty-eight aircraft from this command took off at 0815 hours this foggy morning with Lt. Colonel Kunkle in the lead with the target designated as Berlin. The bombing was intended to be done by pathfinder method. The weather was better than they expected and the bombing was done by visual method. Flak over the target was intense and four ships returned with feathered props. Two ships did not return. They are Lt. Blog in the lead group, 532nd Bomb Squadron and Lt. Sharp, lead element in 533rd Squadron, the high squadron. Lt. Sharp was said to have gone down out of control and I do not have the details on Lt. Blog. Bombing altitude was 26,000 feet and temperature was – 38° C.

B-17 Flight Plan from Major Jones' Mission 28 APRIL 1944

GROUP LEAD	– Maj JONES
GROUP DEPUTY	– Lt PLUEMER
CBW LEAD	– Col PUTNAM
LOW LEAD	– Maj JONES
HIGH LEAD	– Lt JESSOP
HIGH SQDN	– Lt RICKS

CLIMB AT 150 IAS AT 300 FPM
CRUISE AT 155 IAS AT 14,000 FT
BOMB AT 150 IAS AT 14,000 FT
RETURN AT 155 IAS AT 14,000 FT
DESCEND AT 170 IAS AT 14,000 FT
LET DOWN, SPLASHER #7, 360 DEGREES
    GEAR DOWN, 150 IAS, 500 FPM

ORDER OF DEPARTURE:

1ST CBW LEAD; 40TH COMP WING SECOND

INTERVAL BETWEEN CBW's: 3 MINUTES

OTHER EFFORTS:
  5 GROUPS OF + DIVISION WILL ATTACK
CROSSBOW TARGETS AT ZERO PLUS 22 to
ZERO PLUS 34.

ZERO HOUR: 0830
ALTIMETERS: 29.92

FLIGHT PLAN, LOW GROUP

CAMBRIDGE	9,000:	0730
BASSINGBOURN	9,000:	0740
LUTON	9,000:	0745
BARNET	9,000:	0800
CHIPPING ONGAR	9,000:	0820
GRAVESEND	9,000:	0830
SPLASHER 9	9,000:	0857
SELSEY BILL	9,000:	0948
4918-0010W	14,000:	1021
4800-0110E	14,000:	1030
4643-0210E	14,000:	1038
4643-0230E	14,000:	1053
4703-0238E	14,000:	1129
4800-0110E	14,000:	1245
4918-0010W	14,000:	1327
SELSEY BILL	4,000:	1411
LUTON		1420
BASE		1430

CONVOYS: NONE EXPECTED.

TOTAL TIME ON MISSION: 7 HRS 0 MIN.
TOTAL TIME ON OXYGEN: 4 HRS 37 MIN.

SPARES:

LOW GP – (lead) 4H-7084 disp 29
                2A-7023 disp 3
HIGH GROUP   3K-8138 new disp
             58-7330 disp 49

FIGHTER SCHEDULE

4918-0010W	1021
4800-0110E	1030
4643-0230E	1053
4810-0100E	1300

CONTROL POINTS

#1.	SELSEY BILL	1
#2.	4913-0010W	1
#3.	4643-0210E	1
#4.	4300-0110E	1

B-17 Flight Plan from Major Jones' Mission 28 APRIL 1944 (continued)

PILOTS' MTG	0445
STATIONS	0530
START ENG	0545
TAXI	0600
TAKE-OFF	0615
LEAVE FIELD	0715
ALTITUDE	9,000
LAST TIME T/O	0939

— —

LOW GROUP – 1ST COMBAT WING
JONES 535

__HENSLIN__
5P   8061

__GNATZIG__   __WILSON__
5Y   9890   5R   1990

PLUEMER
5Z   1878

__RINGGENBERG__   __NELSON__
5L   9798   3P   2025

LOW – 532   HIGH –
534

__McCRORY__   __CRONIN__
2P   1575   4I   7238

__CAHILL__   __EZZELL__   PENDERGIST   __WARDNECKI__
2L   7969   2E   7088   2F   7760 4A   2585

__THOMAS__   __WILLIAMS__
2D   7100   4P   7174

DEVINE   __CANN__   __CROSSGROVE__   __GARDON__
2R   8079 2B   8103   4K   7076   4F   1291

__SNYDER__
5Q   1067

— —

91ST "B" GROUP, HIGH BOX, 1ST COMBAT WING
HIGH SQUADRON

__RICKS__
3W   1570

__LANCASTER__   __GARRETT__
3L   1614   3N   1698

__RENICK__
3R   9997

__HOLLAND__   __BAILEY__
3U   7454   3V   8194

__TOWNSEND__
3Y   7589

__BLOG__   __PEAK__
2M   2088   4L   7721

<u>19 May 1944</u> (continued):

We had no frostbite. Those wounded were Sgt. Nicholas M. Rotz, WG, and T/Sgt. Floyd C. Hanson, RO, both 535th Squadron men. Sgt. Rotz was wearing a flak helmet and the steel helmet and received a penetrating and lacerated wound of left frontal region of forehead 2" above left eyebrow, mod. sev. Caused by low velocity flak. Sgt. Hanson suffered a wound, penetrating, acute, mod. sev., left mid-axillary line at level of nipple. This also was caused by flak. He was wearing a flak suit, but the missile went in laterally between the two halves of the flak suit. The remainder of the ships returned to this base at 1745 hours.

Missing in action:

<u>532nd Bomb Squadron (H)</u>

B-17G #42-32088 — "Dry Gulcher"

Blog, Harold G.	1st Lt.	P
Dill, Frederick L.	2nd Lt.	CP
Dennis, George W.	F/O	N
Miller, Henry (NMI)	F/O	B
Thompson, Jack L.	T/Sgt.	TTG
Heidebrink, John W.	T/Sgt.	RO
Humphrey, Samuel D.	S/Sgt.	BTG
Poloski, Stanley (NMI)	S/Sgt.	WG
Anderson, Cornelius C.	S/Sgt.	TG

<u>533rd Bomb Squadron (H)</u>

B-17G #42-97454 — "No Name"

Sharp, Earl (NMI)	1st Lt.	P
Garner, Dorrance (NMI)	2nd Lt.	CP
Hardwick, Wayne T.	2nd Lt.	N
Britenbaker, Francis W.	2nd Lt.	B
Schoepf, Jarrett (NMI)	T/Sgt.	TTG
Suchy, William K.	S/Sgt.	RO
Pennybacker, Merrill L.	S/Sgt.	BTG
Rutigliano, Gerald J.	S/Sgt.	WG
Bratton, Follis D.	S/Sgt.	TG

B-17 Flight Plan from Lieutenant Bowen's Mission 30 APRIL 1944

GROUP LEAD   – Lt BOWEN   ZERO HOUR: 0830
GROUP DEPUTY   – Lt RICKS   ALTIMETERS: 29.92
CBW LEAD   – Col COBB (457)
LOW LEAD   – Capt. GARLAND (401)
HIGH LEAD   – Lt BOWEN   FLIGHT PLAN, LEAD A/C 94TH CBW
LOW SQDN   – Lt HELM
HIGH SQDN   – Lt KUEHL (91)   BASSINGBOURN   8,000: 0730
                                      RAMSEY   8,000: 0740
CLIMB AT   150 IAS AT 300 FPM   MARCH   8,000: 0745
CRUISE AT   155 IAS AT 21,000 FT   SPLASHER No. 7   11,000: 0800
BOMB AT   150 IAS AT 21,000 FT   SPLASHER No. 9   15,000: 0820
RETURN AT   155 IAS AT 17,000 FT   SELSEY BILL   15,000: 0830
DESCEND AT   170 IAS AT 500 FPM   4918 – 0007W   20,000:0857
LET DOWN, SPLASHER 7, 360 DEGREES   4710 – 0300E   20,000:0948
    GEAR DOWN, 150 IAS, 500 FPM   4826 – 0422   20,000:1021
                                      4526 – 0458   20,000:1030
ORDER OF DEPARTURE: 4544 – 0456   20,000:1038
                                      4602 – 0404   16,000:1053
41ST LEADING WITH 94TH SECOND   4710 – 0300   16,000:1129
GUIDING LEFT ON 41ST   4918 – 0007W   16,000:1245
                                      SELSEY BILL   5,000:1327
OTHER EFFORTS: BASE   5,000:1411

+ DEPARTING SELSEY BILL AT ZERO PLUS   FIGHTER SCHEDULE
4 AT 14,000 FEET.
                          4918–0007W TYPE 16 CONTR AT 0857
                          4800–0130E TO 4710 – 0300E AT 0923
                          4710–0300E TO 4526 – 0458E AT 0948
                          4526–0458E TO 4710 – 0300E AT 1030
                          4710–0300E TO 4813 – 0130E AT 1129
                          4813–0130E TYPE 16 CONTR AT 1207

CONVOYS: NONE EXPECTED.

TOTAL TIME ON MISSION: 7 HRS 41 MIN.
TOTAL TIME ON OXYGEN: 6 HRS 10 MIN.
                                      FIGHTER CONTROL
POINTS
SPARES: #1. SELSEY BILL 1
LEAD 2F – 7760 NEW 32ND DISP   #2. 4913-0010W   1
     4H – 7084 DISP 24   #3. 4643-0210E   1
     5V – 2102 DISP 39   #4. 4300-0110E   1

B-17 Flight Plan from Lieutenant Bowen's Mission 30 APRIL 1944 (continued)

PILOTS' MTG   0500
STATIONS   0545
START ENG   0600
TAXI   0615   30 APRIL 1944
TAKE-OFF   0630
LEAVE FIELD   0720
ALTITUDE   8,000'
LAST TIME T/O   0755

LEAD AND LOW SQUADRONS OF HIGH GROUP, 94TH CBW

BOWEN (532ND LEAD)

McCRORY 2J 8010

CAHILL 2B 8103   EZZELL 2D 7100

RICKS 3W 1570

WHITEHEAD 4A 2585   KLINKSIEK 2A 7023

LOW – 533

HELM 3K 8188

WAINWRIGHT 3P 2025   GARRETT 3N 1698

JONES 4K 7076

WHITE 4L 7721   MURRAY 4D 2049

FLINT 5L 9798

124

19 May 1944 (continued):

We also received this date a picture of the inspection held on 19 April and the Generals shown in the picture are Lieutenant Generals McNarney, Doolittle and Spaatz, and Major General Kempner. The orderly holding the door of the ambulance open is Captain Cohler.[8]

20 May 1944 — Briefing at 0330 hours and takeoff at 0630. Visibility about 200 yards through heavy haze. The group of thirteen ships was led by Lt. Colonel Shackley. Target was Ville Coublay, France, a large airfield just south of Paris. Bombing altitude was 25,000 feet. The weather was good and bombing results were reported good. All ships returned safely to this base without mishap. There were no wounded or killed and only one case of frostbite.

The body of S/Sgt. Frank J. Kurtz, 32707711, Tail Gunner, 534th Bomb Squadron (H), a former member of Lieut. Henry's crew (see diary entry dated 28 March 1944, par. 2) was washed ashore on Frinton-on-Sea. The body was badly decomposed and there was nothing, but skull above the head. There was a large flak wound in the posterior chest, which confirmed the previous belief that Sgt. Kurtz was dead when the ship was abandoned.

---

[8] Apparently, Dad didn't really like this man very much at the start, even though they eventually did wind up getting along quite well towards the end of their respective tours of duty. Read his footnoted response to Captain Cohler's letter on the applied theory of the "unconscious" mind to him of 9 January 1944 above.

There were numerous articles found in the clothing, but the most interesting of these were maps and photographs, which were partially altered by the sea over the six weeks period. The body was picked up by Lieut. Fick and taken to the American Military Cemetery, Cambridge, England. Funeral services are scheduled for 1430 hours, 21 May 1944.

22 May 1944 — Twenty-eight aircraft from this command took off at 0845 hours with the target the industrial area in Keil, Germany. Bombing was briefed by pathfinder method, but the bombing was done visually with good results. This group was carrying incendiary bombs. All ships returned safely to this base and the only incident that was of note was Lieut. Cann, 532nd Bomb Squadron, who could not keep up with the formation because his #4 engine was feathered. He landed with his tail wheel locked and had to ground loop about 2/3 up the runway. The flak was estimated as light to moderate and a few enemy aircraft were seen, but did not attack. Fighter support was good.

23 May 1944 — Twenty-five aircraft from this command took off at 0515 hours with the primary target an airfield near Metz, France and the secondary target Saarbrücken, France (eastern part). The primary target was overcast and the secondary target could be seen through a hole in the clouds. It was bombed from 22,000 feet and it is though successfully. There were no killed or injured and all ships returned safely to this base. The combat wing was led by Colonel Leber and this wing was one of fourteen that attacked targets in the occupied countries.

24 May 1944 — Thirty-seven aircraft from this command and two PFF's took off today at 0600 hours with the target designated as Berlin. Bombing altitude was 25,000 feet and the temperature was $-38°$ Centigrade. There was six- to eight-tenths cloud cover and bombing was done by visual and PFF methods. Results were thought to be good. There are six ships missing from this operation and they are:

Missing in action:

532nd Bomb Squadron (H)

B-17G #42-38010 — "No Name"

Ezzell, Clarence W.	1st Lt.	P
Nymeyer, John L.	2nd Lt.	CP
Adams, Edward R.	F/O	N
Wilson, William O., Jr.	2nd Lt.	B
Peck, Weslie H.	T/Sgt.	TTG
Baker, Louie K.	T/Sgt.	RO
Beninga, Harm R.	S/Sgt.	BTG
Harvey, Lloyd L.	S/Sgt.	WG
Chaaf, Carl (NMI)	S/Sgt.	TG

B-17 Flight Plan from Major Halsey's Mission 12 MAY 1944

GROUP LEAD — Maj HALSEY
GROUP DEPUTY — Lt HARING
CBW LEAD — Maj HALSEY
LOW LEAD — Capt DAILY (398)
CBW PTS
HIGH LEAD — Capt SAMUELSON (91)

ZERO HOUR: 1030
ALTIMETERS: 29.92

FLIGHT PLAN, LEAD A/C 1ST

BASSINGBOURN	16,000:0951	"A"
CACTON GIBBET	16,000:1024	"B"
SOHAM	16,000:1030	"C"
SPLASHER No. 7	16,000:1041	"D"
CLACTON	16,000:1048	"E"
5107 – 0240	20,000 :	1111
5003 – 0658	20,000 :	1204
5037 – 0840	25,000 :	1305
5057 – 1159	25,000 :	1316
5118 – 1152	25,000 :	1325
5123 – 1137	23,000 :	1330
5025 – 0840	20,000 :	1409
5003 – 0658	20,000 :	1429
5107 – 0240	20,000 :	1534
CLACTON	7,000 :	1558
SPLASHER #7	7,000 :	1609
BASE	7,000 :	1613

CLIMB AT — 150 IAS AT 300 FPM
CRUISE AT — 155 IAS AT 20,000 FT
BOMB AT — 150 IAS AT 25,000 FT
RETURN AT — 155 IAS AT 20,000 FT

DESCEND AT 170 IAS AT 500 FPM
LET DOWN, SPLASHER 7, 330 DEGREES
   GEAR DOWN, 150 IAS, 500 FPM

ORDER OF DEPARTURE:

94A, 94B, 40, 1ST, 41A, 41B

5 MINUTE INTERVALS BETWEEN CBW'S

OTHER EFFORTS:

☐ departing Clacton at 1030

O departing Clacton at 1058

FIGHTER SUPPORT

5107–0250	1107
5017–0600	1146
5024–0830	1222
5036–1100	1254
5032–0900	1359

TOTAL TIME ON MISSION: 7 HRS 46 MIN.
TOTAL TIME ON OXYGEN: 6 HRS 40 MIN.

CONVOYS: NONE EXPECTED.

SPARES:
LEAD 5V – 2060
    2M – 2088
    4M – 8009
    5N – 7313

CONTROL POINTS

1.	CLACTON	1048
2.	5107 – 0250	1113
3.	5024 – 0830	1228
4.	5022 – 0820	1413

LOW RECALL (LOVE-ROGER-CHARLIE)
CBW RECALL (EASY-MIKE-XRAY-QUEEN)

B-17 Flight Plan from Major Halsey's Mission 12 MAY 1944 (continued)

12 MAY 1944

PTS' MTG	0700
STATIONS	0745
START ENG	0800
TAXI	0815
T/O	0830
LEAVE FIELD	0942
ALTITUDE	16,000'
LAST TIME T/O	1016

CBW LEAD

LEAD – 535

HALSEY
CLARK
PFF*B   594   ARMSTEAD

SNYDER   WESTWOOD
5W   0017   PFF-D   562

HARING
50   2102

BARNICLE   PARKMAN
5S   7330   5P   7265

LOW – 533   HIGH – 534

THOMAS   WILLIAMS
2D   7100   4P   7174
BAILEY   BRADNER   PEAK   MYERS
2P   1575 2B   8103   4A   2535 4E   1569
KLINKSIEK   ACKERMAN
2A   7023   4D   2049
DEVINE   CANN   WHITE   MURRAY
2R   8079 2Q   7442   4J   8159 4G   1550
RIGGENBERG
5T   8117

128

24 May 1944 (continued):

533rd Bomb Squadron (H)

B-17G #42-31698 — "No Name"

Wainwright, Clarence D., Jr.	1st Lt.	P
Latton, Howard W.	2nd Lt.	CP
Dorn, Harry T.	2nd Lt.	N
Counts, James R., Jr.	2nd Lt.	B
Stephens, T. J. (IO)	Sgt.	WG
Hoga, Warren K.	S/Sgt.	RO
Kruger, Charles (NMI)	Sgt.	BTG
Kennedy, Lowell D.	S/Sgt.	TTG
Nalley, Floyd M., Jr.	Sgt.	TG

534th Bomb Squadron (H)

B-17G #42-97214 — "Joanne"

Wardercki, John A.	1st Lt.	P
Dayton, Charles R.	2nd Lt.	CP
Morrison, William W., Jr.	2nd Lt.	N
Blackfield, Willard I.	2nd Lt.	B
Bachelin, Warren H.	T/Sgt.	TTG
Miller, Robert E.	S/Sgt.	RO
Andersen, Charles (NMI)	S/Sgt.	BTG
Elliott, George S.	S/Sgt.	WG
Telzerow, Harold R.	S/Sgt.	TG

B-17G #42-31291 — "Avengress"

Gardon, Carl A.	1st Lt.	P
Sorenberger, Archie W.	2nd Lt.	CP
Soltwedel, Edward B.	2nd Lt.	N
Mosely, William C.	2nd Lt.	B
Cornell, Kenneth H.	T/Sgt.	TTG
Schaub, Donald P.	S/Sgt.	ROG
Shaw, Allan E.	S/Sgt.	BTG
Rush, Jacob R.	S/Sgt.	WG
O'Neal, John S.	T/Sgt.	TG
*Ross, Jack M.	S/Sgt.	TG

*(Story on this EM is written below)

535th Bomb Squadron (H)

B-17G #42-31878 — "Spamcan"

Higgins, Walter K.	2nd Lt.	P
Burns, Herbert W., Jr.	2nd Lt.	CP
Beck, James A.	2nd Lt.	N
Hughes, Robert E.	1st Lt.	B
Baird, John S.	T/Sgt.	TTG
Delgado, Eddie (NMI)	T/Sgt.	ROG
Thompson, Robert H.	Sgt.	BTG
Thomas, Donald H.	Sgt.	LWG
Collister, Franklin R.	S/Sgt.	RWG
Smith, Robert F.	Cpl.	TG

B-17G #42-39890 — "Return Ticket"

Dasso, Carl H.	2nd Lt.	P
Watson, William L.	2nd Lt.	CP
Barkett, Phillip J.	2nd Lt.	N
Isom, Norman B.	2nd Lt.	B
Wright, Oscar (NMI)	S/Sgt.	TTG
Madero, Anthony T.	S/Sgt.	ROG
Williams, Paul M.	Cpl.	BTG
Rose, Marshall E.	Sgt.	WG
Herron, Chester E.	Sgt.	TG

It is thought that Lieutenant Wainwright collided with another ship and both exploded. Lieut. Williams, ship #174, flew through the wreckage and blackened his silver plane and the rudder, horizontal stabilizers, and left aileron were partly burned away. The tail gunner, S/Sgt. Jack M. Ross, 38396821, jumped out, apparently thinking the ship was on fire. The ship landed here without event. Lieut. Dasso's ship collided with a fighter, which tore a wing off. I have no detail on the other ships. Lieut. Yates in #017 landed without brakes after having a fire in the nose and cockpit, which burned him and his co-pilot, Lieut. Klutha, slightly. Lieut. Bailey in #990 also landed without brakes and put out a couple of parachutes to slow him down, but were without much effect. He ground looped about two-thirds down the runway. Lieut. Zapinski lost a prop governor at assembly and feathered the engine and tried to stay with the formation, but could not. He salvoed his bombs and still could not keep up. He then turned back and heard a distress call from a fortress and he went on an air-sea rescue mission. He found the ditched crew and also found a small ship in the vicinity and flashed the position of the crew. He landed eleven hours after take-off.

Lieut. Emory H. Baird, the bombardier on Lt. Nelson's crew, 535th Squadron, received a .30 cal. Bullet wound of the right leg.
DIAGNOSIS: 1. Wound, penetrating, leg, right, lateral at mid portion tibia, anteriorly, size of entry ½" in diameter. Incurred while on mission by .30 cal. bullet, low velocity about 1200 hours.

Those burned were: 2nd Lt. Howard R. Yates, 535th Sqdn., who received a mild burn of the right wrist and over the right eyebrow; 2nd Lt. Robert J. Klutho, 535th Sqdn., who received mild burns of neck and both wrists; and S/Sgt. Thomas W. O'Brien, 535th Sqdn. who had a 1st deg. burn of the right thumb.

There was one case of frostbite due to defective electric equipment and Lt. Abraham A. Levine, 535th Squadron reported to the dispensary with mild abrasions of the right cheek due to splintered plexiglass. Sgt. Ross L. Glatfelder, 532nd Squadron, received a very mild wound of the left leg due to low velocity flak. One case of anoxia was reported, Sgt. Oliver E. Brown, 533rd Squadron. The cause of anoxia was the quick-disconnect plug being pulled apart apparently while the gunner was searching for fighters during heavy fighter attack.

The crews seem impressed, but not unduly shaken by their experience and their morale is good. The bulk of the ships returned to the base about 1530 hours.

25 May 1944 — This morning at 0445 hours, Sgt. Robert Q. Pope, 16059173, 535th Bomb Squadron, was hit by a plane part, which was set in motion by a .50 caliber MGB, which was accidentally discharged from a ball turret about 100 yards away. DIAGNOSIS: 1. Wound, penetrating, moderate severity, left costal margin in nipple line. The wound was explored at 121st Station Hospital, Braintree, and the peritoneum was just nicked and an exploratory was not done.

Twenty-six ships from this command took off at 0745 hours with the primary target the airfield at Nancy-Essey, in southern France. Bombing altitude was 22,000 feet, weather was clear and bombing was done visually with good results. The Group was led by Colonel Leber. All the ships returned safely to this base and reported only a few bursts of flak miles behind them. No enemy fighter opposition and friendly fighter support was good. Several crews reported seeing two or three B-17's going down. There were no killed or wounded from this group. The mission was regarded from a strategic standpoint as eminently successful.

27 May 1944 — Nineteen aircraft were dispatched at 0745 hours to fly high group with the 94th combat wing with the primary target the marshalling yards at Ludwigshafen, Germany. In case of undercast, the centers of the cities of Ludwigshafen and Mannheim were to be the target. Bombing altitude was 25,000 feet; weather outlook was favorable for visual bombing. One ship failed to return, Lieut. Stewart and crew, and Lieut. Harding, 534th Squadron, landed about twenty minutes after the formation was in. Lieut. Kelsey was the group leader. Flak was moderate and not too accurate over the target area. This group was fortunate in not receiving any heavy fighter attack, but the group just ahead received considerable opposition. Strike photos showed a bull's eye strike by the lead bombardier, Lieut. Cassidy. There were no killed or wounded.

Missing in action:

533rd Bomb Squadron (H)

131

B-17G #42-107023 — "No Name"

Stuart, Andrew H.	1st Lt.	P
Call, Glenn S.	2nd Lt.	CP
Blyth, Don H.	2nd Lt.	N
Eisen, Charles K.	2nd Lt.	B
Harrison, Frederick W.	S/Sgt.	TTG
Jones, Aurelius W.	S/Sgt.	ROG
Kaplan, Herman H.	Sgt.	BTG
Mickey, Gerald B.	S/Sgt.	WG
Selig, Peter (NMI)	Sgt.	TG

Captain Bland returned last night from seven days SNAFU'ing at the Walhampton House and reported a most wonderful seven days of rest.

28 May 1944 — Thirty-three aircraft took off at 1000 hours with two PFF's. Major Halsey was leading the 1st combat wing flying the first PFF ship. This group was to furnish the lead group and the lead and low squadron for the high composite group for the 1st combat wing. The primary target was missed, the ships being unable to pick it out in time to bomb. Eighteen ships, having bombs remaining, bombed marshalling yards in Frankfurt, Germany as a target of opportunity. They scored hits on the marshalling yards and on a bridge nearby. However, the bombs they were carrying were 500 lb. incendiary, so that this portion of the mission was SNAFU'ed. Flak over Frankfurt was reported as being the most intense encountered over any target, including Berlin, recently.

2nd Lt. Francis J. Treanor, 533rd Bomb Squadron, was evacuated to the 121st Station Hospital because of a perforating flak wound to the right leg. Sgt. William M. Cusick, 534th Squadron, suffered a penetrating wound of the right thigh and was also sent to Braintree. Sgt. George (NMI) Samuelian, 39169144, 532nd Bomb Squadron, was killed in action and his remains are to be sent to Cambridge American Military Cemetery tomorrow. His diagnosis is as follows: Wound, penetrating, marked severity, at lateral anterior aspect, right thigh, at level of hip joint. Size of entrance 2½" x 1¼" with the tract penetrating into the abdominal cavity. Caused by flak, low velocity. There were four other minor flak wounds reported, but those concerned were returned to full flying duty.

29 May 1944 — Briefing at 0500 and takeoff at 0800 this beautiful, clear, and wonderful morning. Designated target was Posen, Poland, a round trip of 1700 miles, one of the longest of the war. Nineteen aircraft were dispatched from this command and their route was over the North Sea and through Denmark. Bombing altitude was 22,000 feet; visual bombing was done with excellent results. Sixteen ships returned to this base. Lieut. Doyle landed at Coltishaw and also Lt. Martin. Lieut. Nelson landed at Foulsham.

30 May 1944 — The bombardier discussed in yesterday's diary entry had a poorly fitting oxygen mask and has been returned to full flying duty.

Thirty ships were dispatched from this command leading the division with Colonel Gross in command. The designated target was the Dessault Aircraft Assembly Plant near Leipzig, Germany. Bombing altitude was 25,000 feet and outside air temperature was −29° Centigrade. The lead and high group got the bombs away right on the nose and the strike photos showed the bombs of the lead group right on the MPI and the bombs of the high group scattered over their MPI. The Group was under hostile attack by ME-109's on the bomb run and two ships were knocked out of formation. They were Lieut. Zapinski and Lieut. Burton. These ships have not returned to this base. Friendly fighters were apparently engaged in enemy activity elsewhere as they were not in evidence in the target area. Lieut. Monahan was heard calling as the ships were coming out of Germany, but his whereabouts are unknown at present. There were no wounded or killed and the remaining ships landed safely at this base.

Missing in action:

533nd Bomb Squadron (H)

B-17G #44-6025 — "So What?"

Zapinski. Leonard P.	1st Lt.	O-753480	P
Widosh, Othmer G.	2nd Lt.	O-759780	CP
Buskirk, Robert (NMI)	2nd Lt.	O-743872	N
Fuller, David P.	2nd Lt.	O-703226	B
Webb, William E.	T/Sgt.	14028463	TTG
Pastre, George J.	T/Sgt.	39554149	ROG
Wilson, James E.	S/Sgt.	39300276	BTG
Harper, Hamilton B.	S/Sgt.	34605139	WG
Harness, Donald A.	S/Sgt.	17160304	TG

533rd Bomb Squadron (H)

B-17G #42-102672 — "Ole' Swayback"

Burton, Merrill O.	1st Lt.	P
Bredeson, David L.	2nd Lt.	CP
Berry, Alvin C.	2nd Lt.	N
Hammond, Robert J.	S/Sgt.	B
Marbry, James E.	S/Sgt.	RO
Eylens, John T., Jr.	T/Sgt.	TTG
Powell, Ralph J.	S/Sgt.	BTG
Pillot, Victor C.	S/Sgt.	RWG
Hittel, Robert (NMI)	Sgt.	TG

B-17G #42-38188 — "Connie"

Monahan, John J.	2nd Lt.	P
Cea, Kenneth C.	2nd Lt.	CP
Haas, Leland M.	2nd Lt.	N

Hoyle, William M.	T/Sgt.	B
Valinski, John (NMI)	S/Sgt.	ROG
Catter, Loebert G.	S/Sgt.	TTG
Granlund, Jerome D.	Sgt.	BTG
Emanuelson, Morris N.	Sgt.	RWG
Bryan, John B., Jr.	Sgt.	TG

Lieutenant Yates, 535th Squadron, was between the IP and the target and engines #1 & #2 were knocked out. #1 was feathered. But #2 windmilled all the way home. The co-pilot, 2nd Lt. Robert E. Klutho, O-815923, and the top turret gunner, S/Sgt. James E. Dixon, 35448138, bailed out right after the ship was hit. The remainder of the crew was under repeated hostile attack and did violent evasive action with two starboard engines and an air speed of about 100 miles an hour. They destroyed three enemy aircraft and probably more. Lieut. Yates used maximum power (2500 RPM and 50 inches of mercury) on his two good engines for 1½ hours and eased it back slowly while over the Channel. Six of the machine guns went out of commission while under attack. The ball turret was salvoed and equipment was thrown out to lighten the ship. He landed wheels down without hydraulics on two engines and ground looped at the end of the runway. Lieut. Yates and crew are excited and shaken, but in good condition. They are being admitted to the sick quarters for sedation this evening.

R E S T R I C T E D

DB #152, Hq AAF Sta. 167, APO 557,
Wednesday, 30 May 1944, cont'd.

OUTSTANDING PERFORMANCES:

Enemy fighter pilots near Dessault yesterday thought they had a sure thing when their first attack killed the #2 engine on the Fortress "Me and My Gal" and knocked the bomber way out of formation. They underestimated her pilot, 2nd Lt. Howard R. Yates, 535th Bomb Sq., and the game crewmen who stuck with him through 20 minutes of almost unbelievable evasive action. While the ME-109's cut in and out with their wing cannon blasting, Yates put his massive buggy through everything in and out of the book, including slow rolls and wing-overs. His control work not only left the Jerries with the worst possible target, but set his gunners up for the kind of shooting that destroyed three of the attackers. When four Lightnings (P-38's) finally showed up to cover him, Yates had both left wing engines out, a windmilling prop on hand, and a three-hour trip home ahead of him. He made the distance on an additional airspeed of 100 MPH.

R E S T R I C T E D

---

31 May 1944 — Briefings at 0430 hours and twenty-five aircraft were put up. Lieut. Colonel Fitzgerald led the combat wing. They put up the high squadron for the composite group, the target being in south eastern France. Upon crossing the Channel, weather was met, which forced the aircraft to 27,000 feet to get over the clouds, and after penetrating into territory over northern and eastern France, they found a large hole in the cloud cover, and, on orders from division, they bombed a target of opportunity, hitting a dispersal point at an airfields in Florennes, France. Only extremely light flak and no enemy fighters were encountered. There were no wounded or killed and all aircraft returned safely to this base landing about 1200 hours.

2 June 1944 — Twenty-four aircraft from this command took off at 0915 hours with the designated targets 50mm gun emplacements just south of Bologne, France. Bombing altitude was 22,000 feet and bombing was done by PFF with ten-tenths undercast. Bombing results are not known. There were no killed or wounded. All ships landed safely at this base. The Group encountered no flak or enemy fighters.

3 June 1944 — Six aircraft from this command took off at 1230 hours with the target designated as a gun emplacement area on the French coast south of Bologne. The mission was PFF. No flak or fighters were encountered. All ships returned safely to this base and there were no killed or wounded. Bombing results are not known.

5 June 1944 — Thirty-nine aircraft from this command took off this date forming a complete combat wing with thirteen planes in each group. Target was the coastal defense area near Caen, France, 2½ miles off the French coast. This mission is undoubtedly in aid of preparation for tomorrow's anticipated festivities and group dance with the *Wehrmacht*. [9]

Briefing was scheduled unexpectedly at 0400 when a cold front lifted. Takeoff was to be at 0530 hours, but was delayed for 50 minutes because the bombs were not loaded. All the ships carried 500 lb., armor-piercing bombs, which was the first time this type of bomb has been carried. Colonel Fitzgerald led the lead group with Lieut. Tarr leading the high group and Lieut. Jones, the low group. Bombing altitude was 25,000 feet and the air temperature was –32° Centigrade. The IP was near Le Havre and fighter escort was good. No flak or fighters were encountered. Visual bombing was done. The only objects noted was a convoy of about 25 German trucks heading south. The second best buzz job of the season was done by Lieut. Bailey who finished up. Lieut. Townsend also buzzed. Strike photos showed bombing results as excellent. There were no killed or wounded and all ships returned safely to this base.

6 June 1944 — (Tuesday) Today was **D--Day!!** The day we have all been waiting for. We were gotten out of the sack at 0300 hours and alerted for enemy action. Everybody on the base was under arms, tense and excited. The station defense was out in force and most of us were more afraid of trigger-happy defense boys than we were of enemy action.

---

[9] So much for "security" from S-2.

Briefing was at 0100 for pilots only and the target was secret. The crews were stationed in the ships and did not know the target until the engines had started. The Group put up forty-eight ships on two different missions and the first group hit coastal targets from 15,000 feet by PFF, and the targets were just north of the Cherbourg area. Crews reported large numbers of invasion craft and small naval ships. No hostile action other than enemy gunfire from the coast was seen. The radio reported intense shelling of the Le Havre area and allied paratroops landing from the Seine Estuary and north to the Dunkirk/Pas-de-Calais area. Warnings were issued to the civil population of occupied countries by General Eisenhower giving instructions about what to do and what not to do. We are all standing by at the moment for anticipated counter invasion and there is to be another briefing later in the day. The irony of it all is that the invasion of Europe had to occur on my day <u>off</u>. It sure is rough in the E.T.O!

Today we received another dentist, making a total of three. His name is Captain Cyril L. Stavinoha. A dental technician, Cpl. Richard Miller, has been assigned to us also.

Also of some interest is the fact that the medical department, which was disarmed by the Geneva Convention, when alerted came out with all kinds of weapons—including a pocket full of rocks.

7 June 1944 — Thirty-three aircraft from this command led by three PFF ships attacked an airfield just north of Lorient, France, which is on the south shore of the Cherbourg Peninsula. Despite the PFF lead, the bombing was visual and German fighter aircraft were taking off the field when bombs were away. Hits were seen and it is thought that the bombing results are good. The flak over the target was fairly intense and accurate, and as the second group made a 360, they went over some more ships in the harbor at Lorient and caught some more flak. All the ships returned safely to this base with the exception of one. There were no killed or wounded. Lieut. Martyniak, 534th Bomb Squadron, flying "I for Item", ship #238, was seen to ditch and his position was reported by two of our aircraft, and acknowledgement received by the ground sector about 2030 hours. He reported that he had lost two engines and did not have sufficient power on the other two. He also reported his position, altitude, and air speed until the time he was within 100 feet of the water.

Aircraft ditched in Channel:

534th Bomb Squadron (H)

B-17G #42-97328 — "I for Item", "Our Captain"

Lieut. Fick and Sgt.'s. Bassett and Johnson attended a meeting of the division Medical Administrative Officers and Chief Clerks at the conference room, 1st Bomb Division. Recent changes in the preparation and submission of medical department reports were discussed and they were advised of pending changes.

8 June 1944 — Thirty-six aircraft from this group took off at 0430 hours with the target a bridge near Tours, France. The weather was poor and assembly was delayed, but was finally made at 25,000 feet. Let down was made to 20,000, which was the bombing altitude. The target was wiped out. All the ships landed safely at this base and there were no killed or wounded. One man was IIA.

Lieut. Martyniak and crew were picked up at 0600 hours this morning and were reported by a naval hospital near Knightsbridge, Sasham. Apparently, they were not much the worse for their experience. They arrived back at this base by plane at 1700.

10 June 1944 — Thirty-six aircraft from this command took off at 0430 hours this morning with the target designated as troop installations in the Bologne area. The bombing was visual at an altitude of 22,000 feet. The bomb load consisted of two, 2,000 pounders. All the ships returned safely to this base and there were no casualties.

11 June 1944 — Briefing was at 0200 and take off at 0400. Nineteen aircraft were dispatched with the target as the Beaumont-Le Roger Airfield about 30-40 miles behind the invasion front. Bombing was done from 15,000 feet. The target area was the only area that was completely overcast and bombing was done by PFF. Results were not observed. A few bursts of flak were observed in the Granville area upon return. No enemy action was encountered and the friendly fighter support was good. There were no killed, wounded or missing.

Yesterday, the author flew down to Stony Cross, the airport just south of Southampton and met some glider pilots who had gone over on D-Day. They had various German souvenirs with them and when one was asked where the hole in the helmet was, he replied, "There ain't no hole in the helmet, I shot him between the eyes!" He also said he shot a lot of Germans there and most of them were dead. He stated that after his glider had landed, he could see other gliders overhead, hear a few bursts of flak, wait a little while, and the inevitable crash followed. The glider pilots said that most of the gliders crash-landed because what they had them briefed on as hedgerows turned out to be tall trees with the top branches clipped to make the aerial photographs appear like a hedge. I found he was glad he was a glider pilot, but his occupation would not seem to be too desirable from the standpoint of personal safety. As we flew over southern England most of the forests were filled with trucks, tanks, jeeps, and other Army vehicles as well as the personnel. All the airdromes and every flat strip of land was covered with aircraft of all types and descriptions—including large numbers of gliders.

The port at Southampton was crammed with ships of all sizes and types, and on every road and railroad there were long convoys and trains conveying equipment to the harbor area. The weight and amount of equipment defies description, but it is TREMENDOUS.

12 June 1944 — Briefing at 0200 hours and takeoff at 0500 following a party at the officers' club. It was pretty damp out and two officers had to be admitted to sick quarters and two had to be relieved from flying for non-operational reasons. The designated target was an airfield near Lille, France. The Group bombed at 15,000 feet. Bombing was visual and results were good. Flak was light and a number of enemy aircraft were seen. There were no killed or wounded, and no MIA. They did not fly over the invasion area so nothing was seen. Thirty-six aircraft were dispatched and the time of return was 1015 hours.

14 June 1944 — Briefing at 0145 and takeoff at 0400 hours. Thirty-eight aircraft took off to bomb a target in Melun, south east of Paris, France. Bombing altitude was 21,000 and outside air temperature was −19° Centigrade. There were no PFF ships; bombing was done visually with good results. Major Halsey and Captain Winter led. Lt. Reese and Lt. Tarr almost did a piggy-back with another ship. Lt. Tarr's #1 engine was feathered and #2 was windmilling, and after he landed, the prop fell off and went through the wing, fuselage, and the horizontal stabilizer. Only one flap was working on the side the engines were on. He had no radio communication, no instruments, hydraulic fluid had to be pumped by hand, and (the ship) had to land because of lack of air speed almost hitting another ship. Flak was moderate and accurate over the target and a few caught it on the way home.

S/Sgt. Fred A. Taylor, 14158833, WG, 532nd Bomb Squadron (H), was killed in action.
DIAGNOSIS: 1. Wounds, multiple, penetrating, right back, chest, & abdomen. 2. Fracture, compound, base of 2nd & 3rd metacarpal, right hand. 3. Wounds, two, penetrating, at lateral aspect, calf, right. Caused by 20mm cannon shell. His body was taken to the American Military Cemetery, Cambridge, England in the afternoon. KIA.

15 June 1944 — Forty-eight aircraft from this command were dispatched at 0400 hours with the target designated as an airfield near Bordeaux, France. Bombing altitude was 22,000 feet. Bombing was done visually and results were thought to be good. There was inaccurate flak over the target and no enemy aircraft were seen. One ship was confirmed as missing in action. All other aircraft returned safely to this base aid there were no killed or wounded.

Missing in Action:

534th. Bomb Squadron (H)

B-17G #42-38009 — "No Name"

Kelly, Charles H.	2nd Lt.	P
Disbrow, Robert C.	2nd Lt.	CP
Champ, Frank A.	F/O	N
Wilczek, Simon J.	S/Sgt.	B
Brooks, Harold C., Jr.	S/Sgt.	ROG
Brashear, Charles F.	S/Sgt.	TTG

Workman, Ralph J.	Sgt.	BTG	
Campbell, Alfred M. Jr.	Sgt.	WG	
Graham, Donald S.	Sgt.	TG	

Today, a medical board consisting of:

Major Ernest Gaillard, Jr.	O-330166	MC	President
Capt. Milton H. Bland	O-565878	MC	Member
Capt. Louis G. Ralston	O-479721	MC	Member
Capt. Bernard J. Cohler	O-382023	MC	Member
1st Lt. Joseph V. Fick	O-1543431	MAC	Recorder
Lt. Col. Michael H. Teitelbaum	O-493784	MC	Consultant

(was) convened to determine the mental status of Corporal Martin W. Rogers [10], 13048800, 535th Bomb Squadron (H). He was found to be a constitutional psychopathic inferior. Recommendation was made that he be held accountable for his acts (see Major Gaillard's report, Reports & Endnotes).

R E S T R I C T E D

OUTSTANDING PERFORMANCES

Quick rescue of the crew of 1st Lt. John A. Martyniak (then 2nd Lt.), 532nd Bomb Sq., from a ditching in to the Channel last Wednesday was furthered by the teamwork displayed by the entire crew. Navigator 2nd Lt. James G. Manion kept radio operator, S/Sgt. Paul E. Stewart, informed of the ship's position as it dropped toward the sea. And Sgt. Stewart maintained constant touch with Air-Sea rescue. Lt. Martyniak called off altitude by radio every 100 feet. All men aboard cooperated in the crash landing and subsequent abandonment of the ditched Fortress.
(See page #137)

---

16 June 1944 — We had a little excitement this morning for an unwelcome change. During the night, Corporal Martin W. Rogers, whose sanity we have just investigated, jabbed himself in the left hand with a stick and a pencil, which he said was a suicide attempt, which we doubt. He remained in sick quarters over night and pulled the old gag of climbing out the latrine window when the guard was standing at the door.

He took off across a pea patch and it looked for a while like he had made good his escape. The author was surprised at the fortitude shown by the individual and, admittedly, a bit amused at the consternation of the military police from whom he had escaped before. However, the amusement was cut short when the author found out the responsibility was just as much his as the M.P.'s. Not being an alarmist, the author called out the station defense, home guard, civilian police, and as many men as the squadrons could supply. The area was searched and after about two hours, the prisoner was returned. Captain Porter, the CO of the military police, was with me and I don't believe I have seen him so happy.

---

[10] This soldier's true name and serial number have been changed to protect his family.

To add further to our misery, someone stole an American Ambulance from the front of station sick quarters at about 2315 hours 15 June 1944, and within 45 minutes, had wrecked and abandoned it. We are carrying out a search for the driver. The damage is estimated at about £300.00.

18 June 1944 — Fifty-four aircraft took off at 0415 hours with the target designated as an oil refinery in Hamburg, Germany. The combat wing was led by Col. Shackley, and the composite group was led by Captain Armstead. Bombing was by PFF. The flak was intense, but no enemy fighters were seen. A German convoy of about 50 ships was seen in the mouth of the Elbe River. All the ships returned safely to this base. There were two with feathered props. The crews look tired and when a briefing is held before 0300 hours, it seems to affect them much more than later briefings. Four hours' sleep seems to be <u>least</u> sleep than is beneficial to the individual.

19 June 1944 — Fifty-one aircraft from this command took off at 0415 hours with the target designated as an airfield near Bordeaux, France. The briefed bombing altitude was 21,000, but because of poor weather conditions, the Group, led by Col. Hall, had to climb to 26,000 feet and then let down to 24,500 feet for their bomb run. The weather was overcast everywhere except in the target area. The bombing was done with good results. One ship aborted, which broke the record of 25 consecutive missions without an abortion. There were no killed or wounded and one aircraft, is missing. Those aboard were:

532nd Bomb Squadron (H)

B-17G #42-107088 — "No Name"

Doyle, John B.	2nd Lt.	O-756201	C
Prokopovitz, Julian K.	2nd Lt.	O-818513	CP
Richards, Richard H., Jr.	F/O	T-124727	N
Leavitt, Bernard S.	2nd Lt.	O-762640	B
Harker, Charles E.	S/Sgt.	32749851	ROG
Wise, Gordon W.	S/Sgt.	39905666	TTG
Thompson, Logan A.	Sgt.	15334265	BTG
Helman, Robert J.	Sgt.	15171209	WG
Matthews, Robert T.	Sgt.	36475633	TG

20 June 1944 — Approximately forty aircraft from this command took off at 0400 hours with target designated as Hamburg, Germany. The bombing altitude was 24,500 feet, and bombing was done visually. All the ships except one returned safely to this base. None of the details of what happened to him are available.

There were three wounded:

1st Lt. Beverly W. Lessenger, O-398312, Pilot, 533rd Bomb Squadron (H).
DIAGNOSIS: 1. Wound, severe, perforating, left knee, wound of entrance medial slightly above patella and medial to knee joint 1½" x 1".

Wound of exit immediately infra patella and 2" x 1½". Course through knee joint. Caused by flak, high velocity. 2. Wound, penetrating, multiple, small, medial aspect, rt. knee. Caused by fragments of low velocity plane parts set in motion by flak. WIA

2nd Lt. Ira K. Zipperman, O-703676, 532nd Bomb Squadron (H).
DIAGNOSIS: 1. Wound, penetrating, left eye, center of cornea, severe. Caused by flak, low velocity. Incurred on operational mission this date. WIA

2nd Lt. Ernest D. Kyser, O-757723, 534th Bomb Squadron (H).
DIAGNOSIS: 1. Wound, penetrating, mild, right wrist, lateral side, base 5th metacarpal, wound ½' long. Caused by flak. WIA

No enemy fighters were encountered. Fighter support was good. Flak was intense over the target area, and the dock area was hit.

Missing in action:

533rd Bomb Squadron (H)

B-17G #42-37612 — "Old Iron Gut"

Dunkel Mark R.	2nd Lt.	O-809938	P
Roehr, Kenneth (NMI)	2nd Lt.	O-551860	CP
Kelly, Frank L.	2nd Lt.	O-708388	N
Evans, Clifford (NMI), Jr.	2nd Lt.	O-762764	B
Stoll, William M.	S/Sgt.	35695145	ROG
Kochel, Aaron R.	S/Sgt.	19070421	TTG
Pillotti, John L.	Sgt.	36457112	BTG
Schmidt, Theodore E.	Sgt.	39695962	WG
Beaman, Roger L.	Sgt.	39045941	TG

21 June 1944 — Briefing at 0215 hours and takeoff at 0445. Target was Berlin, Germany with the route high over the North Sea. Bombing altitude was 27,000 feet and the outside air temperature was –39° Centigrade. Thirty-eight ships from this command were dispatched. Bombing was done visually and the results were thought to be good. The Group was led by Major Halsey and the deputy lead by Captain Armstead. The composite group was led by Lieut. Reese. Large numbers of enemy fighters were encountered near the IP and their attack was persistent. The fighters were mostly ME-210's, which fired rockets and then came on in. The group led by Lt. Reese encountered a large number of JU-88's, most of which were shot down. Lieut. James P. Chisholm, 535th Bomb Squadron (H), Nav., received a lacerated wound, irregular, about 5" long of the left cheek and neck, severe. Caused by flak. "H"

2nd Lt. Peter (NMI) Kowalski, O-761294, B, 533rd Squadron (H)
DIAGNOSIS: 1. Wound, lacerated, left jaw, severe, inferior angle 3" long. 2. Abrasion, middle phalanx, mild, index finger, hand, left. 3. R-1 broken. Caused by flak. "H"

Cpl. Adalbert A. Wszolek, 36035221, 533rd Squadron (H), BTG, suffered the following: DIAGNOSIS: 1. Wound, lacerated, arm, right, triceps region, mod. sev. 2. Wound, perforating of cornea, right with opacity of lens, severe. Caused by fragment of exploded 20mm cannon shell. "H"

There were two other very minor injuries and both men were returned to duty. Three ships failed to return to this base.

Missing in action:

532nd Bomb Squadron (H)

B-17G #42-31980 — "No Name"

Dussault, Roger L.	2nd Lt.	O-756206	P
Segman, Bernard (NMI)	2nd Lt.	O-818229	CP
Magnabasco, Valeria P.	2nd Lt.	O-709480	N
Holcomb, Ralph H.	S/Sgt.	19015267	B
Meier, Elmer C.	S/Sgt.	37408004	TTG
Lawing, Wendell B.	S/Sgt.	14100169	ROG
Corum, Howard L.	Sgt.	16075189	BTG
Ehler, Alonzo L., Jr.	Sgt.	31355689	WG
Mahar, John S., Sr.	Sgt.	18137523	TG

533rd Bomb Squadron (H)

B-17G #42-38194 — "Baboon McGoon"

Bailey, Arthur J.	1st Lt.	O-805726	P
Irwin, Robert H.	2nd Lt.	O-820753	CP
Peterson, Lloyd A.	2nd Lt.	O-814397	N
Brown, Erwin M.	1st Lt.	O-669185	B
Molloy, John J.	S/Sgt.	32486744	ROG
Campbell, Charles J., Jr.	T/Sgt.	18131637	TTG
Forke, Walden W.	S/Sgt.	17130985	BTG
Highsmith, Coral C.	S/Sgt.	36265082	WG
Paoli, Alfred (NMI)	S/Sgt.	16142546	TG

534th Bomb Squadron (H)

B-17G #42-97174 — "Joanne"

Pendergist, Roy H.	1st Lt.	O-805524	P
Lawless, Joseph W.	F/O	T-61670	CP
Harvey, Robert H.	2nd Lt.	O-703897	N
Heniff, Eloy W.	2nd Lt.	O-756978	B
Muir, Malcolm M.	S/Sgt.	374177123	TTG
Salzfieder, Herbert S.	T/Sgt.	16156946	ROG

Wilson, Joseph S.	S/Sgt.	33565765	BTG
Lehman, Harold M.	S/Sgt.	15103687	WG
King, Byron E.	S/Sgt.	17074128	TG

Three ships landed without hydraulic systems and two used parachutes to slow them down after they had landed. Lt. Shobert's ship had a failure of the hydraulic system as he was taxiing around the perimeter track and he crashed into a fence near the bomb dump. Several ships had feathered props and battle damage to a number of ships is fairly heavy. Most of the damage was encountered by flak and fighters over the target. The flak was intense and accurate.

The morale of the crews is lower than it has been for many months. This is due to the decreased number of passes and the decrease in rest home facilities, the frequent change in the definition of an operational tour by higher command, the large number of missions flown in a comparatively short time, and the fact that many of the crewmembers are simply fatigued. We have had an increase in the number of cases that we have seen here showing anxiety reactions and feel that after today's mission, the number we see will be increased. Higher command a short time ago, issued orders concerning pass and leave policies and, at the same time, issued operational orders, which preclude carrying them out. It is felt that if some remedial action is not taken, the number of combat crew failures we have will increase.

About 1500 hours, M/Sgt. Thomas F. Walsh, Jr., 11053045, 533rd Bomb Squadron (H), entered his plane after the mission and found a .45 cal. automatic in the ship that had been left there by a gunner. He accidentally discharged the gun and shot himself through the right leg. His diagnosis is as follows: 1. Wound, perforating, moderate severity, right leg, medial aspect; wound of entrance 3" below lower end of patella; wound of exit lateral and 3" lower than site of entry. He was brought to station sick quarters by ambulance and then evacuated to the 136th Station Hospital.

22 June 1944 — Thirty-six aircraft from this command took off at 1650 hours to hit installations along the coast in the Pas-de-Calais area. Three separate groups were sent, twelve in each group. Bombing altitude was to be 25,000 feet. Due to overcast over the target area the ships returned with their bombs. Flak was light and accurate. There were no killed or wounded, but one ship is missing in action. Lieut. Peak was the pilot of the missing ship and from information received, it seems he received a direct flak hit in the front of the ship near the target area. His plane caught fire, one wing fell off, and it spiraled down and crashed. No chutes were observed leaving the plane.

Missing in action:

534th Bomb Squadron (H)

B-17G #42-97084 — "Spare Charlie"

143

Peak, Samuel L.	1st Lt.	O-3980V4	P
Petroski, Robert F.	1st Lt.	O-801198	CP
Lundberg, John K.	2nd Lt.	O-676081	N
Ostenberg, Allen (NMI)	2nd Lt.	O-741356	B
Simmons, Murl F.	S/Sgt.	32650831	TTG
Wilke, Frank A., Jr.	S/Sgt.	32800468	ROG
Scherff, Robert F.	S/Sgt.	12148493	BTG
Oberlin, Richard D.	S/Sgt.	35547736	WG
Rockey, Max L.	S/Sgt.	364171125	TG

R E S T R I C T E D

OUTSTANDING PERFORMANCES

The courage and determination of 2nd Lt. Peter Kowalski, Bombardier on "Marsha Sue" over Berlin Wednesday, meant the difference between a sortie wasted and a full load of bombs on the Nazi capital. Hit in the jaw by a piece of flak on the bomb run, Lt. Kowalski clung to consciousness just long enough to get his explosives away and close his bomb bay doors. Then he lost consciousness. Measure of Lt. Kowalski's accomplishment became fully apparent when "Marsha Sue" landed here later. The same flak that wounded the bombardier also smashed into the plane's hydraulic system, leaving the bomber without brakes. Her pilot, 2nd Lt. John W. Winter, brought her in on the grass, using parachutes to check her landing speed. (See entry, 21 June 1944)

R E S T R I C T E D

---

23 June 1944 — Eighteen aircraft from this command attacked a tactical target in the Pas-de-Calais area. Bombing was by PFF through a partial cloud cover and bombing results were thought to be good. Bombing altitude was 20,000 feet. All the ships landed safely at this base. There were no killed or wounded.

Major Jollicoeur, Lieut. Keating, and Lieut. Linsky spent the night at the St. James Court Hotel in London and observed many of the pilotless planes going overhead and falling in the vicinity during the night. Shortly after 0800 hours, one of them fell in the very near vicinity, breaking all the glass out of the windows in the room they were staying in, and a piece of glass fell down and cut Lt. Keating in the belly while he was taking a bath. They reported here about 1600 hours sufficiently impressed.

24 June 1944 — Thirty-six ships from this command took off at 0500 hours with the target designated as a railroad bridge near Tours, France. Bombing altitude was 22,500 feet. The bombing results were observed and were excellent and there is no more bridge. One ship was lost and it was thought that none of the crewmembers got out. It was hit by flak. Weather was good; fighter support was excellent. No enemy fighters were encountered. The remaining ships returned to this base and there were two wounded aboard.

2nd Lt. Nelson F. Rekos, O-707323, N, 533rd Squadron
DIAGNOSIS: 1. Wound, abrased, mild, ¼" medial & dorsal aspect, rt. foot, just above the longitudinal arch. Incurred by flak. "Duty"

S/Sgt. Orval E. Page, 39693299, WG, 533rd Squadron (H)
DIAGNOSIS: 1. Wound, lacerated, moderate severity, over first carpometacarpal joint (near radial snuff box) rt. wrist. 2. Wound, lacerated, 1" posterior region, left leg, mod. sev., about 3" above the popliteal fossa and lateral aspect. Caused by low velocity missile. "H"

Missing in action:

534th Bomb Squadron (H)

B-17G #42-102585 — "The-Betty-L"

Romasco, Victor R.	2nd Lt.	O-814558	P
Kellum, Richard L.	2nd Lt.	O-695264	CP
Chandler, James H.	F/O	T-123924	N
Stewart, Roy L.	1st Lt.	O-756920	B
Giddens, Elbert F.	Sgt.	19103322	TTG
Casandier, Paul G.	S/Sgt.	37478335	ROG
Scoggins, Grover L.	Sgt.	38435008	BTG
Owens, Harry E.	S/Sgt.	19180904	WG
Waldow, Ernest L.	S/Sgt.	39327045	TG

25 June 1944 — Thirty-six aircraft from this command took off at 0430 hours with the designated target an airfield in Toulouse, France. The Group was led by Captain Sandman. Bombing altitude was 25,000 feet; outside air temperature was –30° Centigrade. The total length of mission was ten hours and forty minutes, which is a long haul. The bombing results were good on one MPI and fair on the other. No enemy fighters were encountered. Flak was meager and inaccurate over the target area. One area over the battle zone had mobile flak guns and several engines were hit due to their accuracy. All the ships returned to England, but four landed at another base due to battle damage and shortage of gas. There were no killed, wounded, or missing.

28 June 1944 — Thirty-six aircraft from this command were dispatched at 0415 hours to bomb a railway bridge near Fismes, France, which is northwest of Paris and Soissons. Bombing altitude was 24,800 feet. Outside air temperature: –34° Centigrade. The bombing was by visual method and the target was not hit. There was heavy overcast in and out.

Sgt. William F. Bursaw, 533rd Bomb Squadron, TG, was killed in action by a direct flak hit, which tore off the tail of the ship.
DIAGNOSIS: 1. Wound, pen. rt. neck, perforating jugular vein 2. LW, rt. shoulder 3. Wound, perf. lt. foot 4. Wound, LW, rt. knee 5. Wounds, pen. rt. shoulder, minor. (KIA)

The flak was meager and accurate. No hostile fighters were seen and there was ample fighter support. All the ships returned safely to this base. No missing or wounded.

4 July 1944 — Thirty-six aircraft were dispatched today and the designated target was an airfield at Tours, France. Lieut. Bobrof was seen to leave the formation on the way into the target. The airfield was bombed visually and with fair results. The remaining ships returned safely to this base. No killed or wounded and only one was missing.

Missing in action:

535th Bomb Squadron (H)

B-17G #42-38117 — "Touch-the-Button-Nell II"

Bobrof, Bob B.	2nd Lt.	P
Devono, George J.	2nd Lt.	CP
Cole, Charles D.	2nd Lt.	N
Goodman, Bernard (NMI)	2nd Lt.	B
Dell, George W., Jr.	T/Sgt.	TTG
Word, Clinton S., Jr.	T/Sgt.	ROG
Polski, Edward F.	Sgt.	BTG
Hitchcock, Kenneth F.	S/Sgt.	WG
Snyder, Thomas E.	S/Sgt.	TG

6 July 1944 — Thirty-six aircraft from this command took off this AM with the designated target at Reilly, France. Major Halsey led the Group. Bombing altitude was from 24,000 to 26,000 and outside temperature was –25° Centigrade. Ceiling and visibility unlimited in the target area, with a very slight haze. The lead, low and high groups, reported meager, inaccurate high AA fire from he vicinity of Barneville to the right of the formation, and meager, inaccurate high fire from St-Poi-de-Léon area, away from the formation. There was no flak in the target area. Our group made the bomb run after making one 360° and the 91st Bomb Group did five or six 180°s over the target. There were no ships lost, and all returned safely to this base. There were no killed or wounded.

7 July 1944 — Forty-two aircraft from this command took off at 0500 hours with the target designated as the center of the city of Leipzig, Germany. Bombing altitude was 24,000. The lead group was led by Colonel Leber with Capt. Franek as deputy. The low group was led by Lieut. Barnacle. Bombing results were excellent. Enemy activity was minimum. All the ships returned safely to this base. It was on this mission that 36 bombers were shot down, 34 of which were B-24's (Liberators) and the Germans lost 114 fighters.

One EM, Sgt. George J. Formanek, TG, 532nd Bomb Squadron (H) was wounded by plane parts set in motion by flak. He was evacuated to the 121st Station Hospital.
DIAGNOSIS: Wound, left leg, pen., mod., plane parts. (WIA)

Captain Milton H. Bland, MC, O-465678, 535ᵗʰ Bomb Squadron Surgeon, departed this station today for the United States. His absence will be a loss to every man in the department. Besides his ability as a surgeon, he always had a smile and a cheerful word for all who came into contact with him. It is with regret that we saw him leave the Group, but we hope that his presence at home will give aid to his wife in her present illness.

Captain Coppage was here to inspect the chlorinator, which has not been working satisfactorily. The defect has been narrowed down to either poor ortho-tolidene, or the sodium hypochlorite that is used in the chlorinator.

At 0745 this morning we were notified of a crash of 2 B-17's one-and-a-half miles northwest of Haverhill, which is about 13 miles northwest of here. Both ships were from the 384ᵗʰ Bomb Group at Grafton Underwood. Three of the survivors were brought here, Lieut. Bagley, F/C Morton, and T/Sgt. Day. All suffered minor injuries.

A fourth was taken to Little Walden. There were 16 men perished in the crash. The surgeon from Little Walden states that he witnessed the accident and states that the formation was high overhead, an estimated 10,000 feet, when one ship was seen to put its nose down and begin to spin, and was followed shortly by the other. Both planes spun and struck the earth about 1 mile from each other. One of the survivors states that they were flying along straight and level when the other ship approached them from an angle of about 220° and struck them under the fuselage and right wing. Captain Foley from Grafton Underwood came over to pick up the survivors and inquire about the disposition of those who had been killed.

8 July 1944 — Twenty-four aircraft from this command took off on a cross road target this morning at about 0520 hours. The lead group didn't bomb because of a 10/10 overcast. The low group found a hole in the clouds and bombed cross roads elsewhere, a target of opportunity. The only event of the mission was when the bomb shackles broke and they had unpinned bombs rolling around in the bomb bay. They went out over the Channel and finally dropped the bombs safely and returned to the base. There were no killed, missing or wounded.

9 July 1944 — Twelve aircraft from this command took off with the same target as designated yesterday as their destination. They flew through an overcast 20,000 feet thick and did not drop their bombs. All the aircraft returned safely to this base. No killed, missing, or wounded.

11 July 1944 — Eighteen aircraft from this command took off at 0800 hours with the target designated as Munich, Germany. The primary target was bombed by pathfinder method from 27,400 feet. No enemy fighters were encountered and the planes from this group were not damaged by flak. All the aircraft returned safely to this base. There were no killed or wounded.

12 July 1944 — Thirty-six aircraft from this command were dispatched at 0900 hours with the target again designated as Munich, Germany. Colonel Hall led the wing. The bombing was done by PFF and was not observed. All ships returned safely to this base. There were no killed and only one minor injury: 2nd Lt. Emil A. Pane, O-762591, 533rd Bomb Sqdn., Bombardier, suffered a small ¼" laceration of upper rt. thigh. There was a second briefing at 1345 hours, but the mission was scrubbed.

13 July 1944 — Thirty-nine aircraft from this command took off at 0500 hours with poor visibility and clouds down to 17,000 feet. One aircraft, piloted by Lieut. Houston, lost one engine at altitude (10,000). Returning to the field, he made three attempts to land, which were unsuccessful due to poor visibility. Following the third attempt to land, he lost a second engine and attempted to land the aircraft in a wheat field ½ mile south east of the base. The ship was set down successfully and after about 200 yards, rolled into a railroad cut. The Pilot was thrown free of the ship and walked the road where he was picked up and brought to station sick quarters by ambulance. The Co-Pilot was thrown free of

---

R E S T R I C T E D

OUTSTANDING PERFORMANCES

When 1st Lt. Lee V. Wilson's 533rd Fortress, "Honey" pulled out of a 2,000 foot plunge, necessitated to avoid colliding with another bomber during the return trip from France yesterday, four bombs were ripped from their shackles and slammed onto one bomb bay door. Six more swung loosely from badly weakened attachments. Armorer-tail gunner, S/Sgt. Clyde C. Crain, crawled forward to the bay, saw the predicament, (and) realized the four, floored bombs might explode under the slightest jar at any moment. Nevertheless, he began safe-tying the remaining bombs in their shackles, while Wilson headed for the Channel to salvo the deadly load. As he was working, without parachute, a loose bomb knocked Crain down into the bay among the live explosives. He climbed back and, assisted by bombardier 2nd Lt. Richard E. Kennedy, continued with the safe-tying. "Honey" made it to the Channel where her engineer-top turret gunner, Sgt. George N. Meyers, began lowering the bomb bay doors under guidance from the two men in the bay. Not daring to jolt the loose bombs, Meyers eased the hand crank a few threads at a time until, in a tight cluster, they slipped clear and downward to the water. Then, Crain and Kennedy released the remaining explosives, singly and by hand, until the bay was clear. Wilson then turned "Honey" for home, landing safely more than an hour behind the rest of the formation (See entry, 8 July 1944).

---

the ship and dragged to safety by a 7th Station Complement man (name unknown as yet). There was one minor explosion followed by two major explosions about two minutes apart. Ambulances were dispatched to the scene of the accident and the Co-pilot was brought back to sick quarters. Reconnaissance resulted in the picking up of remains of seven bodies, only one of which could be identified by Dental Identification Method. The aircraft was completely destroyed.

The "Toonerville Trolley" (the destroyed Fort) from Great Yeldham will not run for several days due to destruction by 500 lb. bombs. Four 500 lb. bombs were being carried by the aircraft and the balance of the load were 200 lb. incendiaries.

The pilot, 2nd Lt. John L. Houston, O-757387, 534th Squadron (H), received the following injuries:
DIAGNOSIS: 1. Burn, 1st & 2nd deg., thighs, bilateral, wrists, bilateral, face, mild. 2. Wound, mild, rt. infra orbital region. 3. Wound, lacerated rt. supra orbital region. 4. Sprain, ankles, bilateral, mod. sev. 5. Shock, post traumatic, mild.

The Co-pilot, 2nd Lt. William M. Scruggs, Jr., O-818228, 534th Sqdn. (H), suffered the following:
DIAGNOSIS: 1. Burns, 2nd deg., hand, bilateral. 2. Burn, 1st & 2nd deg., face. 3. Abrasion, cornea, rt. mod. sev. 4. Possible fracture of left femur and trochanter or neck.

Both officers were evacuated to the 121st Station Hospital, Braintree.

S/Sgt. Kenneth L. Spatz, 33618577, WG, 534th Squadron (H), was identified by means of Dental Identification Chart.
DIAGNOSIS: 1. Amputation, traumatic, complete, of shoulder girdle and head from rest of body with extensive mutilation of head. Remainder of body unaccounted for. (KIA)

The following named officers and enlisted men were completely mutilated and could not be identified in any way whatsoever. Their remains were gathered and taken to the American Military Cemetery, Cambridge, England by Lieutenant Fick.

534th Bomb Squadron (H)

B-17G #44-6148 — "Toonerville Trolley", "Smashing Thru"

Sullivan, Gerald J.	2nd Lt.	O-761480	N
Walmsley, James A.	2nd Lt.	O-707458	B
Benward, Robert A.	T/Sgt.	37501550	ROG
Murray, Donald B.	T/Sgt.	39199324	TTG
Jackson, Lloyd S.	S/Sgt.	35589038	BTG
Cusick, William M.	S/Sgt.	17113431	TG

All aircraft returned from Munich, Germany after bombing by PFF from 25,000 feet. They reported the flak as heavy and accurate and fighters were seen to attack and disseminate two wings following ours. Damage to this group was minor and no injuries were sustained.

16 July 1944 — Thirty-six aircraft from this command took off in the early hours with the target again designated as Munich, Germany. The target was bombed successfully and all but one ship returned to this base. This ship ditched in the North Sea and all nine crewmembers were rescued. One EM suffered a mild case of anoxia and frostbite.

Lieut. McGregor ditched in the Channel on the side of a rescue ship. His ship lost three engines & they were out of gas. He did such a neat job ditching along side of the rescue ship that the crew didn't even get their feet wet. (Bombing from 26,000')

Aircraft ditched in North Sea:

<u>532nd Bomb Squadron (H)</u>

B-17G #42-102664 — "Happy Bottom" [11]

18 July 1944 — Thirty-eight aircraft from this command took off at 0530 with the target designated as Peenemünde, Germany, which is on the Baltic Sea east of Denmark. The lead group was led by Colonel Fitzgerald, Captain Winter was deputy lead, and Captain Freeze led the low group. The bombing was done visually after preparations had been made for the PFF bombing. A 360° turn was made after it was determined that the bombing would be done visually. Both groups felt that they hit the target, which was a Hydrogen Peroxide plant, which was part of the pilotless plane installation. No enemy fighters were encountered and flak was light and accurate. Lieut. O'Black lost an engine, salvoed his bombs, and it was thought he accompanied the formation over the target, but was unable to keep up and his aircraft was heard acknowledging fighter recognition and heading for Sweden.

It is felt that this is Lieut. O'Black's ship. Bombing was done from 24,000 feet. No killed or wounded and only one ship lost.

Missing in action:

<u>533rd Bomb Squadron (H)</u>

B-17G #42-102663 — "Yardbird"

O'Black, Frank R.	1st Lt.	P
Karch, Robert C.	2nd Lt.	CP
Treanor, Francis J.	2nd Lt.	N
Higginbotham, Herbert, Jr.	2nd Lt.	B
Rich, Wesley K.	S/Sgt.	RO
Beck, Eugene N.	T/Sgt.	TTG
Brown, Oliver E.	S/Sgt.	BTG
Rich, William (NMI)	Sgt.	WG
Freidberg, Bernard G.	S/Sgt.	TG

---

[11] This was Dad's bird—at least his favorite bird to fly in—although doctors were specifically *prohibited* from flying. It was originally christened by the actor, Edward G. Robinson himself, on the base in 1943. He named it after his wife, Gladys, as in "Glad Ass" (too risqué), ergo, dubbed (quite nebulously), "Happy Bottom". Understandably, there was no nose art associated with this particular airplane's moniker (see Photos & Images).

19 July 1944 — Thirty-seven aircraft from this command took off this AM for a target in Augsburg, Germany. Bombing altitude was 22,500 feet. The Group was led by Captain Franek. Bombing results were good, there were no fighters encountered and flak was very mild. No aircraft were lost, and no killed or wounded.

20 July 1944 — Thirty-seven aircraft took off from this command at 0500 hours with the target an aircraft assembly plant at Dessault, Germany. This plant has been assembling ME-109's and the new jet-propelled aircraft that the Germans are developing. There were no killed or wounded. Major Briggs led the Group. Bombing was done visually from 25,000 feet and results were thought to be good. All ships returned safely to this base.

21 July 1944 — Thirty-seven aircraft from this command took off for Schweinfurt, Germany. The Group led the air division and Colonel Leber led the Group. There was stinking weather all the way in and out and the target area alone of the entire trip was clear. The MPI of the lead group was very effectively camouflaged and it was bombed using surrounding landmarks as a means of identification. Bombing was done from 26,000 feet and results were excellent. No enemy aircraft were encountered. Flak was moderate and thoroughly accurate. Four ships returned to this base with feathered props. There were no missing, killed or wounded.

23 July 1944 — Major Gaillard departed this base today for a week's TD with the 312th Station Hospital. His mission is to study psychiatric cases among ground personnel that have been evacuated from the Normandy front and report their similarity to psychiatric disorders occurring among flying personnel.

Private Ralph A. Timonere, clerk of the medical department, reported to this base today and was reunited with his brother, Pfc. Charles J. Timonere, whom he had not seen for two years. "It can happen here!"

The only other thing of note is that Captain Pease has finally attained checker supremacy over Captain Cohler, though even this is in dispute at the moment.

Captain Jones departed this field to join the dental staff of the 3rd Division. He is to have charge of supervising the dental plate work of the entire 3rd Division.

Captain Wistar L. Graham, recently of Georgia, has taken Captain Bland's place as 535th Bomb Squadron Surgeon. While from a physical standpoint we cannot compare him with Captain Bland, there is much resemblance between the classic good humors of both.

24 July 1944 — Last evening, a restriction was placed on all combat personnel forbidding even six-hour passes being given. Briefing during the night was scrubbed and a subsequent briefing took place at 0815 hours. Fifty-two aircraft from this command, the second largest number to be dispatched from this field, took off with the designated target gun emplacements in the St. Lo area, which have been holding up our troops.

151

Approximately 2,000 aircraft were to take part in the attack and the target designated was to be identified by the use of red smoke by the ground artillery. Weather over the target was about six-tenths coverage. Bombing was done visually from 16,500 feet. This group was among the last to bomb and reported sky markers all over the place. Two minutes after the bombs were away radio operators received a message for the Group not to bomb and to return to the base. At the present moment, it is not known whether we bombed our own men or not. All the ships returned safely to the base with only one ship having a feathered prop. There were no killed or wounded.

25 July 1944 — It is hoped that today will be another day marked in history. Thirty-eight groups of aircraft, each numbering fifty-two, bombed ahead of the American troops in the St. Lo area. Low and medium aircraft bombed from 3,000 to 10,000 feet. Our aircraft bombed from 12,000 feet and reported good results. Aircraft were carrying 3800 lb. G.P. bombs per each. The last American aircraft was to drop bombs at 1055; zero hour for the big push was 1100 hours. All aircraft returned to the base, one with a feathered prop. Flak was light, but accurate. One JU-88 was all the enemy aircraft reported, and this was closely followed by one Lightning.

Lieut. Rennick, 533rd Bomb Squadron, has returned from his visit to the States. He weighs approximately 20 pounds more, looks refreshed, and states that the rumor of the U. S. being involved in a war has not yet permeated to the home front. He, also, is delighted to be back, but expresses lack of interest in going on any raids to Munich. Three additional crews were assigned to this station last night, bringing the total to about 23 crews per squadron.

26 July 1944 — No mission was scheduled for today. The buzz bomb situation is becoming acute in that three or four have passed directly over this field.[12] It is hoped Hans continues to put enough petrol in them to get them over this field.

27 July 1944 — Penicillin has been obtained for use in this dispensary, and by peculiar coincidence two brand new cases of gonorrhea have shown up for it. 1,000 units and 10cc of saline were given in one single dose.

The briefing was for Munich and the mission was scrubbed after nine planes had taken off.

28 July 1944 — Thirty-seven planes took off on a mission to Marienburg, Germany, located about 20 miles outside of Leipzig. The target was a synthetic oil plant, which produces about one-tenth of the German synthetic oil supply. In addition, it produces approximately one-third of the ammonia produced in Germany.

---

[12] My mom had a farm near St. Osyth on the coast of Essex to support the war effort. One day, whilst atop stacking huge sheaves with her foreman, Ronnie, she saw **two** V-1 (*Vergeltung Swaffe*) buzz bombs a.k.a. "doodlebugs" heading (from her height) "straight for her" from the North Sea. Conditioned by five years of war, she instinctively jumped to the ground and scurried for cover. After passing harmlessly overhead, Ronnie finally appeased her anxiety and misgivings with *this* rather comforting assurance: "It's alright, mum, the little bastards are bloody-well heading for London".

The flak was reported as being quite heavy by some of the old pilots. There were no fighter attacks on this group, although there were on others. Bombing was by PFF and all ships returned safely without injured aboard.

This group was informed that the 1st Bomb Division had received a Presidential Citation and that all men attached as of July 15th were entitled to wear the blue ribbon on the right side of the blouse.

29 July 1944 — Thirty-six aircraft from this command took off at 0545 hours for Marienburg, Germany, same target as yesterday, and the synthetic oil plant was hit again. The lead group, led by Lt. Colonel Fitzgerald, bombed visually. The high group led by Lt. Barnacle, and the low group led by Lt. Martyniak, bombed by PFF on the smoke of the other group. Twenty 250 lb. bombs were carried. Bombing altitude was 25,000 feet and the outside air temperature was –28° Centigrade. Bombing results are unknown, but are thought to be within the target area. Flak was intense and accurate; no fighters attacked, but were noted by other wings and a few ships were seen to go down with parachutes opening. The ships landed at this with very poor visibility and four ships landed at North Creake, two at Hethel, and one at Attlebridge. Two ships were two hours late and one landed at Attlebridge and the other here. Lieut. Quinn salvoed his bombs and returned early with another group due to the fact he had one engine out. Lieut. Weaver aborted due to mechanical trouble. There were no killed, wounded or missing and only one minor burn was reported.

The P-51 aircraft that recently made the transcontinental record, flown by Howard Hughes, was sent to the E. T. O. with the specific instructions that its performance in combat be observed. The man who flew it over here has just been released from the hospital, the wing of the airplane having fallen off after being airborne less than 20 minutes.

A Mosquito pilot flew a stripped down reconnaissance Mosquito and reported that he had encountered a jet-propelled German aircraft. He reported that it was at least 100 miles an hour faster than his aircraft and estimated its speed at about 500 - 600 miles an hour on the level. Purportedly, this RAF pilot has been placed under some form of sedation.

31 July 1944 — Thirty-seven aircraft from this command took at 0815 hours with the target again designated as an aircraft assembly plant in the vicinity of Munich, Germany. The airfield was named Alach. Bombing altitude was 25,000 feet and the outside air temperature was –28° Centigrade. The Group was led by Captain Sandman. No enemy aircraft were encountered. Flak was light and accurate and bombing results were thought to be good. All but three ships returned to this base, two landing at other bases in England due to engine trouble and the other is missing in action, but is rumored to have made it to Switzerland.

Missing in action:

533rd Bombardment Squadron (H)

B-17G #42-102423 — "My Devotion"

Pearson, Jack B.	2nd Lt.	O-818212	P
Proctor, Joe L.	2nd Lt.	O-819314	CP
Gordon, Sydney H.	2nd Lt.	O-719928	N
Guidotti, Alfred H.	2nd Lt.	O-772047	B
Fontenot, Dewill J.	Sgt.	38483776	TTG
Boyington, William E.	Sgt.	19073637	ROG
Hoover, Harold M.	Sgt.	15113441	BTG
Mizer, Frank S.	Sgt.	35058708	WG
Jones, Charles G.	Sgt.	12O95396	TG

Major Ernest Gaillard, Jr. returned from the 312th Station Hospital, near Stafford, where he attended a course on combat exhaustion. Speaking of exhaustion, the "Jerries" must be getting pretty tired of it, too; the scuttlebutt flying around this station is that Hitler's own men tried to kill him a few days ago. What will they think of next?

1 August 1944 — Thirty-six aircraft from this command took off with the target designated as an airfield near Melun, France. Bombing was done visually with good results from 20,000 feet. All the ships returned safely to this base with no killed or wounded.

3 August 1944 — Thirty-six aircraft from this command, led by Lt. Colonel Hall, attacked the marshalling yards at Mulhouse, France, which is near the Swiss Border. The bombing was visual with excellent results from 20,000 feet. All the ships, except one, piloted by Lieut. Wilcock, returned safely to this base. Lieut. Wilcock was thought to have lost 3 engines over the Channel and to have ordered his crew to bail out.

Capt. Lee W. Scholnik reported here for duty as assistant dental surgeon on 25 July 1944.

Missing in action:

534th Bomb Squadron (H)

B-17G #42-32049 — "Yankee Rebel"

Wilcock, John C.	2nd Lt.	P
Hutchinson, Stanley E.	2nd Lt.	CP
Marsh, Charles R.	2nd Lt.	N
Lucas, Norbert I.	2nd Lt.	B
Ransay, John A.	Sgt.	WG
Printz, Alfred E.	Sgt.	TTG
Friel, Robert F.	Sgt.	RO
Evans, Charles R.	Sgt.	BTG
Fall, Richard, Jr.	Sgt.	TG

4 August 1944 — Thirty-six aircraft from this command took off at 0930 hours with the target again designated as the experimental works at Peenemünde, Germany. The Group was led by Colonel Leber. About 1020 hours we were notified that a ship had caught fire and blown up in mid-air in the vicinity of Weathersfield, nr. Great Saling, Essex, England. After covering most of eastern England due to a succession of bum steers, we finally rounded up the nine survivors and they are:

1st Lt. Hanley G. Cupernall, P, 1. FS, fibula, rt. CW, forehead, mild. "Q"
Capt. Irving (NMI) Moore, CP, – CW, para-vertebral muscles. "Q"
1st Lt. Russell J. Hadley, N, Sprain, rt. ankle, mod. "Q"
1st Lt. James W. Sneed, N, Sprain, lt. ankle, mild. "Q"
1st Lt. Charles W. Yound, B, – FS, lt. ankle. "H"
Capt. Francis G. Hawking, P – CW, occipital region of skull. "Q"
T/Sgt. Earl T. Yankten, TTG, Burn, 1st & 2nd deg., rt. hand; 1st & 2nd deg., face. "Q"
T/Sgt. Frank H. Heinze, RO – No injury. "Q"
S/Sgt. Loren W. Murphy, WG – No injury. "Q"

The tail gunner, S/Sgt. Harold F. Norris, went down with the ship and was killed in action. His diagnosis is as follows: 1. Burn, 3rd deg., entire body; 2. Evisceration of abdominal contents; 3. Avulsion of the cranium and complete evisceration of brain. (KIA)

The body of 2nd Lt. John C. Wilcock was picked up by an Air-Sea rescue boat off Felixstowe, which is on England's eastern sea-board. Captain Wymer picked up the body at Felixstowe and is taking Lt. Wilcock together with Sgt. Norris to Cambridge.

Some more mangled pieces of the bodies were found in the wheat field in the vicinity of the crash and explosion on July 13th. There was no part that could be positively identified. These, too, are being sent to the Cambridge American Military Cemetery.

The bombing results at Peenemünde were excellent and the bombing was done visually from 20,000 feet. All the ships returned safely to this base. There was no enemy fighter opposition and flak was moderate.

5 August 1944 — Briefing at 0600 hours with takeoff at 0835 with the target designated as Niemburg, Germany. The Group was led by Captain Sandman. There was one area of flak that was intense and the lead squadron suffered fairly extensive damage and the deputy lead ship with Lieut's. Palmer and Melomo did not return to the base. 1st Lt. Caleb G. Baxter, O-702361, Nav., 532nd Squadron, on Lt. Rivet's ship, was hit in the left leg by flak and caused considerable tissue damage and fractured the tibia in the middle one-third. The bombing was done visually and the results were good. The remainder of the ships returned safely to this base. Bombing altitude: 18,000 feet.

Missing in action:

533rd Bomb Squadron (H)

B-17G #42-97771 — "No Name"

Melomo, Salavator J.	1st Lt.	O-792049	P
Palmer, Edwin W.	1st Lt.	O-679109	CP
Freeman, Charles S.	2nd Lt.	O-685504	N
Bernstein, William (NMI) (534th Sqdn.)	2nd Lt.	O-692271	B
Lane, David W.	1st Lt.	O-759949	B
Gilbertson, Willard G.	T/Sgt.	39905691	TTG
Vaughn, Leland N.	S/Sgt.	14063199	ROG
Moorhead, James M.	S/Sgt.	37662876	BTG
Hill, Julian E.	S/Sgt.	13016700	WG
Beneke, Louis F.	S/Sgt.	37303280	TG

6 August 1944 — Thirty-six aircraft from this command took off at 0645 hours with the target designated as Brandenburg, Germany, which is just 30- to 40- miles east of Berlin. The Group was led by Major Briggs. Bombing altitude was 25,000 feet and the outside air temperature was –21° Centigrade. Bombing was done visually with good results. Lieut. Webb in the low squadron is missing, having lost an engine over enemy territory and was not seen after that. The remainder of the ships returned to this base, and there were no wounded or killed. Fighter support was good and enemy opposition was negligible, except for flak.

Missing in action:

532nd Bomb Squadron (H)

B-17G #44-6020 — "Under Ground Farmer"

Webb, Allen W.	1st Lt.	O-757633	B
Hates, John W.	2nd Lt.	O-818922	CP
Grossnickle, Earl S.	2nd Lt.	O-716427	N
Gomez, George	2nd Lt.	O-703479	B
Grisham, London L.	T/Sgt.	34287281	TTG
Murkin, Ralph K.	S/Sgt.	17006635	ROG
Burt, William C.	S/Sgt.	17088513	BTG
Gonzales, Adolph M.	S/Sgt.	39277899	WG
Patrick, Jack S.	S/Sgt.	34392540	TG

7 August 1944 — Thirty-six aircraft took off in (3@) twelve-ship flights with the designated target two oil dumps in the neighborhood of Paris. Each dump consisted of 20 – 30 tanks about 30 feet high. Bombing was from 15,000 feet and there was from one- to two-tenths cloud cover. Photographs showed pin-point bombing results. Flak was light and fairly accurate. A few ships returned with holes in the wings and fuselage. There were no injured, missing or killed.

Major Gaillard is spending the next few days at the 121st Station Hospital, Braintree, to assist in taking care of 350 casualties just evacuated from Normandy.

8 August 1944 — Thirty-seven aircraft took off for the designated target south east of Caen, France. Colonel Halsey led and the bombing was about 1,000 yards in front of the invasion forces at an altitude of 14,000 feet. Due to a mechanical failure, one ship failed to bomb. Flak was intense and accurate from the I.P. to the target. Twenty-five ships received major battle damage and five minor damages from the mission. There was good fighter support and only one enemy fighter was seen. Bombing results were excellent. Lieut. Barnacle got a direct flak hit in the wing and the bomb bay. The wing and bomb bay caught fire and they had to jettison the bombs. Lt. Barnacle turned the ship away from the formation and all the crewmembers bailed out from about 10,000 feet landing a little north west of Falaise, France. Lieut. Stuart sprained an ankle; Sgt. Glover received an abrasion of his calf, as did Lt. Long. Lieut. Beackley suffered a sprain of moderate severity of the left elbow. The crewmembers were all rounded up and flown back to England the next morning by ATC and landed in Bishops Stortford, Essex where they were brought to this base by ambulance. After talking with the crewmembers, it was concluded they were a little shaken up by the experience, but none the worse for it. All were admitted to station sick quarters for sedation.

Aircraft lost over Falaise (no MACR):

535th Bomb Squadron (H)

B-17G #43-37704 — "Button Nose"

9 August 1944 — Twenty-four aircraft from this command took from this command with the designated target a large and frequently hit industrial area in Germany. Because of poor weather, the target could not be reached and Saarbrücken, Germany was bombed from 22,500 feet visually with good results. Colonel Kunkle led the Group. No enemy fighters were encountered, but flak was intense and accurate over the target. One gunner, Sgt. Valente, 533rd Squadron, received a minor abrasion of the left forearm due to flak.

11 August 1944 — Thirty-six ships from this command took off this morning to hit tactical targets ahead of the invasion forces. Lieut. McNeil, 532nd Squadron, led the Group. Bombing was done visually from 25,000 feet with good results. No enemy fighters were encountered and our own fighter support was excellent. No flak was noted throughout the entire mission. All the ships returned safely to this base and there were no wounded or killed.

13 August 1944 — Thirty-six ships from this command took off at 0830 hours with the target designated as two bridges and a road junction behind the enemy lines in France. The Group was led by Captain Sandman. Bombing was from 20,000 feet; there was a moderate amount of flak, but no enemy fighters were seen. Friendly fighter support was good.

2nd Lieut. William G. Haines, Jr. O-719938, 535th Navigator, was killed in action as a result of a burst of flak in the nose of the ship, which traumatically amputated his right leg about 2" below the patella almost completely. There were also multiple perforating wounds of the left thigh. Lt. Haines apparently bled to death although all efforts were made to stop the bleeding. A piece of his flak suit was damaged. The radio operator, S/Sgt. Thomas R. Ressler, 33131309, was wounded in the right lumbar region by flak. He was not wearing a flak suit, but the flak came through the top turret floor, struck the flak suit before hitting him, and probably saved his life.

Major Douglas M. Kelly, a psychiatrist from the 312th Station Hospital, was a visitor this date.

The monthly officers' dance was held at the officers' club and, surprisingly enough, the records of neither the guardhouse nor the hospital were increased by the affair. The party was well behaved, well organized and well conducted, and Captain Cohler for the first time in, lo, these many months, took unto himself a female to bring to the party (and beautiful!!!).

14 August 1944 — Thirty-six aircraft from this command took at 0730 with the target designated as an airfield several miles south west of Metz, France. The Group was led by Colonel Halsey and there were two MPI's. Bombing was from 20,000 feet; temperature –16° Centigrade. Bombing was by visual method and the results were excellent. No flak or fighters were encountered and all the ships returned safely to this base.

15 August 1944 — Thirty-seven aircraft from this command took off at 0630 hours for a target designated as an airfield just on the western outskirts of Cologne, Germany. The Group was led by Colonel Hall and bombing was done visually from 26,000 feet with good results. The lead group of the wing encountered intense, accurate flak and suffered much battle damage. Col. Hall had #3 engine shot out along with the hydraulic system. There were no enemy fighters encountered. No killed, wounded or missing. Outside air temperature today was –24° Centigrade.

Major Linn S. Kidd returned to the states this date along with Majors Briggs and Fullick, the latter on a 30-day leave.

16 August 1944 — Thirty-seven aircraft from this command took off at 0700 hours with the target designated as an airfield near Leipzig, Germany. Colonel Fitzgerald was leading and the bombing was done visually with excellent results from the lead and low groups, but the high group over shot. No enemy fighters were encountered and flak was light. Two ships returned with feathered props. One enlisted man, Sgt. John B. Keffer, 33673547, Tail Gunner, 533rd Squadron, was wounded in action by flak. His diagnosis is: 1. Wound, penetrating, left lateral aspect, trochanteric region, mild. He was in good condition upon arriving at sick quarters and was evacuated to the 121st Station Hospital.

21 August 1944 — Major Douglas M. Kelley, MC, formerly of the 312th Station Hospital, and now with the 130th General Hospital, visited this station from 13-21 August. The 130th General Hospital is scheduled to leave for Rennes, France to set up a neurosis center in the next few days. Major Kelley was shown our psychiatric case histories and we attempted to indoctrinate him into the problems the Air Corps personnel have in the air. We also visited Weathersfield, Goss Field, Great Saling, and the Central Medical Establishment of the 9th Air Force. The Surgeon at Great Saling seemed to be well grounded in psychiatry, but the other two fields denied the existence of any psychiatric problems, which, on closer scrutiny, was found to be untrue. The Central Medical Establishment of the 9th Air Force denied any psychiatric problems, yet for the months of June and July had disposed of approximately 130 men each month for psychiatric reasons. An extract of one of their reports is attached (see following pages).

The 9th Air Force has no policy regarding the handling of psychiatric casualties, and anything that is done is done through the efforts of the unit surgeon. In none of the institutions visited was any program of treatment carried out. The 8th Air Force fields that were visited were on the whole better, but, here again in many instances, no preventative or therapeutic measures were carried out in the treatment of psychiatric casualties. While here, Major Kelley gave a couple of mornings to discussing the classification and treatment of ground force personnel to the local officers. I thoroughly enjoyed Major Kelley's visit and feel I have learned quite a bit from him. In civil life, he was an associate professor in psychiatry at the University of California, Berkeley.

24 August 1944 — Thirty-six aircraft from this command took off at 0630 hours with the target designated as Weimer, Germany, which is near Leipzig. Bombing was done from 25,000 feet with good results. The weather was bad all the way. Flak was meager and no fighters were encountered. The Group was led by Major Sandman. There were two wounded and they are: T/Sgt. David (NMI) Caldwell, ASN 33580315, TTG, 534th Bomb Squadron (H). 1. WIA – forearm, right, pen., mod., flak. Horen, Don W., Sgt. – ASN 17131063, ROG, 534th Bomb Squadron (H). 1. WIA – hand, right, pen. Through 5th metacarp-phalangeal joint, mod., FC, head of 5th metacarpal, flak. There were no missing or killed.

25 August 1944 — Thirty-seven aircraft from this command took off this morning with the target designated as FW-190 assembly plants at Neubrandenburg, Germany, which at the present time have been undamaged. Ten 500 RDX B-2 bombs were to be dropped over 4,000 feet and not to be returned to the base. The MPI was hangars and bombing results were good. Captain Winters led and the hangars were missed completely by the lead squadron. Bombing was done from 21,000 - 22,000 feet. Temperature –11° to –13° Centigrade. There were no flak or fighters, and excellent visibility all the way. One casualty — rubber eraser in the left ear of the radio operator.

26 August 1944 — Thirty-seven aircraft, with one PFF, took off this morning with the target designated as Gelsenkirchen, Germany in the middle of the Ruhr Valley. Takeoff was delayed due to fog for two hours.

Colonel Halsey led the Group and a synthetic oil refinery previously bombed by the RAF was the target. Flak was moderate, fighters nil and battle damage minor. Results for high and lead group PA-0 (unobserved) Low group PA-1 (excellent). There were no killed, wounded or missing.

27 August 1944 — Thirty-seven aircraft from this command took off at 1000 hours with the target designated as an aircraft factory south west of Berlin. The route was over the North Sea, but the weather was so bad that the mission could not be accomplished. Most of the wings returned home, but Colonel Fitzgerald, leading this wing, found the city of Emden was just south of course so he called for fighter support, which was granted, and they went in to bomb the city of Emden at 25,000 feet. The bombing was done visually with excellent results and all the ships returned safely to this base. Flak was intense and accurate over the target and there was a fair amount of battle damage to the ships. There was one killed and two wounded. They are:

Ramsdell, Richard B. – ASN 33410302 – Sgt. – 534th Sqdn. TG. KIA – Chest, wound, perforating, site of entry, right side, level of 6th rib, mid-scapular line, posterior, wound 1" in diameter; wound of exit ½ inch in diameter, anterior chest level of 2nd rib 3" lateral (left) of midline. Caused by flak, high velocity.

Defek, John A. – T/Sgt. – ASN 35053993 – 532nd Squadron (H) TTG. 1. Wounds, penetrating, multiple (3) right buttock and over crest of right illium, mod. sev. 2. Wounds, penetrating, multiple, mild, over left buttock. Caused by flak.

LaPierre, Raymond L. – O-759262 – 2nd Lt. 532nd Squadron (H) Pilot – Wounds, penetrating, mod. sev., neck, right side, right shoulder, right arm, rt. and left forearm, rt. and lt. thigh. Caused by low velocity flak.

30 August 1944 — Thirty-six aircraft from this organization led by Colonel Hall took off at 1200 hours with the target designated as Kiel. The continent was overcast ten-tenths all the way in and out. Friendly fighter support was good and no enemy fighters were seen. Flak was moderate and inaccurate. 1st Lt. John W. Carson, O-762753, Bombardier, 535th Squadron (H), received a fairly severe contusion of the forehead when a piece of flak hit his flak helmet. Without question, the flak helmet saved him from death or serious injury. All the ships returned safely to this base. Major McNiel, division dental surgeon, was a visitor this date.

3 September 1944 — Thirty-six aircraft took off at 0725 hours with the target designated as Gelsenkirchen, Germany. The Group was led by Captain Winter. Bombing was done from 26,000 feet and results were unobserved. The target was an oil refinery we have hit several times in the past. Lieut. Penrod's ship lost an engine just after the bomb line was crossed and he turned back toward France. He landed late, but returned safely to the base. Lieut. Stewart lost two engines over the target so landed in France near Paris. Lieut. Tolchinsky had some difficulty with a windmilling prop, but returned safely to the base. No killed or wounded. The flak over the target area was moderate and accurate, but they were tracking the chaff rather than the airplanes. Fighter support was good and no enemy fighters were seen.

**Extract from 9th AAF Central Medical Establishment
(Section 4 of Medical Report)**:

<u>Psychiatric Department</u>:

Functional problems seen at the CME have, in general, fallen into three categories:

  (1) Early severe combat anxiety and panic reactions;
  (2) Chronic maladjustment (psychopathic personality) with superimposed anxiety reactions;
  (3) Anxiety reactions appearing well along in combat. This last category contains the bulk of our cases.

Our general practice has been to recommend permanent disqualification in the first two categories. The third category constitutes the essential problem facing flying personnel.

It can be further broken down into three groups:

  (1) Individuals with anxiety thresholds reduced to the point that they are regarded as finished for combat. Our recommendation has been permanent disqualification. Such recommendations were made.
  (2) Individuals who are not returnable to combat flying after a period of rest, but who may be returnable after a period of two- to four months. Recommendations have been made for reassignment and re-examination at the CME after such time has elapsed.
  (3) Individuals who may be returnable to combat flying after a brief period of rest.

Formerly, such cases were sent to the Narcosis Unit of the 347th Station Hospital following, which they were given a short stay at Rest Homes. Since 8th May, we have not used Narcosis therapy. These cases are now sent to the 1st General Hospital. There, they are given minimal doses of sedation at night to assure restful sleep. Small doses of insulin may be given to stimulate appetite. Any other physical problems are dealt with. They are permitted to rest during the day or be active as they choose. They are kept there for a week of for several weeks depending on their progress. The favorable cases are then sent to Rest Homes. The length of stay in Rest Homes also depends on progress shown.

Hospitalization, not followed by Rest Home, may be instituted for therapeutic reasons in any anxiety-tension state to bring about some reduction in tension before reassignment.

B-17 Flight Plan from Colonel Hall's Mission 15 AUGUST 1944

PILOT'S MTG:	0515	
STATIONS:	0600	
START ENG:	0615	SPARES:
TAXI:	0630	LEAD 5I-7625 (PFF)
TAKE-OFF:	0645	LEAD 4K-7076
LEAVE FIELD:	0820	3T-9997
ALTITUDE:	14,000'	4H-6173
LAST TIME T/O:	0815	

****

LEAD GROUP, 1ST "C" CBW

HALL
KELSEY
PFF 2E 8010

| GIESE | | FREESE-SOALE | |
| 4J 8159 | | PFF 2F 7990 | |

| PENROD | | SCURLOCK | |
| 4A 7852 | | "C" 2L 7969 | |

| BLACK | WILLIAMSON | MILLER | DEVENISH |
| 5R 1990 | 5P 7625 | 2Q 7442 | 2B 8103 |

| MURPHY | WILKENSEN | | INSCHO |
| 4I 2656 | 4G 1550 (DA) | | 4B 7514 |

****

HIGH GROUP, 1ST "C" CBW

BARNICLE, TUZ
5Q 7828

| JARVILL | | ROBERTS | |
| 5N 7313 | | 5M 2590 | |

| DEMAGALSKI | | DAVIS | |
| 5S 7330 | | "C" 21 7543 | |

| STALLINGS | O'CONNOR | NASHOLD | RESEIGH |
| 5V 2060 | 5P 7265 | 2H 2873 | 2P 1575 |

| LANG | | QUINN | |
| 5U 7018 | | 4Q 6115 | |

| HATHERLEY | | LONG | |
| 5R 1990 (DA) | | 5W 0017 | |

****

LOW GROUP, 1ST "C" CBW

RENICK, FENTON
3V 7791

| BONAR | | O'DELL | |
| 3K 7882 | | 3X 7503 | |

| CARROLL | | KLARE | |
| 3S 7059 | | "C" 2N 7675 | |

| TOLCHINSKY | BIGHAM | COPELAND | WORRELL |
| 3W 1570 | 3M 0007 | 2K 6994 | 2D 7100 |

| LACOUTURE | | | |
| 3N 6095 | | | |

| HUBER | | GARDNER | |
| 3R 7560 (DA) | | 3Z 7357 | |

162

8 September 1944 — Thirty-seven ships from this command took off at 0740 hours with the target designated as Ludwigshafen, Germany. Colonel Halsey led the wing and bombing was by combination PFF and visual methods. Bombs were dropped from 27,000 feet and were reported within the target area. All the ships returned safely to this base. Two had engines knocked out and battle damage was light to moderate. No enemy fighters were encountered. The weather was bad all the way and the clouds were up to 28,500 in some places. The crews report that their feeling of security is much greater now that they have so much friendly territory to fly over.

2nd Lt. Harold D. Walker, O-7177548, 534th Bomb Squadron Navigator, received a penetrating wound, mild, top of skull, occipital parietal and parietal temporal region. He was wearing a flak suit and no helmet.

Today, the flying evaluation board met and grounded Lieut. Woolf and recommended that Lieut. Woolf be grounded permanently. He abandoned his aircraft without sufficient reason while on a practice mission.

9 September 1944 — At 0740 hours this clear, cool, and crisp morning, about fifty ships took off with the target designated as Ludwigshafen, Germany. The Group was led by Colonel Fitzgerald and all the assembly enroute was as briefed. Moderate flak was encountered over the target area and the bombing was done by PFF; blind and unobserved. All the ships except one returned safely to this base. The one that did not return was Lt. Gardner's, 533rd Squadron. The ship was fairly badly shot up, had the hydraulic system knocked out, one engine knocked out, and the gasoline was sealed in the Tokyo tanks by the damage done to the wings. The ship landed at Manston, which is on the south coast of the bay that goes into the Thames Estuary.

The toggeler, Sgt. Robert J. Sharp, 19033981, 533rd Squadron, was hit by a piece of flak, which entered just in front of the right hip and came out the right buttocks, and extensively comminuted the trochanter, head and neck of the femur, acetabulm, ischium, and pubic rami. When Captain Wymer and myself arrived, he had received three units of plasma and a liter of blood was running in. He had received too much Morphine and his condition improved considerably while we were there. Later in the evening, a debridement was done and a modified Tobruk plaster was applied. He is to be evacuated to the 91st General Hospital by air tomorrow.

While we were in the station sick quarters, some one taxied the airplane into the mud and the last three hours were spent trying to get the ship out. The airbase there is the largest I have ever seen and had allied ships of all varieties. The east-west runway is at least 1000 feet wide. Aircraft of all types were all over the field. British and American gliders, Mosquitoes, Spitfires, Tempests, Typhoons, Halifaxes, Lancasters, cargo ships, B-24's, B-17's, P-51's & P-47's, to mention most of the types that were predominate. While we were there, three missions of Tempests loaded with rockets, bombs, and 20mm cannons, took off on a combat mission. There was also a regiment of airborne infantry with gliders loaded waiting to take off for France.

HQ 381st BOMBARDMENT GROUP (H) AAF   **M-S-1**
Office of the Surgeon
APO 634
U.S. Army

21 August 1944

C–E–R–T–I–F–I–C–A–T–E

   I certify that on 17 August 1944, I accompanied Major D. M. Kelley[13] on an altitude flight from Ridgewell, Essex, England. Freezing level was at 14,000 feet. Major Kelley's mask was removed at 23,000 feet and Major Kelley remained without oxygen for thirty (30) minutes at this altitude, and we then climbed to 26,000 feet and remained for approximately fifteen (15) minutes and then began the descent at 500 feet per minute.

   During this period, Major Kelley had only mild symptoms of anoxia. His symptoms were cyanosis, respiratory changes, transient periods of euphoria, slurring of speech, and feeling of fatigue.

   Major Kelley's tolerance to decreased barometric pressures is greater than any that I have observed.

Ernest Gaillard, Jr.
Major, MC
Station Flight
Surgeon

---

[13] After war's end, Douglas McGlashan Kelley, MD, 33, was assigned *lead* US Army psychiatrist to examine the whole litany of defendants during the Nürnberg War Crimes Trials. This resulted in the two international bestsellers, *22 Cells in Nuremberg* and *The Case of Rudolf Hess*, recounting his experiences whilst there on a case-by-case basis. Dr. Kelley then returned to his old position as Associate Professor of Psychiatry at UC Berkeley where he died New Year's Day, 1958, at the age of forty-six.

<u>B-17 Flight Plan from Major Halsey's Mission 26 AUGUST 1944</u>

STATIONS:	0555		
START ENG:	0610	<u>26 August 1944</u>	SPARES
TAXI:	0625		LEAD–4K-7076
TAKE-OFF:	0640		3K-7882
LEAVE FIELD:	0810		4P-6163
ALTITUDE:	15,000'		
LAST TIME T/O:	0805		

****

LEAD GROUP, 1ST "C" CBW

HALSEY
__YATES__
5J   8127

__HATHERLEY__   __TODD__
5S   7330   3Z   7357

BARNICLE
__STALLINGS__   __SCURLOCK__
5V   2060   2K   6994

__DAVISON__   __ROBERTS__   __QUINN__   __RESEIGH__
5R   1990 5P   7625   2Q   7442 2 R   8079

__MARBURY__
5N   7313

__SIMMONS__   __MITCHELL__
5X   7267 5W   0017

****

HIGH GROUP, 1ST "C" CBW   __FENTON, LAPIERRE__
5J   8127

__BONAR__   __GARDNER__
3J   7561   3S   7059

__LACOUTURE__   __DAVIS__
30   1761   2H   2873

__ORCUTT__   __WINDSOR__   __BAILEY__   __NASHOLD__
3T   9997 3P   2025 2H   8103 2I   7543

__BERKELEY__   __MILLER__
3N   6095   2N   7675

__O'DELL__   __GERMANO__
3W   1570 3X   7503

****

LOW GROUP, 1ST "C" CBW   __CRONIN, MARTYNIAK__
4D   8158

__SLAVIK__   __SMITH__
4E   1569   4M   8114

__EVANS__   __DURBIN__
4N   2968   2M   2703

__GALLAGHER__   __WILIKENSON__   __WORRELL__   __LAPIERRE__
4G   1550 4H   6173 2D   7100 2P   1575

__FINE__
4Q   6115

__BJORNESS__   __FULTON__
4C   7285 4J   8159

Dad holding Station 167's base mascot, "Peter P. for Pig" [14]
(Photo dated 14 August 1944)

10 September 1944 — Twenty-seven ships, led by Colonel Leber, took off at 0715 hours for Baden, Germany, which is south east of Bremen. The Group carried incendiaries and the bombing was done visually with excellent results. One ship failed to return, Lt. Germano, 533rd Squadron. He lost one engine in the target area and no more details can be obtained. The remaining ships returned safely to this base. There were no killed or wounded. General Gross was a visitor this date.

Missing in action:

533rd Bomb Squadron (H)

B-17G #44-6095 — "Fort Worth Gal – Kathleen"

Germano, Ernest (NMI)	2nd Lt.	O-555010	P
Grey, James M.	2nd Lt.	O-788076	CP
Tierney, Richard A.	2nd Lt.	O-707498	N
Spaniol, Edward J., Jr.	2nd Lt.	O-769911	B
Shelly, William. D., Jr.	S/Sgt.	18042995	TTG
Diedrich, John C.	Sgt.	19113223	ROG
Goody, Cloyde I.	Sgt.	38406212	BTG
Donaldson, Alexander (NMI)	Sgt.	13171816	WG
Siders, Harry (NMI)	Sgt.	35226078	TG

---

[14] All aircraft had call letters; e.g., A for "Able", B for "Baker"...and P for "Peter", etc.— *ergo*, "Peter P. for Pig". Dad had a Medical Dispensary brassard custom tailored for him complete with Red Cross (see photo). The pilots and combat crewmembers so highly regarded this insignificant little porker who saw them off on their missions (and each gently patting his little head on the way out) that they all claimed: "I flew and fought and shot twice as hard as hell just to come back and see that damned pig".

11 September 1944 — Thirty-seven aircraft from this command took off at 0730 hours with the target designated as a synthetic oil refinery near Merseberg, Germany. The Group was led by Captains Winter and Kesley. Bombing was done from 27,000 feet and the outside air temperature was –39° Centigrade. The same target had been bombed by this group some time in July of this year two times. The bombing was done visually and the results were thought to be excellent. One ship failed to return, Lt. Thornton, 535th Squadron, and the details of his trouble are not known, but it is thought he landed in northern France somewhere near Brussels.

There was one man wounded, S/Sgt. Robert F. Irwin, ASN 11098985, TG, 534th Squadron (H). He received a mild penetrating wound of the right great toe due to flak. One man received an insignificant burn from his heated suit and another was scratched by flak in the forearm. The remaining ships landed safely at this base. No enemy fighters were seen, but were reported in the area. Flak was moderate and accurate in the target area. Friendly fighter support was good.

Missing in action: Landed in northern France nr. Belgium. All crewmembers rescued.

535th Bomb Squadron (H)

B-17? #42- Model & Ser. No. not given; believed salvaged after rescue of crew.

Thornton, Jack R.	2nd Lt.	O-758106	P
Quatrain, Ralph E.	2nd Lt.	O-768219	CP
Petersen, George E.	2nd Lt.	O-722355	N
Farley, James R.	2nd Lt.	O-772036	B
Cochrane, Clarence C.	Sgt.	33671279	TTG
Cohen, Abraham I.	Sgt.	36666022	ROG
Klein, Merlin K.	Sgt.	36585963	BTG
Borden, Stanley (NMI)	Sgt.	32229113	WG
Sederwall, William H.	S/Sgt.	36689037	TG

The Reduction of S/Sgt. William O. Stone to grade of private was recommended to his organization this date.

12 September 1944 — Thirty-seven aircraft from this command took off at 0730 hours with the target designated as Brux-on-Most, Czechoslovakia. The lead group, led by Colonel Hall, attacked the primary target, blind and unobserved, and the high and low groups attacked targets of opportunity. There was some enemy fighter activity and numerous fighters were seen. There was considerable battle damage to our aircraft caused by flak. One of our aircraft has not reported in, Lt. McMullen, 533rd Squadron, but it is thought he landed in France with one KIA aboard and a couple frostbites. He was flying 007. Two men were wounded and they are:

S/Sgt. Alvin A. Bacon, ASN 37556937, 532nd Squadron (H), waist gunner.
DIAGNOSIS: 1. Wound, penetrating, abdomen with perforation of ileum and mesosigmoid; site of entry below anterior superior iliac spine. Caused by low velocity flak.

2nd Lt. Maury (NMI) Hill, O-745385, Co-Pilot, 532nd Squadron (H).
DIAGNOSIS: 1. Wound, penetrating, lateral aspect, left thigh, upper 2/3, mod. severity. Caused by flak, low velocity.

"Mickey" operators flying on the mission yesterday flew across the Siegfried Line and Maginot Line in the neighborhood of Patton's 3rd Army. They reported that the radar picked up thousands of tanks on the American side and relatively few on the German side.

15 September 1944 — Lieut. McMullen, 533rd Bomb Squadron (H), was flying with an entirely new crew on 12 September 1944 on a mission into Czechoslovakia, which was designed more to draw up enemy fighters than for any particular bombing mission. The ship, B-17G, had been flying at 28,000 feet for 2½ hours. Oxygen checks were being made every 15 minutes. The radio operator's microphone was not working and he had been relaying his oxygen checks to the waist gunner.

The radioman answered the oxygen check before the IP and then turned around to throw out chaff. He failed to answer the oxygen check 15 minutes later. The waist gunner, Sgt. Meyers J. Barker, ASN 35222168, was dispatched to investigate, and when he failed to report the ball turret man, Sgt. Lydell A. Hayes, 18189699, was ordered to investigate. When in another 5 minutes neither of these men reported, the engineer went back to investigate. He found all three men unconscious.

The radioman, Sgt. Joseph J. Charkowski, 16080932, was lying on the floor by the outlet, into which he throws the chaff, his mask was off, and the face end was disconnected from the oxygen outlet. The engineer put his mask on his face, connected the hose, and turned on (the) emergency oxygen supply. This man made an immediate recovery and, after a short rest period, was able to resume his duties as radio operator. He received a frostbite of the left side of face & cheek, moderate severity.

The waist gunner was lying at the entrance to the radio operator's room and his mask was off his face and completely disconnected from the G-1 oxygen bottle, which was lying beside him. He had taken off his right glove and his hand was frostbitten. The engineer placed his mask on his face, connected him to the oxygen outlet, and he made a full recovery and was placed in the radio room under protective covers.

The engineer's own bottle was running low about this time and he went back and got the tail gunner to help him, and the bombardier came back later. He found the ball turret gunner lying unconscious under the right waist gun, his mask was off his face and disconnected and full of frozen vomitus.

It was disconnected from a full G-1 walk-around bottle lying beside him. A mask was placed on this face. Emergency oxygen given, and artificial respiration, which was continued for approximately 1½ hours on the ship and later on the ground without signs of life returning.

The radioman did not remember what happened after he started forward with the walk-around bottle. The ship left the formation about ten minutes after the discovery of the unconscious men and dove 1700 feet per minute, 250 miles per hour to 4,000 feet, and then returned over the greater part of Germany, including the Siegfried Line, (and) at this altitude without enemy interference.

They landed at a fighter airfield inside of France where the medical officer, after giving artificial respiration to the ball turret gunner, pronounced him dead and then recommended they take these men to another airfield near Paris, which was done.

The radio operator had a frostbite on one side of his face, mod., sev., and the waist gunner had frostbite, severe, of the right hand. It is estimated that the radio operator was unconscious not more than 25 minutes, that the waist gunner was unconscious for not more than 10 minutes, and not more than 15 to 20 minutes elapsed before oxygen and artificial respiration was given to the ball turret gunner. The ball turret gunner had been drinking heavily the night before and had had not more than an hour's sleep prior to the mission.

The cause of these three anoxic incidents was personnel failure. All masks and ship connections had been checked just a few days prior to the mission by the equipment officer. They were all equipped with the new M-45 modification with the quick-disconnect, which makes it virtually impossible for the connections to come apart if inserted at all. The oxygen system of the plane was checked after the ship returned to this base and was found satisfactory. The engineer on this ship who had the same training as the other crewmen was questioned and appeared to have adequate training and possessed adequate knowledge of oxygen equipment and its use.

Lt. McMullen landed his ship at an airfield near Paris and reported that this fighter group was, as the English put it, "highly browned off". It appeared that three of their loaded gas tanks were on the way to the field when some of General Patton's Armored Corps saw them. As a result, gas, gas tanks, etc. were "requisitioned" by "Old Blood and Guts", and have not been seen since. At the present time, gas supplies are being flown in by stripped down B-17's and B-24's.

Additional evidence of personnel failure in this group came to light with the capture of the personnel records of the German *Stalag Luft* where American prisoners are interrogated. From those records it was found that captured members of every one of the squadrons had given extensive information to the Germans regarding our formations, personnel, PW lectures, secret radio information, and allied subjects.

It is interesting that the records revealed that flying personnel from practically every squadron in the E.T.O., and one flyer from the aircraft carrier "Ranger", had divulged significant information to the Germans. There was no reason to believe that personnel had been receiving any pressure when this information was given out.

17 September 1944 — Forty-two aircraft from this command took off at 0645 hours with multiple targets to be bombed by individual squadrons from around 15,000 feet. All of the targets were tactical and were enemy troop concentrations in eastern Belgium and Holland. All of the squadrons hit the targets and the Group returned intact without incidence.

Today was the day that the airbase at Bassingbourne chose to celebrate the completion of 200 combat missions. The affair, which was for the entire base, began at 1100 hours and the entertainments, horseshows, baseball games, tennis exhibitions, and a carnival were held in the afternoon, and there were four dances on the base in the evening.

21 September 1944 — Thirty-seven aircraft from this command took off this morning with the target designated as Mainz, Germany. Captain Winter led the Group. Cumuli were 3/10 to 4/10 with the tops 8 – 10,000 feet at the target. Temperature was –34° Centigrade at the bombing altitude of 27,000 feet. Flak was meager to moderate and generally inaccurate. Fighter opposition was nil. Lieut. Bailey landed in Brussels for reasons unknown and he and his crew are expected back tomorrow. There were no wounded, killed or missing.

22 September 1944 — Thirty-seven aircraft from this command took off this A.M. with the target designated as Kassel, Germany. Colonel Leber led the Group. Bombing was done at 18,000 feet over a ten-tenths cloud cover. Outside air temperature was –34° Centigrade. Flak was meager to moderate and not very accurate. There was no enemy fighter opposition. All the ships returned safely to this base and there were no killed aboard. Sgt. Henry J. Ianni, ASN 32952933, TTG, 534th Bomb Squadron (H), was wounded in action by flak and his diagnosis is as follows: 1. Wound, penetrating, severe, on top of left shoulder, 3" medial to the acromio-clavicular junction. He was evacuated to the 121st Station Hospital; condition good.

25 September 1944 — Thirty-seven aircraft from this command took off at 0739 hours with the target designated as Frankfurt, Germany. The Group was led by Lt. Colonel Fitzgerald and they ran into mild flak over target area.

Two ships landed with feathered props. Bombing was blind and unobserved. Weather in and out was satisfactory for flying. There were no wounded or killed. Bombing was done from 26,000 feet and the temperature was –36° Centigrade. Lt. Gills, 533rd Bomb Squadron (H), went down in the target area; reason unknown. Five chutes were seen to leave the plane.

Missing in action:

533rd Bomb Squadron (H)

B-17G #42-31570 — "Lucky Me!"

Gills, Oscar W.   1st Lt.   O-820997   P

Prenatt, Charles R.	2nd Lt.	O-822084	CP
Adams, Donald K.	2nd Lt.	O-719864	N
Rudisill, William P.	2nd Lt.	O-739217	B
Parks, Paul E.	S/Sgt.	39332969	TTG
Stowe, Minor H.	S/Sgt.	15080602	ROG
Cook, Shelby W.	Sgt.	16187601	BTG
Krainz, Leo V.	Sgt.	36834397	WG
Mourning, Harold A.	Sgt.	16122309	TG

26 September 1944 — Thirty-seven aircraft took off at 1115 hours to hit the marshalling yards at Osnabruck, Germany. The Group was led by Lt. Colonel Shackley and bombing was done visually from 27,000 feet. No enemy fighters were seen and flak was meager and inaccurate. All the ships returned safely to this base and there were no killed or wounded.

27 September 1944 — Thirty-seven aircraft from this command, led by Captain Winter, took off at 0615 hours with the target designated as three factories in the Cologne area. The weather was ten-tenths all the way, so the secondary target was bombed by PFF and it is thought the results were good. The secondary target was the heart of the city of Cologne. The weather above the overcast was good and the bombing altitude was 28,000 feet. There was meager and accurate flak about 26 miles east of Cologne, which is approximately the position of the allied front lines. There were no German fighters seen. All aircraft, except one, landed safely at this base at 1230 hours. Lieut. Schein landed his plane near Brussels and dropped off his tail gunner, Sgt. Keffer, at the 8th British General Hospital, Brussels. As near as can be determined, he is suffering from anoxia, hemorrhage, and convulsions. The crew flew back to England later in the afternoon and everything else seemed in good condition.

Major George K. Sandman departed this date for the 12th RCD on the rehabilitation and return scheme.

28 September 1944 — Thirty-seven aircraft from this command took off at 0730 hours with the target Magdeburg, Germany, which is just south of the city of Berlin. There were two abortions and thirty-five aircraft attacked the target. The Group was led by Captain Tyson. Bombing was by PFF and the results were not observed. Flak was moderate and accurate. There were no enemy aircraft seen. Fighter support was excellent and all aircraft returned safely to this base. The temperature at 26,000 feet today was –39° C.

2 October 1944 — Thirty-seven aircraft from this command took off this morning on the 196th mission of the Group. The target was Kassel, Germany and was attacked from 25,000 feet by PFF method.

The secondary target was the Henschel Plant Supply Depot. The outside air temperature was –38° Centigrade. All aircraft returned safely to this base with no wounded or killed aboard.[15]

5 October 1944 — Thirty-six aircraft from this command took of at 0745 hrs with the target designated as Cologne, where they were to bomb as squadrons with three separate targets, the high-priority target being a plant manufacturing gas converter units with which the Germans hope to transport by November 1. Temperature was minus 43 degrees Centigrade at the bombing altitude of 27,500 feet with a 10/10th coverage.

The ships were forced to bomb on instruments with the target the marshalling yards in the center of Cologne. Flak was reported as moderate and no enemy fighters were encountered by this group, but the 91st BG reported attacks.

On take off, Lt. George Stevens, 533rd, after getting his ship, called "The Railroader", up to about 90 mph, decided it could not take off and jammed on the brakes.

His ship ran into a ditch at the end of the runway and is completely smashed up. It would appear that this is a case of personnel failure since Lt. Stevens reported that the tail of the ship began to whip and was unmanageable. Actually, it would appear that he failed to check trim tabs on take-off and the end rolled up causing the tail to leave the ground prematurely. He stated that he rolled the trim tabs down, the tail hit and bounced and he was unable to handle the ship, so he jammed on the brakes. There were no injuries.

Another ship lost control on the runway, ran off the runway, crossed the field near the perimeter track, and made a successful take off on the second try. Not being satisfied with this, two pilots aborted. The Group commander is very unhappy, and the pilots soon will be.

6 October 1944 — Thirty-seven aircraft took off this morning at 0730 hrs. led by Colonel Leber, the main target being Stralsund, near the Czechoslovakian border. A power plant, bridge and flak installations were hit, then the Group visually bombed the secondary target, which was Keppeln.

A 533rd ship, 1st Lt Robert G. Baker and crew, failed to return and a 535th ship was hit by a jet propelled fighter and the tail gunner, S/Sgt Marion O. Mc Ilman, jumped out over enemy territory; however, the ship returned to base badly damaged.

---

[15] This marks the end of Dad's personal entries; however, I continued on from 5 October through 7 October 1944, as the succeeding commander (and subsequent author of this narrative) mentioned his departure from Station 167 and his transfer to the 91st General Hospital, Cirencester, Gloucestershire where my brother, Garnet Nash Gaillard, was born in 1945.

There were a couple of minor injuries, the most important being 2nd Lt. Richard A. Mitchell, 535th Navigator, suffered a penetration wound of the right forearm, approximately 1/3rd, lateral surface, moderate severe, and was evacuated to the 121st Station Hospital.

Later in the day, Lt. Baker and crew reported missing returned back to base just in time to walk into a rest home reservation, which was previously arranged for him!

Major Ernest Gaillard, Jr., departed this station today per SO 277, 1st Bomb Division, dd October 5. He is to be on TDY at the 91st General Hospital for 30 days. He will not return as a new Group Surgeon has been assigned to this section.

Outstanding Performance: Backed by superb teamwork, 1st Lt. John J. O'Connor, 535th, recently piloted the bomber "Los Angeles City Limits" home alone from inside Germany after flak and fighters had left his ship with two engines dead and a propeller wind-milling violently. Flak got the first engine on the way to the target and the bombardier salvoed the bombs in an attempt to help O'Connor keep up with the formation. Unable to do so, the pilot turned for home.

A few miles later "L.A." was hit by two ME-163 jet-propelled fighters, which O'Connor's gunner successfully fought off until a pair of P-51's showed up. However, cannon fire from one of the enemy planes had silenced a second engine and damaged its prop feathering control. Flying at only 4,000 ft, the bomber ran into tracking flak shortly afterwards. Necessary evasive action left it with even less altitude and a crash landing inside Germany seemed imminent...

Conclusion...

Appropriately, my father's last authoritative, personal entry of 02 October 1944 to this original journal narrative, and just before officially relinquishing command of the 242nd Medical Dispensary of the 381st Bombardment Group to Major Rankin C. Blount, MC, USAAF, was "All aircraft returned safely to this base with no wounded or killed aboard". What a simply splendid way to end a specialized military deployment in the middle of a war: to end it on the upswing of a high note. Unfortunately, the war in Europe would rage on for another eight months. The Allies officially proclaimed the "V-E Day" victory on 08 May 1945 in the wake of both the unconditional surrender of the *Wehrmacht* on 01 May 1945, with Reich Admiral Karl Doenitz assuming conditional, tenant, proxy command of the interim German government, and the civilized world's final riddance of Adolph Hitler's wretched shadow. But the cost—and especially the cost in American lives to save for the second time in twenty-four years all of Western Europe and its war-weary victims—was simply appalling. Of all the United States Army Air Force pilots, crew, and ancillary staff deployed in the E.T.O out of England, the combined total casualty count of MIA, KIA, WIA, and IIA exceeded 100,000 individuals—and that was just the Air Force.

In the first eighteen-plus months of active, American participation by the 8th US Army Air Forces alone, the United States sustained 9,921 MIA, 2,868 WIA, 668 IIA, and 411 KIA for a grand total of 13,868 casualties. This figure comprised some 4.1% of the total numbered USAAF deployment in the E.T.O—and this was just the Eighth—and a decided improvement at that in the modern attrition rate over the previous world war's casualties in Europe. To compare with one of America's earlier conflicts, during the Civil War at the Battle of Cold Harbor 03 June 1864, 7,000 men fell in just twenty minutes for a grand total of 60,000 *Union* casualties alone over a thirty-day period. By today's standards of largely remote control warfare, either of these figures would be considered a bloodbath. Alternatively, during the first Persian Gulf War of 1991, we lost about 148 personnel; the Iraqis lost about 100,000. This is America's finest military kill ratio to date. Somewhere in between, we weren't so lucky with the Germans.

Man for man, weapon for weapon, officer for officer, intelligence for intelligence, and plane for plane (and our heavy bombers, notwithstanding, of which the *Luftwaffe* had few to none), we were both game. America's E.T.O. deployment in the air war over the Third Reich was that classic but lethal match race between two airborne armies of largely Caucasian thoroughbreds. Even the enemy gets his due, and the regular German soldier in the air–as on the ground–was superbly schooled, trained and equipped. The Third Reich lost because we had a better cause and more guys with which to prosecute it—and it was *their* country upon which we were both closing in and ceaselessly dropping ordnance. The Axis didn't stand that proverbial "snowman's chance" against the Allies. We won and we won large.

My generation of so-called "Baby Boomers" owes what remains left of our current rights and freedoms to all those who fought and died there, and, ostensibly, our very lives to those who survived to return home. My mom and dad were two of those who lived on and it is to them I dedicated this modern rendering of the Diary of the Medical Detachment.

To paraphrase what I said earlier in the *Additional Notes to the Reader...* "It was to be savored by all", and by all in remembrance of our brave bomber pilots and crews in that largely ignored battlefield of the big, blue sky; but to also pay homage to those frequently unsung heroes of the ground commands as well—commands who, and after each day's combat sorties, miraculously repaired both the men and their machines for that next morning's raid into Heaven's uncertain firmament.

Reports
&
Endnotes

————WAR DEPARTMENT————
HEADQUARTERS ARMY AIR FORCES
WASHINGTON

<u>MISSING AIR CREW REPORT</u> #1037

IMPORTANT: This report will be compiled in triplicate by each Army Air Forces organization within 48 hours of the time an aircraft is officially reported missing.

1. ORGANIZATION: Location **Ridgewell, England**; Command or Air Force **VIII Bomber Command**; Group **381ˢᵗ Bomb Group (H)**; Squadron **534ᵗʰ Bomb Sq.**; Detachment _____.

2. SPECIFY: Point of Departure: **Ridgewell, England**; Course **To Destination** Intended Destination **Schweinfurt, Germany** Type of Mission **Operational**

3. WEATHER CONDITIONS AND VISIBILITY AT THE TIME OF CRASH OR WHEN LAST REPORTED: **Clouds nil, vis. 6 miles, light haze**

4. GIVE: (a) Date **14 Oct 1943**; Time **14:35** and Location **49° 55' N, 10° 10' E** _____of last known whereabouts of missing aircraft.
    (b) Specify whether (**X**) Last sighted; ( ) Last contacted by Radio; ( ) Forced Down; ( ) Seen to crash; or ( ) Information unavailable.

5. AIRCRAFT WAS LOST, OR IS BELIEVED TO HAVE BEEN LOST, AS A RESULT OF: (Check only one) (**X**) Enemy aircraft; ( ) Enemy Anti-Aircraft; ( ) Other circumstances as follows
    _____.

6. AIRCRAFT: Type, Model and Series **B-17F**; AAF Serial No. **42-29803**

7. ENGINES: Type, Model and Series **R-1820-97**; AAF Serial No. (a) **41-42354** (b) **43-57209** (c) **43-56723** (d) **43-56743**

8. INSTALLED WEAPONS (Furnish below Make, Type and Serial Number.

    13   50 Cal.   Browning Type Machine Guns
    Serial number not available

9. THE PERSONS LISTED BELOW WERE REPORTED AS: (a) Battle Casualty **Yes** or (b) Non-Battle Casualty _____.

10. NUMBER OF PERSONS ABOARD AIRCRAFT: Crew **10**; Passengers _____ (Starting with Pilot, furnish the following particulars: If more than 10 persons were aboard aircraft, list similar particulars on separate sheet and attach original to this form).

Crew Position   Name in Full (Last Name First)   Rank   Serial Number

	Crew Position	Name in Full (Last Name First)	Rank	Serial Number
a.	**Pilot**	**Yorba, Fernando M., Jr.**	**2nd Lt.**	**O-741000**
b.	**Co-Pilot**	**Childers, Gordon L.**	**2nd Lt.**	**O-802250**
c.	**Navigator**	**Dall, Martin M.**	**2nd Lt.**	**O-673488**
d.	**Bombardier**	**Roberson, Wilbur G.**	**2nd Lt.**	**O-676977**
e.	**Top Turret**	**Gorgone, William (NMI)**	**T/Sgt**	**31083156**
f.	**Radio Operator**	**Gracey, Edgar M.**	**S/Sgt**	**33324280**
g.	**Ball Turret**	**Boylan, Robert P.**	**S/Sgt**	**35292918**
h.	**Right Waist**	**Feller, Michael S.**	**Sgt**	**12042502**
i.	**Left Waist**	**Huitt, Kenneth O.**	**Sgt**	**17160104**
j.	**Tail Gunner**	**Johnson, Johnie N.**	**S/Sgt**	**37234120**
k.	___	___	___	

11. IDENTIFY BELOW THOSE PERSONS WHO ARE BELIEVED TO HAVE LAST KNOWLEDGE OF AIRCRAFT, AND CHECK APPROPRIATE COLUMN TO INDICATE BASIS FOR SAME: CHECK ONLY ONE COLUMN

Name in Full (Last Name First)	Rank	Serial Number	Contacted by Radio	Last Sighted	Saw Crash	Saw Forced Landing
A. **O'Sullivan, George D., 2nd Lt., O-796585**				**X**		
B. ___						
C. ___						
D. ___						

12. IF PERSONNEL ARE BELIEVED TO HAVE SURVIVED, ANSWER YES TO ONE OF THE FOLLOWING STATEMENTS: (a) Parachutes were used **Yes**; (b) Persons were seen walking away from scene of crash _____ or (c) Any other reason (Specify) _____.

13. ATTACH AERIAL PHOTOGRAPH, MAP, CHART, OR SKETCH, SHOWING APPROXIMATE LOCATION WHERE AIRCRAFT WAS LAST SEEN.

14. ATTACH EYEWITNESS DESCRIPTION OF CRASH, FORCED LANDING, OR OTHER CIRCUMSTANCES PERTAINING TO MISSING AIRCRAFT.

15. ATTACH A DESCRIPTION OF THE EXTENT OF SEARCH, IF ANY, AND GIVE NAME, RANK AND SERIAL NUMBER OF OFFICER IN CHARGE HERE
_____**None**_____

DATE OF REPORT __**17 October 1943**_____

(Signature of Preparing Officer)   ASN
/T/ Howard N. Kelsey, T/O, Air Corps, T-186686
Sqdn: 534th Bomb Sq.; Group: 381st Bomb Gp. (H)

T O P   S E C R E T

HQ 381st BOMBARDMENT GROUP (H) AAF   M-S-1
Office of the Surgeon
APO 634
U.S. Army

24 October 1943

Combat Crew Failures

The Central Medical Board finds that ninety-five percent of the individuals that are combat crew failures fall into one of the following four categories:

1. Fear Reaction

    a. States fear and quits.

    b. Sobbing, trembling, sickness, etc., before or during mission.

    Cured immediately by grounding and ninety percent occur in first five missions. Always transitory and relieved when stress is relieved.

2. Functional systems due to Combat Stress

    a. Usually develops in first five missions. Symptoms are cumulative and slow to disappear after stress is relieved.

    b. Mental Symptoms

        1) Anxiety or apprehension.

        2) Difficulty in concentration.

        3) Depression.

    c. Physical Symptoms

        1) Cardiovascular.

        2) Gastro-intestinal.

        3) Genito-urinary.

        4) Vasomotor.

T O P S E C R E T

People in these first two groups are lost to combat. Treatment by RAF and 8th AAF has proven of no value. When stress returns, the symptoms return.

3. Psychoneuroses

Reserved for those with history of psychiatric difficulty. These patients will be sent direct to 36th Station Hospital by Central Medical Board.

    a. Anxiety Neuroses.

    b. Hysteria.

    c. Neurasthenia.

        1) Overwhelming Fatigue.

        2) Somatic Symptoms — hypochondriasis.

    d. Obsessive and Compulsive States.

4. Operational Exhaustion

A specific syndrome in fundamentally sound individuals who have broken down after combat and harrowing experiences. Usually occurs between twelve and eighteen missions.

    a. Symptoms

        1) Irritability — sudden, usually very transitory — followed by remorse.

        2) Depression — retardation of mental and physical activity.

        3) Battle Dreams (Nightmares).

        4) Physical Fatigue — poor appearance, no pep.

        5) Weight Loss.

        6) Anorexia — hungry, but filled by a few bites.

        7) Anxiety.

        8) Tremulousness or jitters.

T O P S E C R E T

9) Inefficiency.

10) Poor Concentration.

b. Treatment and Prognosis.

1) Narcosis.

2) Seventy-five percent returned to combat.

5. Emotional Shock

An extremely harrowing experience in normal individual may produce tremor, agitation; individual may be unable to walk or talk, etc.

Treatment — Heavy sedation with six grains of sodium amytal and repeat as necessary. Nursing care and watching the bladder is important. Putting a period of time between incident removes much of its terror.

Disposition of Combat Crew Failures

All combat crew failures suspected of lack of moral fibre, operational exhaustion, or psychiatric disorders are to be sent the Central Medical Board. This action was requested by the reclassification board at Cheltenham.

Procedure:

Officers: Cut a group order placing individual an TD at Station 101, for study by Central Medical Board and upon completion to return to proper station.

A WD AGO Form 64 is done by Central Medical Board, sent to 8th AAF and then to unit. If physically O.K., the unit initiates reclassification. The Adjutant or Group Executive calls 8th AAF to have officer ordered to replacement pool.

Enlisted Men: After found physically qualified by Central Medical Board, enlisted men are demoted to the rank of private and assigned to basic duty or reported to higher headquarters as excess.

T O P S E C R E T

Consultation:

The Central Medical Board can be used for consultation only. The Group cuts the order and patient is sent sick in quarters to Dispensary 302, Station 101, for consultation and upon completion to return to his proper station.

Disposition of Operational Exhaustion:

1. Recovered, approximately seventy-five percent are returned to full combat status. A Form 64 is required. Channels: 5th General Hospital to 8th AAF to Unit. Man is grounded until Form 64 is returned.

2. If not recovered, he is taken off combat status. In unusual cases and upon recommendation of C.O., the individual may be retained on flying status.

If returned from 5th General Hospital and difference of opinion exists as to the fitness for flying, send individual to Central Medical Board.

The operational tour for heavy bombardment in this theatre is twenty-five missions and the Commanding General has decreed that anyone not completing the tour for psychiatric reasons shall not gain by his deficiencies.

3. The reclassification board at Cheltenham may:

a. Exonerate.

b. Dishonorably discharge.

c. Discharge without honor.

d. Have individual resign for the good of the service.

Ernest Gaillard, Jr.
Major, MC
Station Flight Surgeon

T O P   S E C R E T

(REC'D 29 FEBRUARY 1944)

BATTLE CASUALTIES

Casualties reported in this section include personnel missing in action (includes Prisoners of War), killed in action and wounded in action. Those wounded include personnel struck by enemy missiles (GSW), frostbite and injuries received while going to, being engaged in, or returning from an operational mission. Data presented includes the period 1 July 1942 to date, 31 December 1943.

KILLED IN ACTION

A total of 411 individuals have been reported killed in action during the eighteen-month period ending 31 December, 1943. Of these, 112 were killed by enemy gunfire and returned to base in aircraft returning from operational missions. The remaining 299 were killed in aircraft accidents, by drowning, while going to, being engaged in or returning from an operational mission (see Table VIII).

WOUNDED IN ACTION

In the eighteen-month period ending 31 December 1943, there was a total at 3,536 individuals reported as wounded in action. Of this total 1,665 were reported as cases of frostbite, 1,203 were struck by enemy missiles, and 688 incurred other injuries (fractures and burns, etc. See Table VIII).

MISSING IN ACTION

In the eighteen-month period ending 31 December 1943, a total of 9,921 individuals were reported as missing in action from operational daylight missions over enemy and enemy occupied territory. (This includes those subsequently reported as POW, KIA, or Dead).

PERCENT OF CASUALTIES TO COMBAT CREW MEMBERS DISPATCHED

In the eighteen-month period, there was a total of 335,450 combat crew members of the Eighth Air Force dispatched on operational missions. In the same period, a total 13,868 casualties were reported. (MIA, KIA and WIA). Thus, in the period, 4.1% of combat crew members dispatched became casualties. Table VIII shows the percentage of casualties (all types) in relation to individuals exposed. It can readily be seen that of those wounded in action, an individual is more likely to be frostbitten than receive a wound from enemy gunfire.

TOP SECRET

TABLE VIII

Battle Casualties, Eighth Air Force 1 July 1942 – 31 December 1943

CASUALTY DISPATCHED	NUMBER	PERCENT OF COMBAT CREW MEMBERS
Missing in Action	9,921	2.9%
Wounded in Action:		
Frostbite	1,665	0.49%
GSW	1,203	0.35%
Injury	668	0.19%
TOTAL – WIA	3,536	1.03%
Killed in Action:		
Injury, Anoxia	299	0.08%
GSW	112	0.04%
TOTAL – KIA	411	0.12%
GRAND TOTAL	13,868	4.1%

WOUNDS FROM ENEMY MISSILES

The following data is derived from the *Weekly Care of Flyer Report* received in this office from Group Surgeons of the Eighth Air Force. Each individual struck by enemy missiles is reported by name, giving the complete diagnosis, area of the body struck, the type of missile, and the type of wound. In this paper, wounds caused by plane parts (9% of total) set in notion by enemy missiles are included. The data presented covers the period 1 November 1942 – 31 December 1943.

In the period reported, a total of 1,293 individuals were struck by enemy gunfire. This total includes fatalities and non-fatalities.

CAUSES OF WOUNDS

These 1,293 individuals received wounds caused by 1,304 missiles. It was found that wounds caused by flak and cannon shell were approximately the same—531 and 526, respectively. Table X shows the type of missile causing wounds among these individuals.

TABLE X

ENEMY MISSILE	NUMBER	PERCENT OF TOTAL
Flak	531	40%
20mm Cannon	526	40%
Machine Gun	136	11%
Plane Parts**	111	9%
TOTAL	1,304	100%

Flight Surgeon

T O P   S E C R E T

Individuals particularly exposed to wounds caused by plane parts are those in close proximity to Plexiglas windshields. These include the pilot, co-pilot, bombardier, navigator, and tail gunner. Plexiglas fragments set in motion are usually of very low velocity, and cause the majority of wounds on the exposed surfaces of the body, particularly the race and neck. Their course is usually stopped by clothing and other protective equipment used by the flyer. With the introduction of the new type of helmet, it is believed that all plane part wounds of the head will be somewhat reduced.

BODY AREA OF WOUNDS

For statistical convenience and expression, the body was divided into four areas: the Head and Neck, the Thorax, the Abdomen and the Extremities. During the period reported, the 1,293 individuals were struck in 1,577 areas of the body. It was found that the great majority of the wounds were of the extremities (855 – 54%). Table XA shows the area of the body struck by enemy missiles in individuals becoming fatalities as well as those not fatalities.

TABLE XA

AREA OF BODY STRUCK BY ENEMY MISSILES

AREA	NON–FATALITIES		FATALITIES	
	NUMBER	PERCENT	NUMBER	PERCENT
Extremities	835	57%	20	17%
Head and Neck	410	28%	42	35%
Thorax	133	9%	37	31%
Abdomen	80	6%	20	17%
TOTAL	1,458	100%	119	100%

It is evident the majority of non-fatalities have wounds of the extremities, whereas the majority of fatalities have wounds of the head and neck region and thorax. It is realized that the data presented on fatal wounds includes only those individuals being returned in aircraft to base. Although the data is based on a small number of individuals (103), it is hoped that through the analysis of wounds causing fatalities, more adequate protection may be developed to further lower the fatality rate.

In order to obtain a more accurate picture of the individual's liability to be wounded in certain areas of the body, corrections of the data must be made. By analysis, 61 or 15% of the head and neck wounds were caused by plexi-glass, and other plane parts set in motion by enemy missiles; and 50 or 5.5% of extremity wounds were incurred by the same cause. In addition, as described below, 44 individuals were saved from wounds of the thoracic and abdominal regions by wearing the body armor.

T O P S E C R E T

Elimination of the wounds caused by plane parts because their unevenness of distribution, and adding the wounds of thoracic and abdominal regions, which were prevented by use of the armor, the following Table pertains:

TABLE XI

BODY AREAS WOUNDED (FATALITIES AND NON-FATALITIES)

AREA	UNCORRECTED		CORRECTED	
	NUMBER	PERCENT	NUMBER	PERCENT
Extremities	855	54%	805	53%
Head & Neck	452	28%	391	26%
Thorax	170	11%	194	13%
Abdomen	100	7%	120	8%
TOTAL	1,577	100%	1,510	100%

It is seen that the corrected data shows that a total of 21% of all wounds are wounds of the thorax and abdomen. This figure includes non-fatalities and those fatalities being returned in aircraft to base. It must be borne in mind that lack of information concerning individuals wounded in missing planes might make these figures misleading to a limited extent.

TYPES OF WOUNDS

A total of 688 wounds were analyzed in individuals not becoming fatalities in order to determine the general type of wound received from enemy gunfire, and particularly to determine the association of fracture and traumatic amputation with these wounds. Of these wounds analyzed, it was found that approximately 6% are associated with fracture, and 2% with traumatic amputation. A further 105 wounds were analyzed in individuals receiving fatal wounds. In this series, it was found that 15% were associated with fracture, and 3% with traumatic amputation. Table XIV shows the type of wounds received in order of their frequency.

TABLE XIV

TYPE	NON-FATALITIES		FATALITIES	
	NUMBER	PERCENT	NUMBER	PERCENT
Penetrating	373	54%	58	55%
Lacerating	154	22%	8	8%

T O P S E C R E T

Contusions and Abrasions	61	9%		
Perforating	50	7%	18	17%
With Fracture	38	6%	16	15%
With Amputation	12	2%	3	3%
With Evisceration	0	0%	2	2%
TOTAL	688	100%	105	100%

WOUNDS CAUSING DEATH

Data included in this section covers wounds in individuals killed in action or dying as a result of wounds. In this series, 86 individuals were reported as killed in action, and an additional 17 dying as a result of wounds; making a total of 103 fatalities from enemy gunfire, or a case fatality rate of 7.9%. This figure is based on those fatalities being returned to this theater. In determining the case fatality rate by missile and area of wound, only individuals sustaining wounds in single areas of the body were considered, as it was impossible to ascertain the cause of death in those individuals struck in multiple areas of the body.

Table XVI shows the case fatality rate of personnel KIA and dying as a result of wounds of type of missile. It can be seen that machine gun wounds have the highest fatality rate (15%).

TABLE XVI

MISSILE	NUMBER WOUNDED	NUMBER KILLED IN ACTION OR DEAD	CASE FATALITY RATE
Machine Gun	107	16	15.0%
20mm Cannon	364	40	10.9%
Flak	474	13	2.7%
Plane Parts	87	0	0%
TOTAL	1,032	69	28.6%

Table XVII shows the fatality rate by area of the body hit. It can be seen that wounds of the thorax and abdomen, as expected, are the most serious. Wounds of the thorax result in 26.9% fatalities, and wounds of the abdomen 25.6% fatalities.

TABLE XVII

AREA OF	NUMBER OF WOUNDS	NUMBER OF FATALITIES	PERCENTAGE
Thorax	59	16	26.9%

T O P   S E C R E T

Abdomen	39	10	25.6%
Head and Neck	254	30	11.8%
Extremities	680	10	1.4%

WOUNDS BY COMBAT POSITION

It was thought that by analysis of the individuals wounded, by combat position, some insight could be gained into the need for additional armor protection at certain combat positions. This analysis only served to prove that the liability of being wounded in no greater nor less in one combat position than another, except in the case of the ball

turret gunner and the co-pilot who are the least liable to be wounded. Table XVIII shows the number of combat crew members wounded by combat position.

GUNSHOT WOUNDS BY COMBAT POSITION

COMBAT POSITION	NUMBER WOUNDED	PERCENT OF TOTAL
Navigator	156	12%
Tail Gunner	150	12%
Bombardier	144	11%
Radio Operator	131	10%
Waist Gunner (1)	127	10%
Waist Gunner (2)	127	10%
Upper Turret Gunner	102	8%
Pilot	93	7%
Ball Turret Gunner	78	6%
Co-Pilot	68	6%
Gunner – Not Located	117	8%
TOTAL	1,293	100%

REDUCTION OF CASE FATALITY RATE OF THORACIC AND ABDOMINAL WOUNDS THROUGH USE OF BODY ARMOR

In September 1943, the issue of body armor for the use of combat crew members was begun. Since that time, the supply of this item has increased until at the present time, 31 December 1943, all heavy Bomber Groups are supplied with enough body armor to enable very man dispatched to wear one. Since the issue of these suits, this office has record of 62 individuals struck by enemy missiles in the areas of the body covered by the armor (thorax, abdomen, upper thighs). Of these 62 individuals struck, 50 were uninjured, 8 received slight wounds, and 4 have been killed in action. Thus, the case fatality rate of individuals struck while wearing armor in areas covered by the armor was 6.4%. When it is considered that the great majority of these individuals were struck in the thoracic and abdominal region, a great reduction (75%) in the fatality rate is evident.

T O P   S E C R E T

A further proof of the efficacy of the body armor is seen in the comparison of the case fatality rates of wounds prior to 1 September 1943 and since 1 September 1943. In this comparison, all wounds of the body are considered whether the individual was wearing a flak suit or not. In this comparison, the fatality rate of wounds of the thorax and abdomen decreased from 30% (prior to September, 1943) to 22% (since September, 1943). This is shown in Table XIX.

TABLE XIX
CASE FATALITY RATES
BEFORE AND AFTER INTRODUCTION OF BODY ARMOR

	MAY– SEPT 1943			SEPT – DEC 1943		
AREA	WOUNDS	FATALITIES/%		WOUNDS	FATALITIES/%	
Thorax and Abdomen	30	9	30.0%	31	7	22.0%
Head and Neck	90	12	13.3%	112	14	12.5%
Extremities	267	7	2.6%	310	5	1.6%

In the 4 individuals killed in action by enemy missiles perforating the body armor, 2 were killed by wounds of the thorax, and 2 by wounds of the abdomen. It can be definitely stated without exaggeration that of those 62 individuals struck by enemy missiles in areas covered by body armor approximately 93% were saved from death or serious injury through the use of this armor.

TREND OF LOSSES RELATING TO COMBAT CREW EXPERIENCE
HEAVY BOMBER OPERATIONS

A tour of operations in heavy bombers of the Eighth Air Force (B-17 or B-24) consists of 25 operational missions; at which time the individuals be relieved from further combat duty. Experience of the RAF indicates that the liability of loss (killed or missing in action) is greater in the earlier part of the tour than toward the end of the tour. This is attributed to greater experience of combat crew members gained during repeated night operational missions.

In order to make an accurate study of loss trends for daylight heavy bomber missions, a detailed operational history of each individual, making up the whole, must be studied. These individuals must be followed from their initial operational mission until loss through enemy action or otherwise (completed tour, permanent removal for physical disability, or administrative reasons, death in non-operational aircraft accidents, etc.) in the computation of percentage loss per mission, correction must be made for those individuals lost between missions, i.e., those killed in non-operational aircraft accidents, those permanently relieved from flying duty, those repatriated, etc.

T O P   S E C R E T

This paper presents studies made on 2,085 initial combat crew members of the 91st, 94th, 305th, 381st and 384th Bomb Groups of the Eighth Air Force. Each individual was followed through his operational tour until he was permanently disposed of from his combat crew. This permanent disposition included killed in action, missing in action, seriously wounded with permanent relief, repatriations, permanent removal from flying duty for physical disability or administrative reasons, transfers to higher headquarters and out of the combat crew, personnel escaping from enemy occupied territory with further relief from combat duties, etc.

Of the 2,085 initial combat crew members, 34 failed to start their tour of operational flying. Thus, 2,051 were exposed to their first operational mission. Of these, 93, or 4.5%, were killed in action or missing in action on their first operational mission.

Table XXVII shows the number starting each mission, the number killed in action or missing in action per mission, and the percentage killed and missing in action of those exposed.

TABLE XXVII

RATE OF LOSS (KILLED AND MISSING IN ACTION) PER OPERATIONAL HEAVY BOMBER MISSION

MISSION NUMBER	NUMBER STARTING*	NUMBER KIA AND MIA	PERCENTAGE
1	2,051	93	4.5%
2	1,927	139	7.2%
3	1,775	94	5.3%
4	1,651	46	2.8%
5	1,585	117	7.3%
6	1,451	74	5.1%
7	1,360	56	4.1%
8	1,291	75	5.8%
9	1,203	76	6.3%
10	1,117	60	5.3%
11	1.047	54	5.1%
12	990	36	3.6%
13	942	61	6.4%
14	873	28	3.2%
15	831	20	2.4%
16	794	37	4.6%
17	748	31	4.1%
18	708	20	2.8%
19	680	21	3.0%
20	654	20	3.0%

T O P   S E C R E T

21	623	12	1.9%
22	605	6	0.9%
23	588	7	1.2%
24	564	3	0.5%
25	559	9	1.6%
	TOTAL	1,195	3.9%[16]

Figure arrived at by subtracting the number killed and missing plus those otherwise "lost" between missions, from the preceding mission.

Although Table XXVII shows the percentage killed and missing in action by mission, the array might be misleading as it seems to remain practically constant until Mission No. 21 when a rapid decline of % lost takes place. In order to illustrate loss trends more clearly, the average percentage lost by groups of missions, is more illustrative. This is shown in Table XXVIII.

TABLE XXVIII

RATE OF LOSS (KIA AND MIA) BY MISSION GROUPS

MISSION GROUP	AVERAGE PERCENTAGE LOST
1 to 5	5.4%
6 to 10	5.3%
11 to 15	4.1%
16 to 20	3.5%
21 to 25	1.2%

Table XXVIII shows that the rate of loss of heavy bomber crews is practically constant the first 10 missions. Thereafter, the rate of loss decreases at a moderately rapid rate. At first glance, this would appear to bear out the assumption that RAF and Eighth Air Force experience is practically the same relative to experience of combat crews. One further consideration must be taken into account. As crews advance through their operational tours, they increase in rank and are more apt to be found leading flights on missions. This would not account for the rapid decrease of loss, but might have some bearing on the final figures.

FURTHER STATISTICAL DATA

In this series studied, it was found that of 2,085 individuals starting operational tour of missions, approximately 25% complete 25 missions, 57% are killed and missing in action, and 17% are lost from combat crews because of physical disability, lack of moral fibre, death in non-operational aircraft accidents, etc.

---

[16] Mean average percent per mission.

T O P   S E C R E T

FROSTBITE

The tables and statistical data presented in this section include cases of frostbite occurring among heavy bomber combat crew personnel of the Eighth Air Force from 1 November 1942 to 31 December 1943. Only cases of frostbite serious enough to warrant removal of the individual from flying duty are considered. All data is derived from the weekly *Care of Flyer and Statistical Report*, received from Group Surgeons of the Eighth Air Force.

In the period under consideration, a total of 1,634 individuals have been removed from flying duty because of frostbite incurred on high altitude operational day missions. This represents a serious loss as each man removed from flying duty for frostbite loses an average of 10.5 days from combat duties. This condition also results in permanent loss of the individual in many instances. From an analysis of 200 consecutive cases of frostbite removed from flying duty, 14 or 7% were permanently lost, never returning to duty with the Air Force.

As a basis of comparison, in the same period, a total of 1,207 individuals were removed from flying duty because of wounds incurred in action against the enemy. Thus, frostbite is a more serious hazard confronting heavy bomber combat crew members than enemy gunfire.

AREAS OF BODY AFFECTED

Areas of the body affected by frostbite are: the hands and fingers, feet and toes, head, face, neck and ears, and the buttocks and groin. The individuals removed from flying duty for frostbite, in the period reported, (1 November 1942 – 31 December 1943) received frostbites in 1,826 areas of the body, as listed above. Table XX lists the location of frostbite received in the period 1 November 1942 – 31 December 1943. Table XXI shows the location of frostbite prior to 1 July 1943 and since that date. This division has been made to illustrate the decrease in the incidence of frostbite of the hands and fingers, and the great increase in frostbite of the exposed parts of the body: the face, neck and ears. It is readily seen that in the period prior to 1 July 1943, frostbite of the face, neck and ears accounted for 17% of the total, but since 1 July 1943, frostbite of this area accounts for 53% of the total with an average of 45% for the whole period. The decrease in frostbite of the hands and feet is attributable, in part, to improved supply of electrical heating equipment, improvements in equipment, and increased care by regularly assigned equipment offices.

TABLE XX

LOCATION	NUMBER OF CASES	PERCENTAGE OF TOTAL
Face, Neck, Ears	837	45%
Hands, Fingers	613	34%
Feet, Toes	365	20%
Buttocks, Groin	11	1%

T O P   S E C R E T

TABLE XXI

Location of Frostbite prior to 1 July 1943 and since 1 July 1943
(1 July 1943 – 31 December 1943)

LOCATION	PRIOR TO JULY 1943		01 JULY 1943 TO 31 DECEMBER 1943	
	NO. OF CASES/PERCENT		NO. OF CASES/PERCENT	
Hands, Fingers	188	56%	425	28%
Feet, Toes	87	26%	278	16%
Face, Neck, Ears	58	17%	779	53%
Buttocks, Groin	4	1%	7	1%
TOTAL	337	100%	1,489	100%

COMBAT POSITION

In the prevention of frostbite, the combat position of the individual affected is of major importance. In this connection, it seems reasonable to assume that individuals most apt to be affected are those in position of the aircraft exposed to the outside atmosphere, other factors (electrical heating equipment) being normal. In this series, this assumption has been borne out with waist gunners affected more frequently than individuals in other combat positions. This is shown in Table XXII. Furthermore, as shown in Table XXIII, waist gunners and radio operators incur more frostbite of the face, neck and ears (exposed parts) than individuals in other combat positions. These gunners operate at relatively exposed positions in respect to windblast; make them more liable to incur frostbite of the exposed portions of the body.

Concerning frostbite in other areas of the body, only the ball turret gunner and navigator receive more frostbite of the feet than the hands. Other positions reported more frostbite of the hands.

TABLE XXII

Combat Position of Personnel Suffering Frostbite

COMBAT POSITION	NUMBER OF CASES	PERCENTAGE OF TOTAL
Waist Gunner (1) [17]	423	25%
Waist Gunner (2)	423	25%
Tail Gunner	233	14%
Ball Turret Gunner	70	10%
Radio Operator	68	10%
Upper Turret Gunner	59	3%
Bombardier	42	2%

---

[17] A total of 846 waist gunners incurred frostbite. Conversion made for two.

T O P S E C R E T

Pilot	20	1%
Navigator	12	1%
Co-Pilot	10	1%
Gunner—Position Unknown	129	8%
TOTAL	1,689	100%

TABLE XXIII

Location of Frostbite by Combat Position

COMBAT POSITION	HANDS	FEET	FACE & NECK	BUTTOCKS
Waist Gunner	25%	15%	60%	0
Tail Gunner	38%	24%	38%	0
Radio Operator	29%	13%	58%	0
Ball Turret Gunner	34%	45%	17%	4%
Upper Turret Gunner	52%	25%	22%	1%
Bombardier	51%	38%	11%	0
Navigator	33%	55%	12%	0
Pilot	50%	29%	21%	0
Co-Pilot	12%	76%	12%	0

CAUSES OF FROSTBITE

Prior to 1 July 1943, the greatest number of cases of frostbite was due failure of or defective electrical heating equipment. Since 1 July 1943 to 1 January 1944, windblast caused the greatest number of cases. Cases of frostbite of the face, neck and ears are attributed to windblast as these areas are relatively exposed to wind from open windows in the case of waist gunners, and hatches in the case radio operators. In some instances, openings in the aircraft made by enemy gunfire produced enough blast to cause frostbite in otherwise protected individuals, and in the absence of other causes. Table XXIV lists the cause of frostbite reported from 1 November 1942 – 1 January 1944. Table XXV shows the cause prior to 1 July 1943 and since that date. In these two periods, it can be seen that failure of electrical heating equipment, removal of protective equipment and lack of proper equipment, as causes, remained approximately the same, but there occurred a greatly increased incidence of frostbite due to windblast — from 9% to 46% — with an average incidence for the whole period of 39%.

TABLE XXIV

Causes of Frostbite – 1 November 1942 — 1 January 1944

CAUSE	NUMBER OF CASES	PERCENTAGE OF TOTAL
Windblast	668	39%

Flight Surgeon

T O P S E C R E T

Failure of or Defective
Electrical Heating Equipment	415	24%
Lack of Proper Equipment	215	12%
Removal of Protective Equipment	156	9%
No Apparent Reason[18]	147	8%
Urinated in Suit	11	1%
Others and Unknown	96	6%
TOTAL	1,708	100%

TABLE XXV

Causes of Frostbite
Prior to 1 July 1943 and since 1 July 1943 to 1 December 1943)

CAUSE	PRIOR TO JULY 1943		JULY – DECEMBER 1943	
	NO. OF CASES/PERCENT		NO. OF CASES/PERCENT	
Failure Electrical Equipment	88	26%	327	24%
Removal Protective Equipment	43	13%	113	8%
Lack of Proper Equipment	34	10%	181	13%
Windblast	30	9%	638	46%
No Apparent Reason	32	9%	115	8%
Urinated in Suit	4	1%	7	1%
Others and Unknown	96	32%	0	0%
TOTAL	327	100%	1381	100%

FROSTBITE IN INDIVIDUAL GROUPS

In order to evaluate the efficiency of squadron equipment officers, warmth of various types of heavy bombers, the organizations where the greatest amount of prophylactic work, including training of crews, is carried out, comparisons for the various heavy bomb groups in operation in this theater have been made.

The computation has been made in terms of percentage of combat crew members dispatched contracting frostbite. Computation has been made for the period I July 1943 – December 1943 (cumulative). Table XXVI shows the results of such studies.

Of all the groups listed, the 93rd, 44th, and 309th Bomb Groups are well above the

---

[18] Represents individuals sustaining frostbite with electrical equipment apparently satisfactory, no appreciable windblast, with all proper equipment continually worn.

T O P   S E C R E T

average in percentage of frostbite. These groups are B-24 groups, which might explain their high rate. The 401st Bomb Group percentage is based on but a small number of men dispatched (4,100 in November); hence, is statistically insignificant.

TABLE XXVI

Frostbite among individual Heavy Bomb Groups
Percentage based on combat crew members dispatched
01 July 1943 – 31 December 1943

PERCENTAGES[19]---0-0.25% 0.26-0.5% 0.51% 0.75% 0.76%-1.00% Over 1.00%

0-0.25%	0.26-0.5%	0.51%-0.75%	0.76%-1.00%	Over 1.00%
388 BG	390 BG	306 BG	389 BG	93 BG
385 BG	305 BG	379 BG	381 BG	44 BG
96 BG	303 BG	92 BG	401 BG	
	100 BG	95 BG		
	94 BG	351 BG		
	392 BG			
	91 BG			
	384 BG			

FROSTBITE 1ST BOMBARDMENT DIVISION
FOR THE 3–MONTH PERIOD ENDING 12 FEBRUARY 1944

STATION	NUMBER OF CASES
117	102
167	86
128	83
107	72
106	70
111	64
121	56
109	49
105	35
110	21
TOTAL	638

---

[19] Mean average all groups: 0.52%.

T O P   S E C R E T

Tabulation of Frostbite Cases in the Eighth Air Force
For the week ending 4 February 1944

TABLE I

	TIMES		PERCENT
	AFFECTED		OF TOTAL
Head, face and neck	144		70%
Feet	30		15%
Hands	28		14%
Buttocks	3		1%
TOTAL	205		100%

COMBAT POSITION	HEAD, FACE AND NECK	HANDS	FEET	BUTTOCKS
Pilot	NONE	NONE	7%	NONE
Co-pilot	NONE	4%	3%	NONE
Navigator	2%	4%	3%	NONE
Bombardier	3%	NONE	7%	NONE
Radio Operator	8%	21%	3%	NONE
Waist Gunner	71%	25%	34%	33%
Ball Turret Gunner	5%	25%	34%	67%
Upper Turret Gunner	2%	7%	3%	NONE
Tail Gunner	9%	14%	3%	NONE
Photographer	0%	0%	3%	NONE

T O P   S E C R E T

TABLE II

	NUMBER	PERCENT OF TOTAL
Windblast	117	66%
Defective Electrical	34	19%
Lack of Protective Equipment	19	11%
Removal of Protective Equipment	3	2%
No Apparent Reason	3	2%
Urinated in Suit	1	0%
TOTAL	177	100%

TABLE III

BOMB GROUPS	NUMBER OF CASES	% RELATED TO EXPOSURE	% FOR MO OF JANUARY
44th	8	.61	1.3
91st	1	.07	0.24
92nd	22	1.37	0.53
93rd	5	.34	0.32
95th	4	.23	0.40
96th	1	.06	0.06
100th	1	.06	0.07
303rd	6	.39	0.43
305th	2	.12	0.22
306th	4	.24	0.26
379th	22	1.37	1.2
381st	6	.43	1.09
384th	17	1.07	0.43
385th	16	1.04	0.35
388th	1	.05	0.06
389th	5	.36	0.45
390th	10	.61	0.55
392nd	15	.80	0.60
445th	2	.17	1.1
446th	20	1.53	1.18
447th	22	1.38	0.86
448th	8	.74	0.68
482nd	2	.32	0.18
TOTAL	200		

HEADQUARTERS   (M-C-2)
1ˢᵀ BOMBARDMENT DIVISION
Office of the Surgeon
APO 557

20 April 1944

C E R T I F I C A T E

On April 10, 1944, while on a scheduled Combat Mission over enemy-occupied Europe, 2ⁿᵈ Lt. Honor G. Windes, a co-pilot, was hit by an exploding, 20mm shell. The wounds were slight, consisting of multiple small lacerations about the left face and a small, penetrating wound of the leg. A huge hole had been blown into the side of the steel helmet worn by Lt. Windes, and it is a miracle that he had not been killed. There is no question in our minds that the helmet worn by Lt. Windes saved his life.

/s/ THELBERT R. WILSON
/t/ THELBERT R. WILSON

HEADQUARTERS
1ST BOMBARDMENT DIVISION
Office of the Surgeon
APO 557

(M-C-2)

07 June 1944

SUBJECT: Group Photographs

TO: Surgeon, All Stations, is Bombardment Division, APO 557

1. Enclosed are pictures taken at the last Group Surgeons Meeting.

2. Identification is as follows:

Front Row	Second Row
Left to Right:	Left to Right:
Major Mulmed, Earl I.	1st Lt. Hicks, Gordon T.
Major Gaillard, Ernest (NMI)	Capt. Stroud, Henry H.
Major Bergner, Karl L.	Major Zampetti, Herman A.
Major Longworth, Edmund F.	Major Wise, Ralph W. E.
Lt. Col. Shuller, Thurman (NMI)	Major Munal, Harold D., Jr.
Major Walker, John C.	Major Black, Abraham (NMI)
Major Henry, Joseph R.	Major Schumacher, George O.
Major Haggard, Gordon H.	Major Nowack, Louis W.

C O N F I D E N T I A L

History of Rogers, Martin W., Cpl., 13048800, 533rd Sqdn., 381st Bomb Gp. (H)

HEADQUARTERS **AAF Station 167** **Office of Surgeon** **APO 557**	M-S-1

14 June 1944

Case History of Cpl. Martin W. Rogers[20], 13048800, Age 25, 533rd Bombardment Squadron, 381st Bombardment Group (H) AAF.

1. Personal History as given by patient:

This 25-year-old white male was born February 21, 1919 in Bridgeville, Pennsylvania, a population of about 4,500. His life until the time of enlistment was spent in Bridgeville.

Childhood:

This individual showed no unusual tendencies during childhood. He apparently socialized well, was an average student, participated in athletics, and has no criminal record. He was AWOL from a YMCA camp, returning because he was homesick. Patient is the youngest of three boys and was well treated by his parents. Parents are of average circumstances.

Education:

Graduated from high school in the middle third of his class and states he got along well with his teachers and fellow students. Rogers had no conflict with the law prior to his entering the service.

Military Service:

Subject enlisted voluntarily January 6, 1942 and was signed for aerial gunnery. He was told that he would have to become an armorer before he could become an aerial gunner. After compliance, he was informed that in as much as he was an armorer, he would remain an armorer. He resented this misrepresentation and feels that his not being allowed to go to gunnery school is in a large part responsible for his present difficulty. He arrived in the E.T.O. in December 1942. He was accepted for O.C.S. in March, but did not attend because of hospitalization for varicose veins from March 25 to April 17, 1943. He was returned to the hospital three days later with suspected meningitis, which was not confirmed. He left the hospital late in July undiagnosed and with persistent

---

[20] Once again, this soldier's true name and serial number have been changed to protect his family.

C O N F I D E N T I A L

History of Rogers, Martin W., Cpl., 13048800, 533rd Sqdn., 381st Bomb Gp. (H)

tinnitus aurium. Patient states that during his hospitalization for meningitis, he could not walk. Psychiatric examination consultation helped considerably and he was able to walk from the hospital. He was sent from the hospital to the 12th R.C.D. where he remained for two months as block chief.

Here he met gunners who were returning home after completion of their missions. He learned much of the talk of the trade and learned of harrowing experiences that these gunners had been through. He states that he obtained flying equipment, parts of escape kits, and decorations from the returning gunners. He was transferred to the 533rd Bomb Squadron, 381st Bomb Group (H) in September and, on the way from the R.C.D., wore a sergeant's uniform with many decorations and a pair of gunner's wings. He states that at the time he felt he was truly a gunner. A search was made for flying equipment and he was made to give up the equipment in his possession. Courts Martial was threatened by Captain Tutsock, Adjutant, 533rd Squadron, if any more flying equipment was found in his possession.

He worked in the Armament Section until about December 1, 1943 when he was put on base detail by Captain Tutsock. After one week of base detail, he was ordered to another week of detail and inquired why, asking Capt. Tutsock if it was for personal reasons. Subject stated that Capt. Tutsock lost his temper and again inspected his barracks bags and this time found French money, escape kits, first aid kits, and .45 cal. ammunition. He was informed that he was on Capt. Tutsock's shit list for the duration and that any dirty base detail would be reserved for him. Rogers states that he had never hated anyone as much as he hates Capt. Tutsock and that he threatened to kill him on one occasion. When inquired as to whether he really would kill Capt. Tutsock, he said he did not believe he would be able to. Rogers also expressed suicidal tendencies in several documents, but states although miserable, he had no intention of carrying them out.

Instead of going on base detail for the second week, Rogers packed and left. He states that he was "all mixed up" and "something made him". He was aware that AWOL is not correct, but did not know that it would be classed as desertion. He states that he went to Bury St. Edmunds and he is vague as to what happened after that. He gives no detailed account of his actions between December and March and states he cannot think clearly about some of the things he has done. He was picked up in March by the Bury St. Edmunds' U.S.M.P.'s, and, when picked up, was wearing a British battle jacket and Naval wings. His explanation was that he was given the battle jacket by a British soldier and wore it because it was comfortable. He was returned to the guardhouse, AAF Station 167 where he remained for one month.

A medical consultation was requested and, after he was dressed to be brought to the station sick quarters, he found the guard house door open and

C O N F I D E N T I A L

History of Rogers, Martin W., Cpl., 13048800, 533rd Sqdn., 381st Bomb Gp. (H)

something said, "walk out". Which he did. He went to Bury St. Edmunds and here again is hazy about his activities. On May 2, 1944, he found himself on a train in northern England heading for Edinburgh, Scotland where he remained registered at the ARC Club in his own name. He remained at the ARC Club for ten days and then with relatives for a week. He forged a leave pass and went to Portsmouth by way of Liverpool and Bristol. He met enlisted men and officers at an ordnance base and states that no pass or identity card was requested at any place. He states he was staying with friends and relatives. At Portsmouth, he posed himself as a 1st Lieutenant in the Air Corps with pilot's wings, D.F.C., Purple Heart, and Air Medal, and informed his associates he had completed his operational tour.

He also had some cards printed stating he was a member of the Military Intelligence Division. He heard about an altercation between British sailors and American soldiers and went to the police station, presented his credentials, and volunteered his services.

Some time later, a Major Butler (ordnance or quartermaster) requested proof of identity and did not accept proof of the M.I.D. card as sufficient evidence. He was then arrested. He states he impersonated the officer because it enabled him to get around better with less questioning. He bought the uniform at Bury St. Edmunds and states he had 80 pounds of his own money sent to him by his parents.

Thought content as given by Cpl. Rogers:

Rogers states that he has hallucinations, believing he was a member of the U.S. Navy & traveling all over the world. During this time, he wore the Navy uniform and talked and lived with the sailors. Later, he believed he was a pilot in the Royal British Navy and wore the wings. Later, he believed he was an officer of the Military Intelligence, conducted himself as such, and attempted to assist in an investigation. He further believes he is an aerial gunner and has completed his operational tour and has been decorated with the D.F.C., Purple Heart, and Air Medal. Rogers states he believes he is insane to a certain extent, and, if he wasn't, he would not do the things like the above. Rogers states he has hazy recollections and a lack of knowledge about past events as stated in the history above. He further states no one cares for him and no one would do anything for him. He believes everyone will do everything in their power to keep him going downward. He is unable to elucidate specific instances.

2. Information from other sources:

Captain Louis G. Ralston, 533rd Bomb Squadron Surgeon has the following entries on the case history at station sick quarters during admission

C O N F I D E N T I A L

History of Rogers, Martin W., Cpl., 13048800, 533rd Sqdn., 381st Bomb Gp. (H)

November 13 – 18 1943. Patient was admitted for an injured left knee and no pathology was found. He states he was in the Pacific, and further stated he had flown five missions in B-26's and was grounded for poor vision. The following record was written by Capt. Ralston when patient was dismissed from station sick quarters:

"This man's service record was checked and failed to show that he had ever been on flying status. Also, a check showed that he was dissatisfied with this present job and had been reporting to the orderly room and claiming that he had leg trouble. It was noted that when he was under observation he would limp markedly, but at times when he was not aware that he was watched, he would walk quite normally.

"He was confronted with the above plus an analysis of his attempts to convince the medical officer of his disability and finally admitted that he had no actual leg injury. He stated that he had not been satisfied in his previous outfit, that he desired combat training, and was not able to get it, and thought that he might get it if transferred. His month's hospital time was by his own admission largely malingering. He stated that he actually fell down as claimed this time, but after he had injured himself slightly, decided to profit by it if he could and so pretended greater injury for his own benefit."

"He was discharged to full duty and walked out of the hospital without any limp".

/s/Louis G. Ralston
/t/Capt. LOUIS G. RALSTON, MC

The Lowery Field Revmeter, undated, in possession of courts and boards, shows a picture of Private Martin W. Rogers being decorated for China service and is accompanied by a long line of prevarications eulogizing Rogers.

Forgeries of cards of Military Intelligence Department, forgery of two C.D.D.'s using two different names, forgery of an official telegram, forgery of rank on a pay voucher, and papers substantiating assumption of rank of 2nd Lieutenant are component parts of the evidence collected against Rogers for courts martial purposes, and the sworn statements by officers, M.D.'s, and enlisted men merely substantiate details of the histories and the forgeries outlined.

3. Medical Examination:

History:

C O N F I D E N T I A L

History of Rogers, Martin W., Cpl., 13048800, 533ʳᵈ Sqdn., 381ˢᵗ Bomb Gp. H)

Patient had pneumonia, mumps, and scarlet fever during childhood and the age at which he had mumps is unknown. Scarlet Fever and Pneumonia were uncomplicated. Patient also states that he suffered sunstroke, but is unable to elaborate. He has been unconscious five or six times following injuries. Fifteen minutes is the longest period of time he has been unconscious. There is no history of pavor, nocturnus, enuresis, nail biting, temper tantrums, mood swings, etc. For the past year, he states he has had headaches located behind the eyes and radiating to the occipital region and the attacks are occasionally associated with dizzy spells and weakness. In April 1943, he had a short, saphenous ligation for varicosities at the 2ⁿᵈ Evacuation Hospital and was admitted three days after discharge with suspected meningitis. The meningitis was not confirmed and the patient states that he remained hospitalized running a temperature from 99° – 103° F, and he was unable to walk for a period of three months during which time he was hospitalized (see above statement by Captain Ralston) [21].

Family History:

Father living and well. Mother living and well except for sequelae of cholescystectomy and appendectomy. Three brothers all living and well. There was a history of a 3ʳᵈ cousin dying of a mental condition at the age of 37. No other instances of mental disease in the family.

Physical Examination:

A well-nourished, mildly obese, white male, not ill. He shows a feminine distribution of fat and is small boned.
BP 100/60   P 68   R 16
Eyes – pupils equal – react to light and accommodation
Neck – thyroid not palpable
ENT – negative
Chest – Heart and lungs normal. No pectoral hair
Abdomen – Spleen, skin, and kidney not palpable
Female distribution of pubic hair
Scrotum – Testes undescended, bilateral. Not palpable in inguinal canals
Penis – infantile
Extremities – Normal
Reflexes – Normal, no pathological reflexes present

4. Psychiatric Findings:

---

[21] Captain Ralston passed away at his Pennsylvania home, suddenly and unexpectedly, in 1967 at the age of fifty-three.

C O N F I D E N T I A L

History of Rogers, Martin W., Cpl., 13048800, 533ʳᵈ Sqdn., 381ˢᵗ Bomb Gp. (H)

- a. General classification test III, which is above average. Malingering as shown by hospital record and patient's own statement.
- b. Pathological lying.
- c. Identification.
- d. Poor judgment.
- e. Acts on impulses.
- f. Unable to profit by experiences.
- g. Feels he must be partly insane.
- h. Feels everyone is against him.
- i. Questionable fixation, narcissistic level.
- j. Physical findings – Female distribution of fat and pubic hair. Hypo-genitalism, cryptorchidism, and fair skin are consistent with a mild Froelich's syndrome.

5. Physical Evaluation:

This individual socialized fairly well in a small town environment and probably was protected by relatives and friends. Upon entering the army, he found himself to be a very small part of a tremendous undertaking and his first bid for attention that we know of was when he was spuriously decorated for heroism while at Lowery Field. His wish to be an aerial gunner was thwarted and he used hospitalization with minor surgery and malingering in an effort to satisfy his desires. Later upon being assigned to this bomb group, he had difficulty with his superiors, possibly with some justification, and went AWOL as a means of escape, which I feel demonstrates an inability to accommodate himself to his social environment without conflict. His sense of responsibility and appreciation of proper values has been lost for, without question, he knows that being AWOL for any period of time is considered as desertion and he is aware of the sentence that can be given deserters.[22] He apparently had no sense of obligation, no sense of guilt, and he failed to appreciate the punishment of incarceration when he was apprehended.

The only demands that he has satisfied are those of his own desires, which have been satisfied without any thought of right or wrong, or any real fear of punishment. His judgment was poor as demonstrated by his many forgeries, his

---

[22] Note: Private Eddie Slovik had yet to be executed (31 January 1945) at Ste-Marie aux Mines, France for the abandonment of his unit right after the Battle of the Hurtengen Forest, October 1944 — the first such execution for desertion from the field of battle since the Civil War. Even twenty years later, Ike never talked about issuing the final death warrant and order; this, according to his then-assistant presidential physician, the late Major General Walter Robert Tkach, MD, USAF MC, my brother-in-law.

C O N F I D E N T I A L

History of Rogers, Martin W., Cpl., 13048800, 533ʳᵈ Sqdn., 381ˢᵗ Bomb Gp. (H)

intruding upon a legal case where he would most certainly be found out, his breaking of arrest and the conduct of his whole thought and behavior pattern. I do not regard his hazy recollections or his acts, which he states are compulsive as of any psychiatric significance, but feel they are the result of conscious desire.

His lying is seemingly wish fulfillment and is not unlike the phantasies (*sic*) of children and apparently has grown by elaboration and the addition of material in the effort to have his story remain plausible. He has demonstrated no true schizoid, paranoid, or manic tendencies, and there is no discrepancy between thought behavior and emotional content.

Malingering is the only thing he has shown that is consistent with minor psychiatric manifestations. His primary pathology is that of a defective state in which the individual is unable to profit by his experience, acts on impulses, shows poor judgment, pathological lying, and identification.

Contrary to the useful behavior pattern in this type of case, the individual tends to socialize at a higher rather than a lower level. The labeling of the individual as a narcissistic may be questioned. He shows phantasy, self-consciousness, and conceit. Against the narcissism is his hetero-sexual experience. In the absence of any truly psychotic or minor psychotic manifestations, it is felt that this individual must be a constitutional and psychopathic inferior.

6. Diagnosis:

    a. Constitutional and psychopathic inferior.

7. Recommendations:

    It is recommended that this individual be legally held responsible for his acts.[23]

MAJOR ERNEST GAILLARD, Jr.
Major, MC
Station Surgeon

Major Gaillard,

You are to be congratulated upon a very thorough examination and well written report. The report was also of great interest to the J.A.G. section and they now have the case under consideration. It has raised some questions in their minds, which I am watching with great amusement.

Thanks,
Lieutenant Fuller

---

[23] Cpl. Rogers passed away peacefully at his home in Minnesota on 26 February 2002 at the age of eighty-three.

HEADQUARTERS   M-S-1
AAF Station 167
Office of the Surgeon
APO 557

22 July 1944

SUBJECT: Efficiency of the ground personnel.

      TO: Surgeon, Hq. Eighth Air Force, APO 634, U.S. Army

1.   The evaluation of the mental and physical status of the large group of individuals that comprise the ground personnel of this station is divided in two parts for the purposes of this report. First, the opinions of doctors and other officers and, secondly, information gained from interviewing a representative cross section of the enlisted personnel.

2.   It is the consensus of officer opinion that both men and officers are doing their work in a very proficient manner due to the level of experience. Every man knows his work well and is able to perform it in a proficient manner. It is also the consensus of opinion that a large proportion of the personnel on this base, both officer and enlisted, are becoming fed-up, war-weary, stagnant, disinterested and indifferent to their work, and this opinion is based on a general feeling of unrest, increased irritability, increased use of tobacco and alcohol, and statements indicating that the personnel would like to "get way from it all for a while". It was also noted that ground personnel have sufficient interest in the war effort and their part in it to continue to work well.

3.   Physical fatigue is not nearly as great a problem. On occasions when the work is unusually heavy, the ground crews do suffer some physical exhaustion, but this is on comparatively infrequent occasions and is not thought to be of sufficient importance to warrant any remedial action. It is felt further by this investigating group that a system of leaves and passes that could be fairly rigidly adhered to would be the most beneficial action that could be taken to alleviate mental stress that the ground personnel has developed.

4.   The second phase of this duty is given to the presentation of facts and the results of interrogating a representative cross section of personnel. The personnel interviewed have been in the E.T.O. from nine to thirty-two months, with an average of fourteen months. Personnel from ordnance, armament, chemical warfare service, headquarters, mess halls, the flying line, machine shops, auto mechanics, medical personnel, and others selected at random were interviewed and the following facts were established:

    a. There has been an increase in the number of Courts Martials at this base. There were more in the month of June than in any previous three months.

    b. Men working in static jobs, working regular hours, have little if any complaint. They work an average of eight hours daily.

c. Twenty to forty per cent of the personnel receiving 24-hour passes remain on the base. The reason for remaining is they are tired and could not go to any place of interest because of time and travel restrictions.

d. Fifty per cent stated that his work was becoming more monotonous and they had increasing difficulty carrying on with it, despite the fact that they were more efficient. The working day varies from eight to fifteen hours.

e. Twenty per cent stated that they were now drinking more than they had six months ago. Others stated that the only thing that keeps them from drinking more is the shortage of supply.

f. All of the men stated that they had little interest in going on pass because there is insufficient entertainment within a radius of 25 miles.

g. Forty-four per cent complained of increasing nervousness and irritability.

h. Almost without exception, the smokers state that they are smoking ½ pack more than they did six months ago.

i. Five per cent stated that they had had weight loss and fifteen per cent stated they did not know.

j. To the question, "What do you think would be the best single thing that could be instituted to better your lot?", 80% replied that they would like to have more time to spend as they desired to get away from the base, army of discipline, and overcrowded mess halls.

5.   Comment: — The efficiency of ground personnel at this base is unimpaired because of their mental and physical fatigue. However, a large proportion of individuals have lost interest and do work mechanically, live only from day to day, are becoming more nervous and irritable, find their range of interest considerably restricted, and look forward only to the time they will return to the States. It is my considered opinion that we will see psychiatric problems and have a loss of technical efficiency of the group in the not too distant future unless some type of remedial action is instituted.

                                        Ernest Gaillard, Jr.
                                        Major, MC
                                        Station Flight Surgeon

HEADQUARTERS   M-S-1
AAF Station 167
Office of the Surgeon
APO 557

1 August 1944

MENTAL DEFECTIVES

1. <u>Purpose</u>: – The purpose of this discussion is to aid in the recognition, classification, and disposition of mental defectives.

2. <u>Etiology</u>:

   a. Heredity – If the heredity of the individual is poor from the mental standpoint, the individual will probably be poor intellectually.
   b. Deformities and birth injuries – This group is fairly obvious and requires but little elucidation. It is this group that mental defectives with normal parents usually occur.
   c. Seventy per cent of the mental defectives have no demonstrable pathology.
   d. Phenyl pyruvic oligophenia – A rare condition that is characterized by the execration of phenyl pyruvic acid in the urine and the mental deficiency associated with this abnormal execration is thought to be due to a disturbance of physio-chemical metabolism, which adversely affects nervous tissue.

3. <u>A.G.C.T.</u>

a.	5%	Superior	150—130	Up
b.	15%	Above Average	130 – 110	16
c.	70%	Average	110 – 90	14
d.	10%	Below Average	90 – 70	10
e.	5%	Defective	70 – --	Down

4. <u>Intelligence</u>:

   a. Intelligence is the ability to solve problems and is not influenced to any great extent by learning or previous experience. It has been found that the development of intelligence ceases at about the 16th year, but may continue into the early 20's. However, late maturity does not necessarily mean superior intelligence, but may mean only retarded development. The mentally defective group lives in a very limited sphere and consciously or unconsciously reject or repel outside influences. When the pressure of life begins to overwhelm the individual, they develop anxiety, which most frequently is projected into somatic symptoms. This group has been difficult to train, gets into trouble, into stupid errors, and often winds up on K.P. or other details.

b. Mental age 8 – 10 years – defective, but stable. The Army can use. Diagnose and place.

c. Defective, but unstable – remove from Army by Section VIII.

d. Less than 8 years – This group is removed from the Army whether they are stable or unstable. Their symptoms are important only to rule out organic disease. This individual is seldom benefited by treatment, but his symptoms not infrequently clear over a period of time if the stress is removed.

e. All mental defectives are LOD No, EPTI or EPTE, unless they have been broken by combat.

5. <u>Diagnosis</u>:

a. Longitudinal life history, including schooling. Here, it is important to learn what grade they finished in school, the age at which they finished, whether or not they attended regularly, and whether or not any effort was put forward.

b. A.G.C.T. – A verbal extemporaneous questioning based on the experience, opportunity, and familiarity of the individual and this is followed by a performance test. The intelligence test depends on cooperation and physical status of the individual. The Army uses a modified Bellevue-Wechler Intelligence Test and the following excerpts are particularly valuable in this mental age group.

   1) The numbers forward test, i.e., repeat after me.
   2) Vocabulary test.
   3) General information based on experience.
   4) Evaluation – 4 numbers repeated twice equals mental age of 7 years times; 5 repeated two times equals mental age of 9 years; 6 repeated two times equals mental age of 11 years.
   5) The following test words are used:

Apple	Cushion	Tent
Donkey	Schilling	Armory
Join	Gamble	Fable
Diamond	Bacon	Brim
Nuisance	Nail	Guillotine
Fur	Cedar	Plural

Definition of 9–12 words equals mental age of 8 years and progressively to 16 equals a mental age of 10 years or more.

General information in that they should know where they are, why they are, why they are here, Capital, the ocean they crossed to get here, who we are fighting and the heads of governments are asked. Another useful test is to have the individual make change in the currency with which he in most familiar. For example, give him 50¢ and have him buy 2 articles, one costing 6¢ and one costing 9¢, then ask him how much change he would receive. Mental defectives take abnormal time in arriving at the correct answer or miss it entirely. They not infrequently pay their bills by holding out their hands and depend upon the shopkeeper's honesty or they take someone with them to pay their bills.

6. <u>Constitutional Psychopathic State</u>:

   a. Emotional instability   /
   b. Criminalism   /
   c. Nomadism   /   Inadequate personality
   d. Psychopathic liar   /
   e. Paranoid personality   /
   f. Sexual psychopath   /

   g. This group has three things in common:

      1) Inherent
      2) Heredity and environment is usually poor
      3) All LOD No, and not aggravated by Military Service.

   h. It is axiomatic that a constitutional psychopath never was good as a psychoneurotic (ground force terminology) who is a "has been". This group is composed of the people who sponge on society and many criminals, hobos, swindlers, racetrack operators, carnival barkers, fast-talking salesmen, as well as a large number of chronic complainers and failures. Sargeant, the British investigator who introduced narco-synthesis, has been doing some experimental work with Benzedrine with this group and he finds that the emotionally unstable usually have an increased Benzedrine tolerance that is almost diagnostic.

   Some of these people can be helped by treatment, which includes psychotherapy, education, reassignment, etc. Another characteristic of the combat psychopath is that he does not learn by experience or by punishment, even though the punishment is severe, and in conversation they usually have a low emotional tone regarding their deficiencies and their indifference is characteristic. In order to understand this group, the individual is best considered from three viewpoints:

   1) <u>Intellect</u>:

   Intelligence is not the deciding factor in this group. They may be quite bright, or dull.

   2) <u>Personality</u>:

   The personality is inadequate as is best brought out by a longitudinal history.

   3) <u>Emotion</u>:

   Unstable, characterized by fear, rage, depression, etc.

By using the development of a normal child as an example, the constitutional psychopath is merely a child's emotional set-up in an adult body. The antisocial and the unstable CPS is sent to the recovery center, which is termed "The school of the unwilling soldier" – and it is tough. The recovery rate is surprisingly high. For the first time in their lives they have been made to accept society rather than to sponge off of it. In evaluating the personality of this group, the individual is considered from the standpoint of his constitution, which considers his heredity, intra-uterine development and birth, his past development from a physical and psychological viewpoint, and evaluates the present stress from a physical and psychological standpoint. The following diagram depicts the individual structure and the stress.

Another method used in evaluating personalities is to use the chart shown below in a chronological manner:

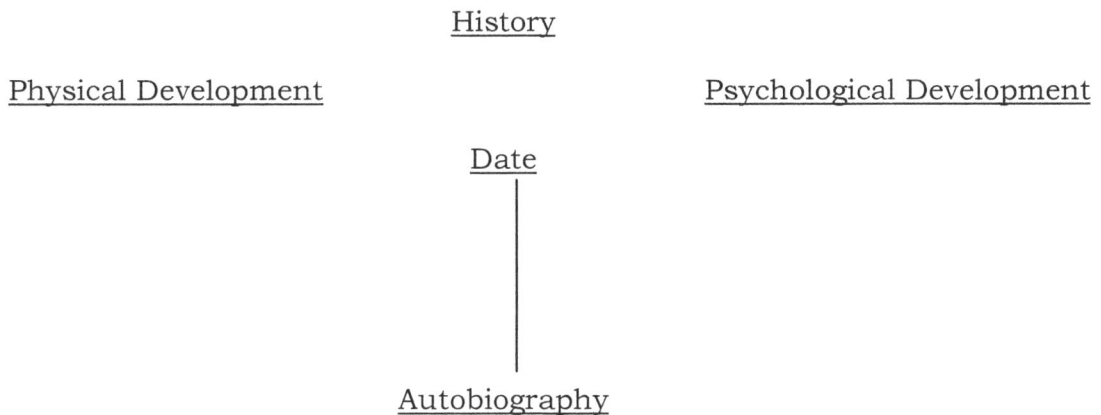

History

Physical Development   Psychological Development

Date

|

Autobiography

i. At the 312ᵗʰ Station Hospital, those individuals are treated, studied as described above, and an attempt is made to educate them to an adult level. They may or may not receive Benzedrine and they are frequently returned to useful duty.

7. Neurosis:

    a. Definition – "Too much reaction to stimuli or prolonged reaction to stimuli". Any individual may develop a neurosis. The unstable individuals or those with predisposition will develop the neurosis much earlier, but even the most stable and courageous individual will develop a neurosis if the stress is severe enough or if the stress is prolonged. An excellent example is the development of a 100% neurosis among the Marines at Guadalcanal. These individuals were highly trained and a carefully selected group who were in front line combat under constant and unremitting attack for a period of four months. When finally relieved, 100% of them had a neurosis and many of them are not rehabilitable *(sic)*. The increase of stress or pressure on the normal individual will cause a break if severe enough.

215

There are also instances where special weaknesses may cause a break down. If an individual has had a particularly harrowing experience in previous life and some trivial incident associates his present circumstances with that harrowing experience, a break down may be precipitated.

The individual with a poor background frequently breaks irrefutably and the individual with a sound background can easily be cured if seen before a neurosis is too well organized.

b. Conditioning: – The chief thing that distinguishes man from the lower animals is the ability to reason. For example, any animal fears fire because of the heat, which produces pain. Man, by reasoning, has controlled fire and put it to useful purpose. When man was first burned, he also continued to fear fire, but can now approach fire without fear of being burned. However, when a fire is out of control, man again experiences fear. This points out the development of reasoning and also man's ability to evaluate difficult situations. However, (1) frequently man has been prejudiced by a situation and (2) and unconsciously develops prejudice against a situation. For example, if a man has a hatred for an individual by the name Gerald, the next Gerald that he meets he will be unconsciously suspicious of. The same is true in a similarity in features, expressions, habits, etc. In the explanation of conditioning, the following diagram may be of help:

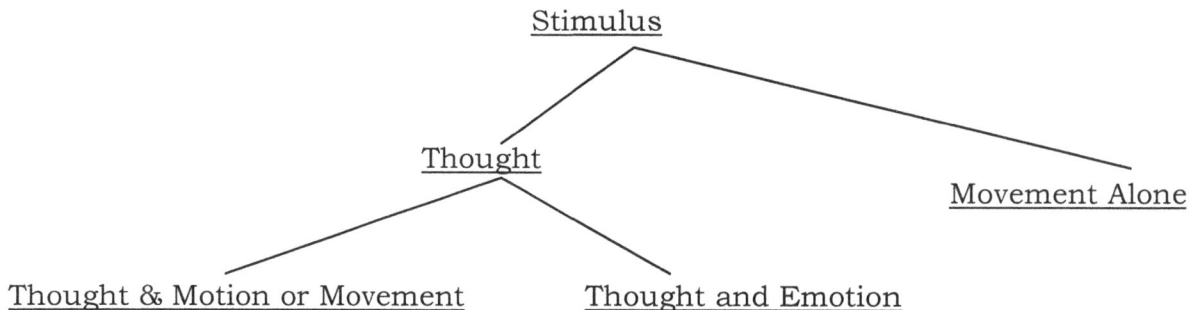

Stimulus

Thought

Movement Alone

Thought & Motion or Movement

Thought and Emotion

As can be seen from the diagram, any stimulus may result in: (1) Thought, (2) Thought and Motion or Movement, (3) Thought and Emotion, and, (4) Movement Alone. Most symptomatology that is seen in the neurosis results from previous conditions (even in the normal subject) and must be dug from the patient. Symptoms are (1) suggested, (2) acquired by operation or illness, and, (3) learned from the environment. The reason man is able to develop an extremely complex condition as distinguished from, for example, the genus of great apes, is shown in the following descriptive diagram.

Ape #1 is trained to brake at the red light, stopping in rather than at the intersection. Ape #2 crashes into him, but Ape #1 keeps repeating the accident because he can't use his cerebral cortex. Man's refusal to evaluate situation #2 is on the same intellectual plane as the ape in situation #2. Treatment is by explanation and breaking up is by narcosis. Treatment in the 312th Station Hospital is by history (see chart below).

216

<u>History</u>

<u>Physical Development</u>   <u>Psychological Development</u>

<u>Date</u>

<u>Autobiography</u>

An autobiography plus explanation of conditioning. This is done after the treatment.

8. <u>Fear</u>:

> a. Prudence and self-restraint.
> b. Concentration and caution.
> c. Anxiety – Visceral and motor symptoms as result of lack inhibition of frontal lobe and symptoms are produced.
> d. Perception level – anguish.
> e. Panic and later stupor – thalamus only. Decorfication fatigue accelerates breakdown.
> f. Death – at level of pons or medulla.

9. <u>Anxiety</u>:

> a.   If you can run or fight the adrenalin off, not so many break.
> b.   Stimulus one (1) is wiped out in consciousness and the reason is ascribed to symptom two (2).
> c.   If the emotion can be reproduced and the original stimulus identified by patient, he is usually cured.
> d.   The stimulus – emotion and secondary stimulus is broken up by narcosis and physiochemical shift is toward normal.
> e.   Insulin decreases blood sugar, but also shakes up metabolism benefits digestion, etc. It is not anti-sympathetic.
> f.   Ergotamine tartrate sometimes relieves shakes, allows to patient to sleep better than controls.
> g.   The treat symptoms medically – agree that they have symptoms – explain mechanism of production and they cooperate after some relief has been obtained.

10. <u>Prodromal symptoms of anxiety</u>:

> a.   Irritability – fatigue – collapse – flatness is result of fatigue.
> b.   Shifting of personality – quiet becomes overt, etc. Should be rested.

c.   Failure in efficiency due to straight fatigue

d.   Shift in basic rhythm, weight loss, insomnia, anorexia (Treat here with insulin).

11. <u>Hysteria</u>:

> a.   Disorder produced by suggestion and cured by persuasion. Found in child-like borderline intellect in emotionally unstable. Anxiety is converted to symptom. Coward – goes against social pressures – may show fear indistinguishable from neurosis. Rx does not change coward's outlook – neurosis can be put into anxiety by pressure. Hysteria Rx must be brought back through the anxiety state.
>
> b.   Suggestion plays an important part in etiology of hysteria. Mechanism is disassociation of the mind. A mind is able to concentrate on one point only. Hysteria is unconscious disassociation.
>
> c.   End point of hysteria is an organic shift secondary to symptom as atrophy and stasis. Reeducation of arm or leg, or other movement by physiotherapy as well as psycho.
>
> d.   Onset – secondary to acute disorder and comes on fast.
>
> e.   Lack of organic findings.
>
> f.   Shift in suggestion, i.e., shifting of areas of anesthesia.
>
> g.   Hysteria is 20% of NP BC.

<u>Rx</u> – Suggestion:

Suggestion and drugs $CaCl_2$. Suggestion and cortical inhibition (pentothal or ether) twilight sleep – he must return to consciousness cured, i.e., walking talking, etc. Then work it out psychologically and explain mechanism to patient.

For barbiturate intoxication – Metrazol 2–5cc one time. 2cc stat and 1cc per minute for 2-3 minutes.

Coramine – Nikotamide – give IV until effect and later when barbiturate takes over. Also, give glucose to prevent liver damage.

Rx of acute alcoholism – severe.

100mg B IV
50cc 50% glucose
30-40m Insulin

MAJOR ERNEST GAILLARD, Jr.
Major, MC
Station Surgeon

12. <u>References</u>:

1)   Army Med. Bul. #66, April 1943.   Summary of important data in

AR.

2)   Surgeon ETO, Cir. Ltr. #56, dd 11 April 1944.

3)   Homosexuality, Cir. #3, WD Washington, dd 3 Jan. 1944.

4)   ETO Cir. #3, OCS, "Handling of combat forces in field.

5)   OCS, ETO, Cir. #4. Disposition of psychotic patients in ETO.

6)   AR 600-500. Care and disposition of insane.

7)   Suicides – AR 600-5--, Par. 35 a,b,c. Par. 63 (apt. of board).

8)   AR 35-1040 – Individual unable to sign name.

9)   AR 35-6680 – Officer with fund goes insane.

10)   AR 615-350 – Discharge methods.

11)   AR 605-110 – Maint. And test for physical fitness for officers.

12)   AR 605-230 – Reclassification of commissioned officers.

13)   Physical – AR 40-100 – 40-105 – 40-110.

14)   Index to AR 1-5 Heading of "insane".

15)   AR 40-1025 LOD Status. Chapter 1, par. 18, dd Aug. '42.

16)   182nd General Hospital, Sudbury, Staffs. (Capt. Kapernik).

'They're taking all my toys!'

Let the whole story of the V1 Victory be told!
Here is part of it—the important part which the Ack–Ack played

London Daily Express
07 September 1944

by Basil Cardew

THE story of the flying bomb can and should now be told. Victory of our armies in the field has swept the Germans clear of the main areas from which they launched it. Those few that do reach the shores today come from bases far, far away.

Of the Army's brilliant success everyone knows, but the tale of what has gone on in this country, on the assumption that our troops would not make such progress, has not been printed.

For security reasons, I cannot tell the whole story yet; I cannot tell you of the efforts made by the fighter squadrons, some of which have remarkable scores; I cannot tell you of the contributions of the balloons. But I can tell you something of the work of the Anti-Aircraft Command.

Two men

MANY people thought that the defences were caught off their guard at the very beginning. History may explain that in an entirely different way.

The final report may show that at first the fighters were the (our) main defensive weapon and that later the ground gunners destroyed many more than they did at the start.

Whether we had a secret weapon, as the Germans stated in a broadcast, must rest till after the war. But credit is due straight away to two men.

One is a General Sir Frederick Pile, son of an ex-Lord Mayor of Dublin, one of our senior generals and, despite his 60 years, one of our youngest. He is the nation's commander–in–chief of general Anti-Aircraft Command.

The other is Air Marshal Sir Roderic Hill, the 50-year-old head of the Air Defence of Great Britain, a man who controlled all of the fighters, a former test pilot who has flown every operational airplane in the RAF

Of Hill's men we have heard that one, solo squadron-leader alone destroyed more than 50 bombs, and that several shot down three in a single sortie.

But nothing has been said of the 24-hour-shift efforts of the men and women under General Pile. Pile was on half-pay for a year before war broke out, spending most of his time marking examination papers for the Army. He had been Director of Mechanisation at the War Office, where he produced a good but expensive tank. He was a commander of a tank corps, an infantry man in the last war.

221

A small, neat and compact figure, he directed his national A.A. command with little fuss and great efficiency for four and a half years while the Luftwaffe was powerful. He saw it battered and defeated.

Nearly three months ago he had thrust upon him the main task of combating the first Battle of the Robot.

The battle, as well he realised, was sure to be recorded in the future history books of the world. Here, for the first time in warfare, an insidious automation was now being tested out against the largest and richest target in the world—London.

The issue was clear-cut the flying bomb with a ton of high explosive and no man to pilot it v. the defences.

Confidence

IN those early weeks I have seen Pile at forward gun sites while his own men and women who, although sleepless through constant vigil, have sweated and struggled to keep the firing fast and accurate.

In those momentous weeks the general never lost confidence in his men or in himself, remaining quick but gentle, firm and dominant.

At once he found that the flying bombs presented the most difficult targets his gunners had been called upon to tackle. Their high speed and the smallness of their 16 feet overall outline demanded precision and a fast rate of fire which reduced the shooting down of crewed Luftwaffe planes to simple practice.

One German aircraft did venture within their sights during the flying bomb offensive. It was shot down in seconds.

Pile collected round him some rather enthusiastic and brilliant experts. One, Brigadier John Burls, of Royal Electrical and Mechanical Engineers, had the task of finding new platforms for the heavier anti-aircraft guns which could be quickly erected to serve our static units. The night he was given the job he worked out a plan and a drawing on his knee in the car that drove him home.

Next day a "mattress" was installed. It failed to give the guns the necessary firm foundation.

Again, Burls set to with pencil and paper, and the following day his new design was tested and successful.

Brand–new American equipment was tried out on the guns. Gear was rushed across the Atlantic to stem the German menace.

Thousands of men and women were trained afresh on wonder apparatus and in new methods which made their older drill almost archaic.

And how about the balloons?

Through experiment and trial, using the searchlights in new roles and the guns in experimental battle array, more flying bombs began to be destroyed. Over four times the belt of batteries was simply uprooted and sent to new positions.

New tactics

Meanwhile, the sly Germans began to feature the flying-bomb attack at the top of their daily war communiqué, above the news of France and Russia, which testified to the importance they gave it.

Constantly, they changed their tactics. First the bombs were sent over with a round-the-clock regularity. Then the Germans tried semi-saturation, sending gaggles of bombs within five or ten minutes.

Later, they then synchronized their attacks, launching a dozen or so robots simultaneously.

Each time, General Pile anticipated their move, and countered, mostly with success.

In the last three weeks results have been still better. Now the V1 offensive has petered out with an official total of just a touch under 9,000 launchings, of which 370 were despatched against us last week. Final week saw an average of only 53 flying bombs sent over in every night and day period.

People in Bomb Alley in London can go and measure for themselves all of the successes of the defences with these figures in mind.

Battle won

Throughout these 10½ weeks of attack, Pile has never once been satisfied. I have been permitted to attend his most secret conferences with his experts, held in a country mansion on the coast, while often the windows have rattled and even the black-out blew down as the ground gunners destroyed the fly bombs in high flight.

"Gentlemen", Pile always said when starting these round table affairs, "we are here not to discuss the flying bombs destroyed, but those that got through. They must all be stopped".

And now it is ended and the battle won.

Apart altogether from the march of our armies in capturing the enemy's flying-bomb areas, I believe that our defences had *already* won the first battle in the history of warfare against the robot.

Glossary
of
Terms
&
Acronyms

224

Glossary of Terms & Acronyms

AA – Acronym for ack-ack.
AAEG – Armored Aircraft Engineer/Gunner (*)[24]
AAF – Army Air Forces
AAG – Armored Aircraft Gunner (*)
Ablution – Bathing area or bath soap.
AC – Air Corps
Ack-Ack – Ground-based anti-aircraft guns (Allied).
AEG – Aircraft Engineer Gunner (*)
AFCE – Automatic Flight Control Equipment; i.e., Automatic Pilot.
AG – Air Gunner (non-com); otherwise, Adjutant General (*).
ANC – Army Nursing Corps
Anoxia – Medical condition arising from acute oxygen deprivation at high altitude.
APO – Army Post Office
A.R.C./ARC – American Red Cross
AROG – Aircraft Radio Operator/Gunner (*)
ASN – Army Serial Number
ATC – Air Transport Command
B – Bombardier [25]
BG – Bomb/Bombardment Group
Brassard – White cloth upper armband emblazoned with a Red Cross to distinguish medical personnel from other enlisted men, largely, to keep the MP's from beating them up with their Billy clubs.
BS – Bomb/Bombardment Squadron
BTG – Ball Turret Gunner
CBW – Composite Bomb Wing
Chaff – Foil-backed strips of paper randomly dumped out of an airplane in order to confuse ground-based, enemy anti-aircraft radar.
CMB – Central Medical Board
CME – Central Medical Establishment
CO – Commanding Officer
Comminuted – shattered, pulverized.
Compounded – fracture associated with lacerated soft tissue and bone protruding through the skin.
CP – Co-pilot
"D" – Duty (returned to duty after medical release by the flight surgeon).
DC – Dental Corps
E.T.O./ETO – European Theater of Operations
E.V.S./EVS – Enlisted Volunteer Service (nursing).

---

[24] (*) Early, various terms for acronyms (educated approximations, actually) for airborne gunners that were eventually replaced by the far more uniform, succinct and efficient TTG/BTG/LWG/RWG/TG/ROG/CTG, etc.

[25] The Bombardier, when not later taking control of the aircraft with the Norden Bomb Sight and/or dropping ordnance on the designated target, also doubled, and along with the Navigator, as either the nose-, cheek-, or chin turret gunner, depending on the model type and manufacturer of his particular B-17 Flying Fortress.

EM – Enlisted Man/Emergency Medical (rare for the time).

EP – Enlisted Personnel

F/O – Flight Officer

Feathered engine – Cut RPM and reduced power; propeller rotated to straight fore and aft orientation (with the air stream) when an engine has been knocked out (dead) by flak or other enemy gunfire.

Feather merchant – American military jargon for a civilian government employee.

FLAK – 1938 German (Axis) synonymous acronym for Ack-Ack (**FL**ieger **A**bwehr **K**anonen = Air Defense Cannons).

Ground Loop – When the aircraft in motion on the ground begins to rotate around the vertical axis. If not corrected immediately, it "snowballs" until the aircraft has ground-looped. Large aircraft with tail wheels, not unlike the B-17 bomber, can do this fairly easily. Sometimes it was even done on purpose. Think of it as the aircraft "spinning out" on the runway—as in today's equivalent of an automobile freeway "solo spin-out"—except angled up on one front tire.

GSW – Gun Shot Wound

(H) – Heavy—as in Bomb Group "Heavy"/Bombardment Squadron "Heavy".

"H" – Hospital (hospitalized for wounds or injuries after medical examination).

I.P./IP – Initial Point/Initiation Point (aerial point of commencing a bomb run).

IIA – Injured in Action

J.A.G./JAG – Judge Advocate General (military legal counsel).

K.P./KP – Kitchen Police

KIA – Killed in Action

Luetic – Syphilitic: affected with, caused by or pertaining to syphilis.

LWG – Left Waist Gunner

M.P./MP's – Military Police

M.P.I./MPI – Mean Point of Impact, sp., the bomb target area.

MAC – Military Airlift Command

MACR – Missing Air Crew Report

M.C./MC – Medical Corps

MGB – Machine Gun Blast

MIA – Missing in Action

Mickey Operator – USAAF slang for the operator of the H2X Radar Bombing System (nicknamed the "Mickey") where the radar beam was pointed at the intended target, and through a bombing computer used in conjunction with the Norden bombsight, picked the precise release point for dropping ordnance. [26]

M.O.D./MOD – Medical Officer of the Day

N – Navigator

Nacelle – Enclosed, rounded, sheet metal shelter on an aircraft wing or nose billeting the engine.

NCO/"Non-Com" – Noncommissioned officer

Neil-Robertson litter (stretcher) – Emergency patient medical stretcher made of semi-rigid canvas and several sewn-in, longitudinal wooden slats. It enables the wounded or injured to be tightly wrapped mummy-fashion, and then extracted from confined holds and through restricted access hatchways too narrow to

---

[26] The same American mastermind who designed, invented and developed the H2X "Mickey" Radar Bombing System later went on to think up and devise the maser, which subsequently evolved into today's laser.

permit the use of a regular stretcher. This particular litter was named after John Neil Robertson, MB, CM, Fleet Surgeon, Royal Navy (1873-1913) who had, and on his own, adapted it from an earlier *Japanese* Navy design, however, with sewn-in *bamboo*—not wood—slats.

Nissen hut – A prefabricated building of corrugated steel in the shape of a half cylinder (after Peter Norman Nissen (1871-1930), British army officer and mining engineer).

(NMI) – No Middle Initial

Norden Bombsight – American-made bombsight (after Swiss immigrant inventor, Carl Lucas Norden (1880-1965)) that eventually supplemented the PFF to drop bombs accurately within a 100-foot ground diameter from four miles up out of the aircraft bomb bays, utilizing a computer, and supplemented by and also comprising a sophisticated system of gyros, motors, gears, mirrors, levels—and a powerful telescope.

Ordnance – Bombs, ammunition and artillery shells—and their conveyances.

P – Pilot

PFF – Pathfinder Force: bombing tactic and technology developed originally by the British Royal Air Force 15 August 1942 and later adopted by the USAAF.

"Piccadilly flak" – British slang for gonorrhea (named for the Piccadilly Circus area of London notorious for drugs, gambling, and prostitution).

Picquet hut – Half-buried, fortified hut named for François Picquet (1708-1781), French missionary of Montreal who built several small, attack-proof fortifications against "pagan" Indian tribes to protect his converted Christian tribes. "Abbe Picquet was worth several regiments", said Governor Duquesne of him (1754).

PX – Post Exchange (military convenience store on base).

Q.M./QM – Quartermaster

"Q" – Quarters (confined to quarters; usu. after minor wound or injury).

Quonset hut – Same as Nissen hut ("Quonset" = proper trademark name, however, *American*).

QSM – "Shall I repeat the last message which you sent me?" (International "Q" Code).

R.A.F./RAF – Royal Air Force

R.A.S.C./RASC – Royal Army Service Corps

RCD – Recruit Corps Depot

RO – Radio Operator

ROG – Radio Operator/Gunner (alternate waist gunner from assigned WG).

RWG – Right Waist Gunner

S.O.S. – Special Operations Squadron or "Services of Supply" (Allied).

SC – Southern Command/Special Command

Tannoy – Loudspeakers; public address system (English manufacturer's brand name, as applied).

TD/TDY – Temporary Duty

TG – Tail Gunner

Thomas' leg splint – Primarily a *knee* splint (after Liverpool surgeon, Hugh Owen Thomas (1834-1891)) for removing the pressure of the weight of the body from the knee joint by transferring the incidence of that pressure to the upper portion of the hip and floor of the pelvis.

Tobruk plaster – An immobilizing split plaster cast applied from the foot to the groin; with skin traction tapes through openings in the plaster and buttressed with a Thomas' splint (after General Sir Bernard Law "Monty" Montgomery's decisive military victory over Field Marshal Erwin "The Desert Fox" Rommel's *Afrika Korps* at the port city of Tobruk, Libya on 13 November 1942, and where first utilized).

Toggeler – Alternatively, "togglier" or "toggeleer"—the functional replacement for the bombardier on many ships. Later on during the war, there was no need to always have a fully trained, commissioned-officer bombardier in every crew, so the toggeler–usually a sergeant–would simply "toggle" (drop) ordnance on the lead ship bombardier's cue or command.

Tokyo Tanks — External fuel tanks retrofitted to the undersides of the wings of both heavy and medium bombers (and, also, some escort fighters) to increase their effective reach on long-range bombing missions deep into enemy territory. (named for General James Harold "Jimmy" Doolittle's 18 April 1942 twilight raid on Tokyo in his B-25 Mitchell bombers launched from the decks of the *USS Hornet* and *USS Enterprise* some 650 miles off the Japanese coast).

Tommy/Tommies – British foot soldier

"T.T." – Top Turret

TTG – Top Turret Gunner

VC – Volunteer Corps

WG – Waist Gunner

W/O – Warrant Officer (exalted non-com, but not quite commissioned officer; however, holding a warrant from the President).

WAAF – Women's Army Air Forces

WIA – Wounded in Action

Lightning Source UK Ltd.
Milton Keynes UK
UKOW07f1941270515

252365UK00005B/215/P

9 781410 746719